The Nature of Moral Judgement

The Nature of Moral Judgement

A study in contemporary moral philosophy

Patrick McGrath

UNIVERSITY OF NOTRE DAME PRESS

First American Edition 1969
University of Notre Dame Press
Notre Dame, Indiana 46556

First Published 1967
Sheed and Ward Ltd., 33 Maiden Lane, London WC2, and
Sheed and Ward Pty. Ltd., 28 Bourke Street, Melbourne

Library of Congress Catalog Card Number: 69-14815
Printed in the United States of America

Contents

Part 3

Part 4

Preface

Moral judgements form a constant feature of everyday discourse—'Euthanasia is never morally justified', 'Hitler was an evil man', 'You ought to apologise for what you said'. We commonly make remarks of this kind, yet we would be in immediate difficulties if someone were to ask us what they mean. Like St Augustine with regard to time, we know what *good* and *ought* mean until asked how to define them. The nature of moral judgement is perhaps the most fundamental problem in moral philosophy since the answer to it determines the character of a moral system, yet hitherto it has been curiously neglected. All the great moralists *have* a theory of moral judgement, but they seldom expound it in any detail and even less often provide any evidence to show that it is true.

In our day the situation has been reversed. The linguistic analysis movement has placed the problem of moral judgement at the forefront of philosophical discussion to the exclusion of some of the traditional problems of ethics. In this work I

1*

have tried to present this discussion as it has developed since the publication of Ayer's *Language, Truth and Logic* in 1936. Since it would be impossible to deal with all the writings on the subject since then, seven authors have been selected for consideration whose writings appear to have made the greatest contribution to the discussion. This book has been conceived, however, more as a work of philosophy proper than as a study in the history of philosophy. My primary concern has been not so much with the details of what has been said about the problem of moral judgement as with finding of a satisfactory solution to it. Consequently more space has been devoted to the evaluation of these writers' theories than to the presentation of them. In the final section I have tried to use what has been learned from these discussions to formulate a satisfactory theory of moral judgement.

I wish to acknowledge my indebtedness to Professor J. D. Bastable of Maynooth, Professor A. Wylleman of Louvain, and Miss Elizabeth Anscombe of Somerville College, Oxford, each of whom read portions of the manuscript at various stages of its development and offered helpful comments. I am also indebted to Professor Bastable in his capacity as editor of *Philosophical Studies* for permission to reproduce chapters 3 and 6, both of which originally appeared as articles in that journal. Finally, acknowledgements are also due to the following publishers for permission to reproduce copyright material: Oxford University Press, for permission to use extracts from *The Language of Morals* and *Freedom and Reason* by

R. M. Hare; Victor Gollancz Ltd, for permission to use extracts from *Language, Truth and Logic* by A. J. Ayer; Macmillan & Co. Ltd, for permission to use extracts from *Philosophical Essays* by A. J. Ayer; Cambridge University Press, for permission to use extracts from *The Place of Reason in Ethics* by Stephen Toulmin; Cornell University Press, for permission to use extracts from *The Moral Point of View* by Kurt Baier, and from *Ethics and Language* by C. L. Stephenson; and Doubleday & Co. Inc, for permission to use extracts from *The Two Sources of Morality and Religion* by Henri Bergson.

Part 1

The emotive theory of moral judgement

1
The background
to the
emotive theory

1. Moore's refutation of naturalism

The emotive theory made its first appearance—a brief and rather tentative one—in *The Meaning of Meaning* (London 1922) by Ogden and Richards. But it did not gain general currency or receive anything like a complete formulation until it was put forward by A. J. Ayer in *Language, Truth and Logic* (London 1936). It is an outgrowth of the ultra empiricist movement known as 'logical positivism', but it is not however a necessary consequence of the application of empiricist theories to ethics. Empiricism has had a long history, but in the past even its most extreme exponents, such as Hume and Mill, had treated moral judgements as factual rather than emotive. The change was due to the influence of G. E. Moore, and in particular to his book *Principia Ethica*, which was published in 1903.

Moore produced two books and several articles on ethical topics, but his influence on subsequent ethical thought was due almost entirely to the first chapter of *Principia Ethica*, where he considers 'the most fundamental question in all ethics': What is goodness? What does the term *good* mean? The question for him is real rather than verbal. It is concerned not so much with the meaning of a word as with the nature of the object or idea which the word denotes.

My business is solely with that object or idea which I hold, rightly or wrongly, that the word is generally used to stand for. What I want to discover is the nature of that object.[1]

What, then, is goodness? The answer proposed is something of an anticlimax.

If I am asked 'What is good?' my answer is that good is good and that is the end of the matter. Or if I am asked 'How is good to be defined?' my answer is that it cannot be defined, and that is all I have to say about it. [*Principia Ethica*, 1.]

The attempt to define *good* Moore termed the 'naturalistic fallacy'. This terminology is doubly unfortunate, for the error is not a fallacy in the strict sense, and, secondly, it is incurred not only by those who define *good* in naturalistic terms, but by those who define it in supra-naturalistic or metaphysical terms as well. However, it is now standard philosophical terminology, and its inaptness is no longer likely to mislead.

The argument put forward in support of this view, like the famous argument of St Anselm, is

[1] G. E. Moore, *Principia Ethica*, Cambridge 1903, 6.

simple in outline but extremely difficult to evaluate.

> The hypothesis that disagreement about the meaning of good is disagreement with regard to the correct analysis of a given whole, may be most plainly seen to be incorrect by consideration of the fact that, whatever definition be offered, it may be always asked, with significance of the complex so defined, whether it is itself good. [*Principia Ethica*, 5.]

By the phrase: 'it may always be asked, with significance of the complex so defined', Moore means that the question will be one of fact, not a mere verbal question about the meaning of certain terms. The argument, then, may be stated in simpler form, as follows: The question, Is x good?, no matter what value we choose to give x, is always a question of fact. Hence x cannot be part of the meaning of *good*. *Good*, therefore is indefinable.

The next point in Moore's argument is that, since *good* is indefinable, it must refer to some simple characteristic.

> My point is that 'good' is a simple notion just as 'yellow' is a simple notion; that just as you cannot, by any manner of means, explain to one who does not already know it, what yellow is, so you cannot explain what good is. [*Principia Ethica*, 7.]

Moore seems to have thought that this followed immediately from his first conclusion, and his manner of framing the previous argument obscures the fact that it is not an immediate inference.

> Definitions of the kind that I was asking for, definitions which describe the real nature of the object or notion denoted by a word, and which do not merely tell us what the word is used to mean, are only possible when the object or notion in question is something complex. [*Principia Ethica*, 7.]

Words and things are distinct, however, and even should we grant that, if *good* is definable, what it denotes must be complex, it still does not follow that, if *good* is indefinable, what it denotes is something simple. For it has been argued that *good* does not denote anything at all; or again that, besides denoting, *good* performs another linguistic function and that, since its definition concerns only what it denotes, this second function is sufficient to explain the lack of equivalence between the definition and definiendum. This is not to prejudge the value of these arguments, but their very existence is sufficient to show that the transition from 'indefinable' to 'denoting something simple' is not an immediate inference.

Moore's treatment of goodness may be outlined in the following schema of propositions:

a. *Good* is the fundamental ethical concept.
b. It is indefinable.
c. *Good* is a descriptive term.
d. It denotes a simple quality or characteristic.[1]

[1] Moore described goodness as a 'non-natural' quality. He never defined this term, but part of what he means by it is that goodness is not perceived by the senses.

It is perhaps an indication of Moore's influence that the development of English ethical thought in this century can be summarised in terms of these four propositions. Moore's immediate successors, deontological intuitionists such as Prichard, Carrit and Ross, denied (a). They held that the concept of right cannot be derived from that of good, but is equally fundamental, and that *right*, like *good*, denotes a simple characteristic. The emotive theory is based on a denial of (c) and (d), and the successors of the emotivists, while admitting (c) to be true in some sense, denied (d).

2. Logical atomism
The year 1903 is the most significant date in modern English philosophy. It saw the publication of three important pieces of philosophical writing—*Principia Ethica* and *The Refutation of Idealism* by G. E. Moore, and *The Principles of Mathematics* by Bertrand Russell. These marked the beginning of the end for the pantheistic idealism which dominated English thought in the second half of the nineteenth century, and the beginning of a new movement, known by different names at different periods of its development, but whose most appropriate title is perhaps 'logical empiricism'. Russell's *The Principles of Mathematics*, though not intended as a work of philosophy, was probably the most influential of the three, for it removed a long standing reproach to empiricism, and—even more important—provided a model for a new system of philosophy, an entirely new approach to reality. But these two accomplishments certainly did not form part of

Russell's intention in the writing of this book, which is concerned solely with the problem of mathematical knowledge.

What are we talking about when we say, for instance, that two plus two equals four? We do not seem to be referring to the world of experience: when two objects—drops of liquid, say—added to two other objects fail to produce four objects, we don't claim that a theorem of mathematics has been refuted. But if mathematical truths refer to a supra-empirical world, how is our mathematical knowledge to be accounted for? There are almost as many answers to this question as there are systems of philosophy, but nearly all agree in postulating a source of knowledge other than that of experience to account for our grasp of mathematical truth.

Russell's answer to the problem is given in his preface to *The Principles of Mathematics*:

> All pure mathematics deals exclusively with concepts definable in terms of a very small number of fundamental logical concepts, and ...all its propositions are deducible from a very small number of fundamental logical principles.[1]

This contrasts with the theories of Plato, Descartes, and Kant. Each of these had accounted for mathematics by placing it in a general philosophical framework. Russell's immediate predecessors, Hilbert, Peano, and Frege, concentrated instead on finding out what kind of thing a

[1] B. Russell, *The Principles of Mathematics*, Cambridge 1903, xv.

mathematical statement really is. A picture gradually emerged of mathematics as a purely deductive science. Like Euclidean geometry, the entire corpus of mathematical truth may be derived, by a strict logical process, from some elementary axioms or postulates. Frege's definition of number in purely logical terms made clear that these axioms are all principles of formal logic. Mathematics is, therefore, a branch of logic.

This could hardly be said to be an empirical interpretation of mathematics, but by removing the 'other-worldly' character from mathematical truth, it rendered mathematics much more amenable to an empirical interpretation.

The second point about *The Principles of Mathematics* was that it provided a model for a new approach to reality. Mathematical propositions, according to Russell, are compound propositions; they are in fact truth functions of the simple propositions of which they are composed, that is to say, their truth or falsity is determined by the truth or falsity of their components. To establish the truth of a mathematical proposition one must show that it is deducible from the fundamental logical principles which, for Russell, are the basis of all mathematical truth. If we apply this conception to our non-mathematical knowledge we arrive at the following position: Since all our non-mathematical knowledge is derived from experience, every non-mathematical proposition is either a simple proposition which describes immediate experience or a truth-function of such propositions. The simple empirical propositions have here the same function as the principles of logic in the sphere of mathematics. They provide the foundation for all our non-mathematical knowledge. What we need, therefore, is a method for reducing complex propositions to the simple propositions of which they are composed. This would enable us to decide, with regard to any contingent proposition, whether it is deducible from the data of immediate experience. Those which are not so deducible may be disregarded, for even if we do not know with certainty that they are false, there is no reason for believing them to be true.

Russell's famous 'theory of descriptions' showed how the truth-functional conception could be applied to non-mathematical discourse by providing a technique for reducing compound propositions to the primitive empirical propositions of which they are composed.[1] The basis of the theory is the distinction between complete and incomplete symbols. A complete symbol is a proper name. An incomplete symbol is a word or phrase with the same grammatical function as a proper name, but which does not name anything. It is really a linguistic convenience, a sort of shorthand. Propositions with incomplete symbols as grammatical subjects are truth-functional. Thus, in the proposition 'The author of *Waverley*

[1] The theory of descriptions was first expounded by Russell in his article 'On Denoting', *Mind* XIV (1905) and reprinted in *Logic and Knowledge*, ed. R. C. Marsh, London 1956, 41–56; but the best and clearest account is that given by him in *Introduction to Mathematical Philosophy*, London 1919, 167–80.

was Scotch', the phrase 'the author of *Waverley*' is an incomplete symbol, and the entire proposition, which seems simple, is in reality complex. It is equivalent to the conjunction of the following three propositions: 'at least one person wrote *Waverley*'; 'at most one person wrote *Waverley*'; and 'whoever wrote *Waverley* was Scotch'. What this paraphrase brings out is that the phrase 'the author of *Waverley*' does not *denote* the individual who actually wrote *Waverley*, and hence the proposition 'The author of *Waverley* was Scotch' does not require the existence of such an individual in order to be significant. It does not presuppose his existence in the way in which a proper name presupposes the existence of its bearer. Thus, if there was no such individual as Mr Krushchev, the proposition 'Mr Krushchev is bald' would be devoid of significance.

From all this Russell was led eventually to postulate two theories—one about meaning, the other about reality. If all incomplete symbols are ultimately reducible to complete symbols or proper names, then it follows that proper names are the bricks out of which language is built up. Now the meaning of a proper name for Russell is the object which the name denotes. Meaning, therefore, is purely extensional.

In a logically perfect language the words in a proposition would correspond one by one with the components of the corresponding fact, with the exception of such words as 'or' 'not' 'if' 'then', which have a different function. In a logically perfect language there will be one word and no more for every simple object, and everything that is not simple will be expressed by a combination, derived, of course, from the words for the simple things that enter in, one word for each simple component.[1]

In a logically perfect language there would be one term, and only one, for each separate item in reality, and the meaning of a term would be the reality it denotes.

Russell's second theory, the ontological counterpart of his nominalism, was to the effect that the world is radically pluralistic. Since our language has meaning, there must be an object, a particular, corresponding to each of the proper names out of which language is composed. And as language is ultimately composed of logically independent proper names, so reality must be ultimately composed of ontologically independent particulars.

What are these particulars? They are those things with which we are, or can be, acquainted.[2] This follows immediately from the theory that the meaning of a term is the object it denotes, for if, in a logically perfect language, there is a term

[1] B. Russell, 'The Philosophy of Logical Atomism', *Monist* XXVIII and XXIX (1918–19), reprinted in *Logic and Knowledge*, 197.

[2] 'I say that I am acquainted with an object when I have a direct cognitive relation to that object, i.e, when I am directly aware of the object itself.' (B. Russell, 'Knowledge by Acquaintance and Knowledge by Description', *Proceedings of the Aristotelian Society* XI [1910–11]; reprinted in *Mysticism and Logic*, London 1918 [Penguin edition 1953, 197]).

corresponding to each separate item in reality, each term will have meaning only for someone acquainted with the particular to which it corresponds. Now, according to Russell, the only objects with which we are, or can be, acquainted —the only objects of our direct experience—are sense-data and mental states.[1] These are the atoms out of which the world is composed, the only objects which can properly be named. The more familiar objects of everyday life—things such as tables, chairs, and persons—are 'logical constructions', that is to say, they are not separate objects but collections of entities: terms such as *table* or *chair* are incomplete symbols. 'A thing may be defined as a certain series of appearances, connected with each other by continuity and by certain causal laws.'[2] The self is defined as 'an assemblage of particulars, namely, what would be called states of mind, which would belong together in virtue of some specific common quality'.[3] Russell did not deny the possibility of constant individual entities underlying these appearances or mental states, but he saw no reason for supposing that such entities existed. 'The assumption

[1] There is some doubt whether Russell, when writing 'The Philosophy of Logical Atomism', had already abandoned his old view that we are acquainted with universals. The references to it in the text seem to conflict, and his reticence on the subject probably indicates that he was as yet undecided.

[2] B. Russell, *Our Knowledge of the External World*, London 1914, 106.

[3] B. Russell, 'The Ultimate Constituents of Matter', *Monist* xv (1915); reprinted in *Mysticism and Logic*, 126.

that there is a constant entity is a piece of gratuitous metaphysics.'[1] The wisest course, therefore, is to ignore them.

By the principle of Occam's razor if the class of appearances will fulfil the purposes for the sake of which the thing was invented by the prehistoric metaphysicians to whom common sense is due, economy demands that we should identify the thing with the class of its appearances.[2]

Russell's logical atomism, then, is not merely pluralistic: it is also ultra empirical.

The classic formulation of logical atomism was given in the *Tractatus-Logico Philosophicus* of Russell's friend and pupil, Ludwig Wittgenstein. Besides being more systematic and developed, this differs in some important respects from the account presented by Russell. For Wittgenstein the unit of meaning is the proposition rather than the single term. A proposition is a picture of reality: it represents a state of affairs or fact. A word has meaning only as part of a proposition. To represent something, a picture must possess the same form as the object depicted: thus a spatial picture can represent spatial reality, a coloured picture a coloured reality. Similarly, a proposition can represent a reality whose *logical* form it possesses. But the proposition cannot depict this logical form: if it were to do so it would no longer be a picture of reality, and hence

[1] *Our Knowledge of the External World*, 106.
[2] B. Russell, 'The Relation of Sense-Data to Physics', *Scientia* 1914; reprinted in *Mysticism and Logic*, 148.

no longer a genuine proposition. 'A picture cannot, however, depict its pictorial form: it displays it.'[1]

Apart from this shift of emphasis from terms to propositions, Wittgenstein's theory of meaning does not differ significantly from Russell's:

> 3.202 The simple signs employed in propositions are called names.
>
> 3.203 A name means an object. The object is its meaning.

As Wittgenstein takes the proposition, rather than the simple term, as the unit of meaning, so, for him, the unit of reality in not the particular but the fact. Names have meaning only in propositions, so particulars exist only in facts. We cannot conceive of them except as elements in facts.

> 2.0131 A speck in the visual field, though it need not be red, must have some colour: it is, so to speak, surrounded by colour-space. Tones must have *some* pitch, objects of the sense of touch *some* degree of hardness, and so on.

Their having a particular colour, or pitch, or degree of hardness is obviously a fact. Existence, then, is to be attributed to facts rather than to particulars.

The last quotation may give the impression that

[1] L. Wittgenstein, *Tractatus Logico-Philosophicus,* London 1922, para. 2.172. (The *Tractatus* is set out in numbered paragraphs. In subsequent quotations the paragraph number is given with the text. The translation used is that by D. F. Pears and B. F. McGuiness, London 1961.)

Wittgenstein's primitive facts are to be interpreted in the same empirical fashion as Russell's, that is, in terms of sense-data and mental states. But there is nothing else in the *Tractatus* to support this interpretation, and we now know that it was not intended by Wittgenstein.[1] However, one who already holds an empiricist theory of knowledge would, if he sympathised with the philosophy of the *Tractatus*, be bound to interpret it in an empiricist manner: that is its most natural interpretation, and it was the one given it by those on whom it had the greatest influence.

Moreover, even if the philosophy of the *Tractatus* is not necessarily empiricist, it is certainly incompatible with any system of philosophy which infers the existence of a transcendental reality from the facts of experience. The atomic facts of Wittgenstein's world exist independently.

> 5.135   There is no possible way of making an inference from the existence of one situation to the existence of another, entirely different situation.
>
> 5.136   There is no causal nexus to justify such an inference.
>
> 5.1361 ... Belief in the causal nexus is *superstition*.

[1] See Norman Malcolm, *Ludwig Wittgenstein*, Oxford 1958, 86: 'I asked Wittgenstein whether, when he wrote the *Tractatus*, he had ever decided upon anything as an *example* of a 'simple object'. His reply was that at that time his thought had been that he was a *logician*; and that it was not his business, as a logician, to try to decide whether this thing or that was a simple thing or a complex thing, that being a purely empirical matter.'

One cannot bridge the gap between the world of experience and the supra-empirical world by means of self-evident propositions, for these are necessarily true only because they are devoid of content: they cannot be false simply because they say nothing. The truth of factual propositions, on the other hand, is always contingent:

> 2.223 In order to tell whether a picture is true or false we must compare it with reality.
> 2.224 It is impossible to tell from the picture alone whether it is true or false.
> 2.225 There are no pictures that are true *a priori*.

The traditional problems of philosophy are pseudo-problems which arose from a failure to understand the logic of our language. The propositions of philosophy are not false but senseless. Philosophy provides no special knowledge; it merely clarifies our language.

> 4.112 ... Philosophy is not a body of doctrine but an activity. A philosophical work consists essentially of elucidations. Philosophy does not result in 'philosophical propositions', but rather in the clarification of propositions.

What Wittgenstein's analysis of language and reality ultimately amounts to, therefore, is positivism. He philosophises so as to banish philosophy.

> 4.11 The totality of true propositions is the whole of natural science.

There can be no valid philosophical arguments:

there cannot even be a significant philosophical statement.

> 3.328 If a sign is *useless*, it is meaningless. That is the point of Occam's maxim.

3. Logical positivism

The *Tractatus Logico-Philosophicus* had, at first, most influence in its author's native Austria, especially amongst the little group, later known as the 'Vienna Circle', which gathered under the leadership of Moritz Schlick. They accepted its idea of philosophy as a discipline whose sole purpose is the clarification of propositions. But the manner in which it had eliminated metaphysics was looked on with less approval. The *Tractatus*, while declaring metaphysics to be nonsense, had propounded a system of logical atomism which was itself a metaphysic. In order to draw the line between what was senseless and what was not, Wittgenstein had to talk 'nonsense' himself. His theory of the relation of language to reality was an attempt to state something which, on his own theory, language could only display, and his proof that metaphysical utterances do not express anything was itself based on such metaphysical assertions as 'the world is the totality of facts'. Wittgenstein was, of course, aware of the paradoxical nature of his position:

> 6.54 My propositions serve as eludications in the following way: anyone who understands me eventually recognizes them as nonsensical, when he has used them—as steps—to climb up beyond them. (He

must, so to speak, throw away the ladder
after he has climbed up it.)
He must transcend these propositions, and
then he will see the world aright.

But this is only a half-hearted condemnation of
metaphysics. If one needs the metaphysics of the
Tractatus to see the world aright, perhaps other
metaphysical theories may increase one's understanding. Furthermore, Wittgenstein's conception
of 'the mystical' showed that the limits proposed
in the *Tractatus* were of language rather than of
thought.

> 6.522 There are, indeed, things that cannot be
> put into words. They *make themselves
> manifest*. They are what is mystical.

The genuine positivist position on this matter
was expressed by Frank Ramsey in the remark:
'What we can't say we can't say, and we can't
whistle it either.'[1] But what was most significant
for Wittgenstein was what could not be expressed.

> 6.52 We feel that even when *all possible* scien-
> tific questions have been answered, the
> problems of life remain completely un-
> touched.

And his final remark in the *Tractatus* is the cryp-
tic 'What we cannot speak about we must consign
to silence'.

This conception of 'das mystische' was wholly
opposed to the positivist bias of the Vienna Circle.

[1] Quoted by A. J. Ayer, 'The Vienna Circle', *The
Revolution in Philosophy*, ed. Gilbert Ryle, London
1956, 75.

Their problem was to eliminate metaphysics without introducing surreptitious metaphysics into their own theory. The logical atomism of Russell and Wittgenstein had to be transformed into a logical positivism. An alternative proof of the meaninglessness of metaphysics was demanded. This was achieved by means of the famous principle of verification. As formulated by Ayer, this declared that propositions are meaningful only if they are capable of being verified. It was now no longer necessary to speak of the world as composed solely of atomic facts. By applying the principle of verification to metaphysical statements it could be shown that they were all unverifiable, and therefore meaningless.

We now possess all the data necessary for an understanding of Ayer's general philosophical outlook in his book *Language, Truth and Logic*. This work was largely a synthesis of the theories of Russell and Wittgenstein with the metaphysical elements discarded. The objects of the external world and the self are regarded, with Russell, as logical constructions from sense-data, while a-priori propositions are considered, with Wittgenstein, to be devoid of content. There is no special knowledge to be gained from philosophy: its purpose is simply the analysis and clarification of the propositions of everyday life and, more particularly, of the sciences. Genuine propositions can all be divided into two classes—empirical statements of fact, and the purely formal propositions of mathematics and logic. Metaphysical statements are devoid of all significance and may be discarded as meaningless.

2
A. J. Ayer

1. The emotive analysis of ethical terms

The sole function of philosophy, according to
Ayer, is the analysis of language. Moral philosophy is simply the analysis of moral language,
that is, of statements containing terms which
are usually regarded as having moral or ethical
significance—terms such as *good, right, ought,*
and *duty*. If these statements express genuine
propositions, they must consist either of tautologies or of statements of empirical fact. The first
alternative, however, is hardly worth considering.
The disputes which occur on ethical issues would
scarcely arise if they concerned merely the way
in which certain terms are to be defined, nor can
moral perplexity be plausibly presented as simply
a doubt concerning the meaning of, say *right* or
duty. Are ethical propositions, then, statements
of empirical fact? To answer this question Ayer
has merely to apply the principle of verification.
Ethical statements, he finds, are not, even in

principle, capable of being verified: they cannot be regarded, therefore, as genuine propositions.

It must be noted that this view is not a direct consequence of belief in the principle of verification. There are several well-known ethical theories, all of them compatible with empiricism, which enable one to interpret ethical statements in such a way as to leave them capable of being verified. Subjectivism and utilitarianism are the best known of these. But the tradition of the Vienna Circle was against any such interpretation. Wittgenstein had declared in the *Tractatus* (para. 6.421) that ethics cannot be expressed; moral problems are among those which remain when all possible scientific questions have been answered. And Rudolf Carnap declared that ethical statements are commands or imperatives.

The real reason, however, for Ayer's reluctance to adopt a less revolutionary theory of ethics was not the tradition of the Circle, but the work of G. E. Moore. Subjectivism and utilitarianism offer definitions of the principal ethical terms: *good* according to subjectivism means 'that which I approve of', and according to hedonistic utilitarianism 'that which causes pleasure'. Now Moore's refutation of naturalism had, it was claimed, shown all such definitions to be faulty, since it had proved that the term *good* cannot be defined.

Ayer's case against naturalistic ethics in *Language, Truth and Logic* is a restatement of Moore's argument in *Principia Ethica*:

We reject the subjectivist view that to call an

22

action right, or a thing good, is to say that it is generally approved of, because it is not self-contradictory to assert that some actions which are generally approved of are not right, or that some things which are generally approved of are not good ... And since it is not self-contradictory to say that some pleasant things are not good or that some bad things are desired, it cannot be the case that the sentence 'x is good' is equivalent to 'x is pleasant' or to 'x is desired'.[1]

This is clearly an application of Moore's dictum that 'whatever definition may be offered, it may always be asked, with significance, of the complex so defined, whether it is itself good'. If it is not self-contradictory to say that some pleasant things are not good, then the question: Is pleasure good?, must be significant.

Ethical statements are unverifiable, but this does not mean that they are to be regarded, like the statements of metaphysics, as meaningless. The term *meaningless* is applicable only to utterances which are intended to convey information. But ethical statements appear to have a different function. Rudolf Carnap had suggested that they are really imperatives.[2] On this theory the statement 'You ought to keep your promise' is equivalent to 'Keep your promise'. But clearly some aspects of ethical statements cannot be fitted into

[1] *Language, Truth and Logic*, London 1946[2], 104–5.

[2] See, for example, R. Carnap, *Philosophy and Logical Syntax*, London 1935, 24–5: 'A value statement is nothing else than a command in a misleading grammatical form ... it is neither true nor false. It does not assert anything and can neither be proved nor disproved.'

the imperative form. Imperatives refer always to actions to be performed in the future, whereas ethical statements refer just as often to actions already performed. 'You ought not to have told a lie', for example, cannot plausibly be reduced to an imperative. Again, if 'That is good' and 'You ought to do that' are both equivalent to 'Do that', how are we to interpret a statement such as 'That is good: nevertheless, I don't think you ought do it'? This statement is in accordance with ordinary usage but makes no sense on Carnap's theory. The conclusion is that Carnap's theory is not a correct analysis of ethical terminology.

Ayer, who was a student at Oxford during the controversy concerning the Right and the Good, must have been aware of the impossibility of reducing every type of ethical statement to the one imperative form. At any rate he produced a theory which allowed for a distinction between *good* and *ought* and which, to some extent, avoided the difficulties inherent in Carnap's view. Ethical statements, he asserted, are simply the expressions of moral approval or disapproval. The force of the term *expression* must be noted. Ethical statements do not *assert* feelings, as the subjectivists hold. If they did, they would be verifiable, and hence be genuine propositions. They *express* feelings, just as a yawn expresses boredom or a sigh expresses grief.

In every case in which one would commonly be said to be making an ethical judgement the function of the relevant ethical word is purely 'emotive'. It is used to express feeling about certain objects, but not to make any assertions about them. [*Language, Truth and Logic*, 108.]

But this analysis is obviously incomplete. The function of 'you ought to do that' is not merely to express one's feelings about the actions in question; it also, like a command, tells a person how he should act. Ayer concedes that Carnap's view is at least partly true, and recognises a double function for ethical statements.

Ethical terms do not serve only to express feeling. They are calculated also to arouse feelings, and so to stimulate action. Indeed some of them are used in such a way as to give sentences in which they occur the effect of commands. Thus the sentence 'It is your duty to tell the truth' may be regarded as the expression of a certain sort of ethical feeling about truthfulness and as the expression of the command 'Tell the truth'. The sentence 'You ought to tell the truth' also involves the command 'Tell the truth', but here the tone of the command is less emphatic. In the sentence 'It is good to tell the truth' the command has become little more than a suggestion. And thus the 'meaning' of the word 'good', in its ethical usage, is differentiated from that of the word 'duty' or the word 'ought'. [*Language, Truth and Logic*, 108.]

Ayer points out that once we have discovered the true nature of ethical statements no further analysis of them is possible.

We find that ethical philosophy consists simply

in saying that ethical concepts are pseudo-concepts and therefore unanalysable. The further task of describing the different feelings that the different ethical terms are used to express, and the different reactions that they customarily provoke, is a task for the psychologist. There cannot be such a thing as ethical science, if by ethical science one means the elaboration of a 'true' system of morals. Since ethical judgements are mere expressions of feeling, there can be no way of determining the validity of an ethical system, and, indeed, no sense in asking whether any such system is true. [*Language, Truth and Logic*, 112.]

2. The principle of verification

Ayer's analysis of moral judgement derives most of its plausibility from his theory of meaning. For there appears to be no means of conclusively verifying the truth of a moral judgement. When someone disagrees with us on a moral issue, we do not, to demonstrate the truth of our view, ask him to undertake some observation or experiment. We simply argue with him, and if neither side succeeds in convincing the other, there is nothing to do but 'agree to disagree'. It follows, on Ayer's reasoning, that moral judgements are not factual; they assert nothing which is either true or false.

If we examine this argument more closely, however, its weaknesses soon become apparent. It is not clear, in the first place, that all moral judgements are unverifiable. On Ayer's definition of the principle, a proposition is unverifiable, not if its truth cannot be conclusively established by experience, but only if no observation would be relevant to its truth or falsehood. (*Language, Truth and Logic*, 38.) Now, in this sense many particular moral judgements are in fact verifiable. If I say, for example, 'You did wrong to drive through the town at that speed', the truth of my statement depends on certain factors which could be established by observation—that you did drive very quickly, that conditions at the time made such speed dangerous, that there was no serious reason for driving so quickly. If any one of these factors is absent, my statement is false. And this shows that it is verifiable, in Ayer's sense of the term, and hence not amenable to an emotive interpretation.

The second defect in Ayer's arguments is that the principle of verification is a wholly unsatisfactory criterion of meaning. This became evident shortly after it was first formulated. For the principle overlooks the essential fact that the judgement that a particular statement is or is not verifiable presupposes an understanding of its meaning. If I come across a sentence in an unknown language, I must first of all understand what it means before I can tell whether or not it is verifiable. The fact that it turns out to be unverifiable cannot entail that it is meaningless, for I could never know that it was unverifiable unless I had first understood its meaning. Meaning and verifiability are therefore quite distinct.

If, to avoid this difficulty, one says that the principle of verification is really a prescriptive theory of meaning, a statement of how the term *meaning* ought to be used rather than how it actually is used, the principle immediately loses all its bite. To say that the statements of ethics or metaphysics are meaningless in this sense is to say nothing more than that they are unverifiable. And there is now no reason for believing that, because they are unverifiable, they are in any way defective.

The principle of verification was, of course, originally put forward as an analysis of the actual meaning of meaning. But in his Introduction to the second (1946) edition of *Language, Truth and Logic* Ayer qualifies this claim considerably:

> In putting forward the principle of verification as a criterion of meaning, I do not overlook the fact that the word 'meaning' is commonly used in a variety of senses, and I do not wish to deny that in some of these senses a statement may properly be said to be meaningful even though it is neither analytic nor empirically verifiable. I should, however, claim that there was at least one proper use of the word 'meaning' in which it would be incorrect to say that a statement was meaningful unless it satisfied the principle of verification . . . Furthermore, I suggest that it is only if it is literally meaningful in this sense, that a statement can properly be said to be either true or false. Thus, while I wish the principle of verification itself to be regarded, not as an empirical hypothesis, but as a definition, it is not supposed to be entirely arbitrary. [*Language, Truth and Logic*, 15–16.]

Nevertheless, I do not see how the term *meaning*,

as it is ordinarily understood, could have a sense according to which it would be incorrect to say that a statement is meaningful unless it satisfies the principle of verification. For to judge the verifiability of a statement we must, as we have just seen, first understand it. And there is no sense of *meaning* which allows us to say that we understand an expression without knowing what it means.

Again, even if we grant that, in one sense, meaning and verifiability are identical, one could hardly conclude that it is only if it is meaningful in this sense that a statement can properly be said to be true or false. *Truth* is a predicate which is applicable to any meaningful assertion. If, as Ayer claims, there is more than one kind of meaning, then there should be more than one kind of truth.

But is it not possible to defend the verification principle not as an analysis of the term *meaning*, but as a factual statement about meaning? No: the principle itself forbids this. It is not itself verifiable: hence, if one takes it as a factual statement, it is either meaningless or false.

Ayer made some attempts to defend the principle against the criticisms. In 1956 we find him writing as follows:

A favourite argument of those who wish to defend metaphysics against the logical positivists' attack is that the verification principle is itself not verifiable. And, of course, it is not: it was not meant to be. It was put forward as a definition, not as an empirical statement of fact.

But it is not an arbitrary definition. It purports to lay down the conditions which actually govern our acceptance, or indeed our understanding, of common sense and scientific statements.[1]

This is to give the verification principle the status of an analytical statement, but the function of an empirical one. The operative term here is *actually*. A principle which lays down the conditions which actually govern our understanding of factual propositions must be itself a statement of fact. But an analytic proposition, according to Ayer, 'provides no information whatsoever . . . about any matter of fact' (*Language, Truth and Logic*, 79). Clearly no such statement could lay down the conditions which actually govern a process like the understanding of a proposition.

This difficulty concerning the status of the verification principle is another instance of the problem which confronts all positivists, namely, how to banish philosophy without philosophising oneself. If there are no significant statements other than empirical propositions and tautologies, what of the propositions which go to make up *Language, Truth and Logic*? Hume's demand in his *Inquiry concerning Human Understanding* (1748), that every volume of divinity or school metaphysics be committed to the flames, should, if he were consistent, have been extended to his own books.[2]

[1] A. J. Ayer, 'The Vienna Circle', *The Revolution in Philosophy*, ed. G. Ryle, 75.

[2] D. Hume, *An Inquiry concerning Human Understanding*, ed. L. A. Selby-Bigge, Oxford 1888, 165: 'If we

Ayer has at length perhaps recognised the self-destructive character of positivism. At any rate, in his more recent writings he has abandoned the verifiability principle as a general criterion of meaning.

> The most that has been proved is that metaphysical statements do not fall into the same category as the laws of logic, or as scientific hypotheses, or as historical narratives, or judgements of perception or any other common sense descriptions of the natural world. Surely it does not follow that they are neither true nor false, still less that they are nonsensical.[1]

3. The logical positivist theory of meaning

The significance of this change of view should not be exaggerated. The verification principle was intended as a test of meaningfulness. To abandon it as unverifiable is not the same thing as to abandon the theory of meaning of which it was merely one expression. It is to this conception of meaning, not to the verification principle, that Ayer appeals when, in a recent essay, he argues that ethical statements are not factual. To prove his point Ayer asks us to consider some imaginary murder case. He enumerates the details which

---

take in our hand any volume: of divinity or school metaphysics, for instance; let us ask, Does it contain any abstract reasoning concerning quantity or number? No. Does it contain any experimental reasoning concerning matter of fact and existence? No. Commit it then to the flames, for it can contain nothing but sophistry and illusion.'

[1] A. J. Ayer, *Logical Positivism*, Glencoe 1960, 15–16.

would be of interest to an observer—the time of the action, the motives of the criminal, the methods used, and so on. When all the facts have been outlined, when we have a complete description of the case, let us suppose that someone applies an ethical predicate to it:

> Suppose then that we say that the man acted rightly. The point that I wish to make is that in saying this we are not elaborating it or modifying our description of the situation in the way that we should be elaborating it if we gave further police-court details, or in the way that we should be modifying it if we showed that the agent's motives were different from what they had been thought to be. To say that his motives were good, or that they were bad, is not to say what they were. To say that the man acted rightly or that he acted wrongly, is not to say what he did. And when one has said what he did, when one has described the situation in the way that I have outlined, then to add that he was justified, or alternatively that he was not, is not to say any more about what he did; it does not add a further detail to the story. It is for this reason that these ethical predicates are not factual; they do not describe any features of the situation to which they are applied.[1]

It is certainly true that the ascription of an ethical predicate adds nothing to the description

[1] A. J. Ayer, 'On the Analysis of Moral Judgements', *Horizon* xx, 117 (1949); reprinted in *Philosophical Essays*, London 1954, 231.

of the action. But it hardly seems to follow that the value judgement is therefore non-factual. The ethical judgement is *based* on the natural features of the action and this would seem to be sufficient to guarantee its factual character. Ayer considers this objection in some detail.

To begin with, it is, or should be, clear that the connection is not logical. Let us assume that two observers agree about all the circumstances of the case, including the agent's motives, but that they disagree in their evaluation of it. Then neither of them is contradicting himself. Otherwise the use of the ethical term would add nothing to the circumstantial description: it would serve merely as a repetition, or partial repetition of it. But neither, as I hope to show, is the connection factual. There is nothing that counts as observing the *designata* of the ethical predicates, apart from observing the natural features of the situation. But what alternative is left? Certainly it can be said that the ethical features in some way depend upon the natural. We can and do give reasons for our moral judgements, just as we do give reasons for our aesthetic judgements, where the same argument applies. We fasten on motives, point to consequences, ask what would happen if everyone were to behave in such a way, and so forth. But the question is: In what way do these reasons support the judgements? Not in a logical sense. Ethical argument is not formal demonstration. And not in a scientific sense either. For then the goodness or badness of the situation, the rightness or wrongness of the action, would have to be something apart from the situation, something independently verifiable, for which the facts adduced as the reasons for the moral judgement were evidence. But in these moral cases the two coincide. There is no procedure of examining the value of the facts, as distinctive from examining the facts themselves. We may say that we have evidence for our moral judgements, but we cannot distinguish between pointing to the evidence itself and pointing to that for which it is supposed to be evidence. Which means that in the scientific sense it is not evidence at all. [*Philosophical Essays*, 256–7.]

This is an important argument. It brings out—in a way in which the appeal to the verification principle does not—the basic assumptions of Ayer's position.

The central premiss of the argument is that, for the ethical judgement to be factual, there must be observable factors in the situation which are the *designata* of the ethical predicate. This is a repetition of the purely extensionalist conception of meaning which has already been mentioned in connection with Russell and Wittgenstein.[1] It could be summarised as saying that, apart from logical constants, every significant linguistic symbol is either simple or complex. If it is simple, it designates some element of experience; if it is complex, then any statement which contains it

[1] For an explicit statement of the theory by Ayer, see *Language, Truth and Logic*, 136.

may be analysed into equivalent statements which contain only simple symbols.

I would like to argue here that Ayer's argument fails because the conception of meaning on which it rests is inadequate. I do not wish to consider the broader issue as to what precise validity, if any, this conception possesses. All I am concerned with showing is that it is at least *partially* inadequate, that it fails to account for one class of terms whose descriptive meaning is doubted by no-one, not even the most rigid empiricist.

The purely extensionalist conception of meaning asserts a direct relation between language and reality; *to mean* is, in essence, *to name*; the meaning of a word is the reality for which it stands. It takes no account of the possibility that language as descriptive reflects not reality tout court, but an interpretation of reality: that, in other words, there are three elements involved—language, reality, and mind. Now there is one class of terms whose meaningfulness cannot even begin to be understood unless the role of the mind is considered. This is the class of relational predicates —terms such as *large, small, tall, short*, etc. These express a comparison between the entity to which they are ascribed and something else. The mental operation of comparing is essential to them: to attempt to explain them in terms of a simple 'mirroring of reality' is to leave them inexplicable.

Suppose one says that a particular animal, a horse for example, is small. Everything which Ayer says about ethical predicates in the passage quoted above could be said with equal justice about *smallness*. Once we have described the animal's dimensions we do not add anything to this description by saying that he is a small horse; there is nothing that counts as observing the *designata* of his smallness apart from observing his other attributes; these other attributes provide reasons for asserting that he is small, but these reasons cannot support the judgement of smallness in a logical sense, nor, apparently, in a scientific sense, for then his smallness 'would have to be something apart from the situation, something independently verifiable', which of course it is not; there is no process for examining the smallness of the animal's dimensions apart from examining the dimensions themselves. In short, the conclusion of Ayer's argument should be that not only *good* but every relational predicate is devoid of descriptive meaning. Since this is absurd, the theory of meaning from which it is derived must be false.

But is there any reason for regarding *good* as a relational predicate? A strong prima-facie case can, I think, be presented.[1] Consider the two statements: 'That is a black horse', and: 'That is a small horse'. They differ in this, that while the first implies the two separate statements 'That is black' and 'That is a horse', this is not true of the second. A horse is small only when considered as a horse. He is not small when considered as an animal, or as a living being, or simply as an object. This is so because *small*, being a relational predicate, is based on a comparison between this

[1] I am indebted for this point to an article by P. T. Geach: 'Good and Evil', *Analysis* XVII (1956), 33–42.

particular animal's dimensions and the average dimensions of all animals of the same type. A black horse is black under whatever heading you consider him; his blackness has nothing to do with the sort of animal he is. But a horse's smallness is intimately connected with the fact that he is a horse. The term *good* functions in precisely the same way. If a man is a good writer, it does not follow that the statements 'He is a writer' and 'He is good', are both true. He is good only qua writer: he may be a bad citizen, a bad father, or a bad man. You cannot ascribe goodness to something without first knowing what it is, for its goodness depends on its being the sort of thing it is. This suggests very strongly that *good*, like *small*, is a relational predicate. If so, Ayer's argument is beside the point. All it proves is that *good* is a different sort of term from, say, *red* or *yellow*, but this is not to say that it is 'non-factual' or 'non-descriptive'.

4. An assessment of emotivism

So far we have been concerned with the arguments for the emotive theory. What of the theory itself? One thing to be noted about it is that it allows for very little distinction between the different types of ethical statements. For example, the statements: 'You ought to tell the truth', and: 'It is good to tell the truth', differ, on Ayer's analysis, only in this, that whereas the first commands one to tell the truth, the second merely suggests it. This, I think, is demonstrably incorrect. Consider the statement: 'That is good, but I don't think you ought to do it all the same'. There are numerous circumstances in which this remark would be apposite. On Ayer's analysis, however, it is quite incoherent, since it suggests that you do a certain action and, at the same time, commands you not to do it. Again, suppose someone is trying to decide between two incompatible courses of action. To tell him that each of the proposed courses is good is, according to Ayer, to suggest that he engage in both.

Ayer's contention that to say that something ought to be done, that it is good, and that it is one's duty are, apart from their imperative tone, simply different ways of expressing approval of the action, is equally implausible. For the negation of these statements should then express equivalent lack of approval, and this is clearly not the case. To say that something is not good and that it is not one's duty are not at all equivalent, since an action which goes beyond the demands of duty may be the most highly approved of. Again, consider the statement: 'You do not have a duty to do that, although it would be a very good thing to do'. This is quite intelligible in ordinary discourse, but on Ayer's account it is nonsense, since it expresses both approval and disapproval of the same action.

Ayer's conception of the double function of ethical statements also needs to be examined:

Ethical terms do not serve only to express feeling. They are calculated also to arouse feeling, and so to stimulate action. Indeed some of them are used in such a way as to give the sentences in which they occur the effect of commands. [*Language, Truth and Logic*, 108.]

Several comments are called for here. First, the fact that an ethical statement tends to arouse feeling does not give it the character of a command. A command has nothing to do with arousing feeling. When a sergeant-major bellows: 'Attention', he is not trying to evoke amongst the recruits the feeling of wanting to fall into line—he is simply telling them to do so. One may, of course, try to get a person to do something by endeavouring to make him want to do it. But this is not at all the same thing as ordering him to do it. Persuading and commanding, though they have the same purpose, are themselves radically distinct.

Secondly, it is not clear why statements which express feeling should tend to arouse feeling. They don't naturally do so. When someone expresses his annoyance by saying: 'Damn', his remark does not tend to arouse similar feelings of annoyance in others. The shouts of 'Hurrah' from supporters of the winning team have no power to evoke delight amongst the supporters of the losing side. The fact that ethical statements express feeling cannot be the *reason* why they evoke feeling. Ayer has, in fact, provided us with no explanation of why they should do so.

Thirdly, Ayer's analysis seems to be derived from an examination of statements made in debates on ethical issues between two or more people rather than of statements made in the context of personal moral decision. But suppose someone, after much doubt as to what is the right thing to do, finally decides that he ought to do x. Can one plausibly analyse his statement 'I ought to do x' into an expression of feeling and a tendency to evoke similar feeling? The evocative tendency must clearly be omitted if we conceive his statement as a personal remark, addressed merely to himself; he cannot be attempting to evoke in himself a feeling which he already possesses. But is it then merely an expression of feeling? If so, then his decision was a decision to have a particular feeling. But we do not normally *decide* to have feelings. We do not weigh up the various circumstances of the case and then decide to feel in this particular way towards whatever is the question. If, however, one who is trying to decide what he ought to do is not concerned with his feelings, then his statement 'I ought to do x' cannot be simply an expression of feeling. In this case Ayer's analysis would seem to have broken down completely.

It should be clear that ethical statements are far too complex to be accommodated within Ayer's *simpliste* account. There is, however, a later version of emotivism which is more subtle and developed than Ayer's. This will be the subject of my next chapter.

3
C. L. Stevenson

1. Ethical disagreement

A notable difficulty concerning the emotive theory had been expressed many years before by G. E. Moore. Moore was arguing here against subjectivism in ethics, but his remarks apply equally well to the emotive theory:

> If, when one man says, 'This action is right', and another answers, 'No, it is not right', each of them is always merely making an assertion about *his own* feelings, it plainly follows that there is never really any difference of opinion between them; the one of them is never really contradicting what the other is asserting. They are no more contradicting one another than if, when one had said, 'I like sugar', the other had answered, 'I don't like sugar.'. . . [This] involves, therefore, the very curious consequence that no two men can ever differ in opinion as to whether an action is right or wrong. And

41

surely the fact that it involves this consequence is sufficient to condemn it.[1]

Ayer's reply to this objection in *Language, Truth and Logic* is that we never do, in fact, differ in opinion about questions of value.

> This may seem, at first sight, to be a very paradoxical assertion. For we certainly do engage in disputes which are ordinarily regarded as disputes about questions of value. But in all such cases, we find, if we consider the matter closely, that the dispute is not really about a question of value, but about a question of fact. [*Language, Truth and Logic*, 63.]

This could hardly be regarded as a satisfactory answer, however, for even if we grant the highly debatable point that we never dispute about questions of value unless we are in disagreement concerning some related matter of fact, it is obvious that the factual disagreement will come to light only in the course of the dispute on the value question. The dispute will normally have already arisen before the protagonists are aware of the purely factual disagreement. What gives rise to the dispute, therefore, is the disagreement on value and, on Ayer's theory, this remains inexplicable.

A second attempt to answer Moore's argument on behalf of emotivism was made in 1937 by Charles L. Stevenson in an article entitled 'The

[1] G. E. Moore, *Ethics*, Cambridge 1912, 63.

Emotive Meaning of *Ethical* Terms'.[1] Stevenson did not deny that when A says that an action is right and B says that it is wrong, there is real disagreement between them. But he denied that this was necessarily disagreement in belief. Moore's emphasis on the purely cognitive aspects of moral judgements had led him to hold that there is only one type of disagreement. According to Stevenson, disagreement in *attitude* is as pervasive as, and, for ethics, even more important than, disagreement in *belief*. Here is how he distinguishes the two. When there is disagreement in belief:

> One man believes that p is the answer and another that not-p, or some proposition incompatible with p, is the answer; and in the course of discussion each tries to give some manner of proof for his view, or revise it in the light of further information. . . . [But] there are other cases, differing sharply from these, which may yet be called 'disagreements' with equal propriety. They involve an opposition, sometimes tentative and gentle, sometimes strong, which is not of beliefs, but rather of attitudes—that is to say, an opposition of purposes, aspirations, wants, preferences, desires, and so on. [*Ethics and Language*, 2–3.]

A disagreement in attitude can lead to a dispute just as easily as a disagreement in belief. Two

[1] C. L. Stevenson, 'The Emotive Meaning of *Ethical* Terms', *Mind* XLVI (1937). His views were later expressed at much greater length in his book *Ethics and Language*, New Haven 1944.

43

people going out to dine, for example, often argue about their choice of restaurant, though there may be no difference of opinion between them. The purpose of their argument is not to bring about agreement in belief, but agreement in attitude.

Moral disagreement, according to Stevenson, always involves disagreement in attitude. It may, of course, also involve disagreement in belief; the moral disagreement may, in fact, be rooted in disagreement in belief, so that when it is solved there may no longer be any further disagreement. But if the moral disagreement remains when all disagreements of belief have been resolved, then the disagreement is purely one of attitude.

Conflicting moral judgements, then, express not a disagreement in belief, but a disagreement in attitude. When we say that a particular action is right, we are not attributing a certain characteristic to it, but rather asserting that we possess a certain attitude towards it. But this can only be part of what we mean. For if, when A says that an action is right and B says that it is wrong, they are merely describing their own attitudes, there would be no matter for dispute between them. A difference in attitude does not necessarily involve a disagreement. What causes the dispute is the desire to change the attitude of the other. When people argue about ethical issues, what they are trying to do is to bring the other person's attitude into line with their own. Ethical judgements, then, not only describe the attitude of the speaker, but strive to mould the attitude of the hearer.

To the question, 'What distinguishes ethical statements from scientific ones?' it has been answered: 'Ethical statements have a meaning that is approximately, and in part, imperative'. [*Ethics and Language*, 26.]

2. The meaning of ethical statements

Stevenson's analysis of the more common types of ethical statements is as follows: 'This is wrong' means 'I disapprove of this: do so as well'. 'He ought to do this' means 'I disapprove of his leaving this undone: do so as well'. 'This is good' means 'I approve of this: do so as well'.

The analysis in each case consists of two elements—an assertion, which is really a description of the attitude of the hearer, and an imperative or exhortation to the hearer to adopt a similar attitude. These are intended as 'working models' rather than as strict definitions. What ethical statements assert is normally too vague to be strictly defined and, in any case, the emotive meaning of a term can rarely be reproduced by another: 'do so as well' in this instance is merely a rough characterisation. The working models do, however, give us the essentials of ethical meaning.

Stevenson's analysis differs from Ayer's on two points. Ethical statements are now regarded as genuine assertions, not mere expressions of feeling; and, secondly, their emotive content is now regarded as part of their meaning, whereas with Ayer meaning was rigidly restricted to descriptive content.

These differences should not be unduly stressed, however, for even if ethical statements can rightly be regarded as asserting something which is either true or false, their truth, on Stevenson's analysis, is of little moment. We do not normally err about our attitudes. Hence the only situation in which it would make sense to challenge the truth of an ethical statement is when one suspects the speaker of deception. Moreover, it seems clear that what prevented Ayer from adopting the view that ethical statements are assertions, rather than expressions, of feeling was Moore's refutation of the naturalistic fallacy. Stevenson has now shown how, by extending the concept of meaning, one can circumvent Moore. *Good* cannot be adequately defined because its definition will lack the emotive meaning of the original term. The question: 'Is *x good*?', is always significant, therefore, not because *good* denotes a simple, unanalysable quality, but because its meaning is both descriptive and emotive.

But how are we to understand *meaning* if it is to refer both to the descriptive and to the emotive content of terms? The difficulty is that *meaning* is usually regarded as a comparatively stable quality, whereas the emotive function of terms may vary widely from one context to another. A place-name, for example, however much feeling it may evoke in a native, is, to a stranger, usually a purely descriptive term. To overcome this difficulty, Stevenson appeals to the concept of potency or permanent disposition. The emotive meaning of a term is measured, not by the feeling which it evokes in a particular situation, but by the feeling which it has a permanent disposition or tendency to evoke. To maintain the view that descriptive and emotive meaning are two species belonging to the same genus, Stevenson defines descriptive meaning in somewhat similar terms:

> A sign's descriptive meaning is its disposition to produce *cognitive* mental processes, where 'cognitive' is to be taken as a general term, designating such specific kinds of mental activity as believing, thinking, supposing and so on. [*Ethics and Language*, 62.]

These dispositions to evoke emotion or produce cognition are not, of course, natural qualities of terms: they are acquired in use.

> A sign's disposition to affect a hearer is to be called a 'meaning' only if it it has been caused by, and would not have been developed without, an elaborate process of conditioning which has attended the sign's use in communications. [*Ethics and Language*, 57.]

One critic has suspected that this involves circularity, since a sign could not be used in communication unless it already had a meaning.[1] It seems, however, that Stevenson could answer this by distinguishing between the de facto power to evoke emotion or produce cognition in a particular situation and the permanent ability to do so. A term might have the first but not the second, so that it would be used in communication without possessing meaning in the sense of the term in which he is interested. Besides, what Stevenson is looking for is not a definitive theory

[1] A. Duncan-Jones, 'Critical Notice of *Ethics and Language*', *Mind* LIV (1945), 346.

of meaning, but a valid sense of the term that will permit the predication of meaning to terms whose function is purely emotive. In his own words, he is concerned merely 'with certain aspects of meaning', and, in this sense, his remarks on the subject are, I think, unexceptionable.

The emotive meaning of ethical terms is characterised in the working models by the phrase 'do so as well'. This, however, is not intended as anything more than a rough characterisation. There are very few terms with exact emotive counterparts:

> One need only attempt to interchange 'Hurrah' and 'How exciting' to see that the terms are only roughly synonymous. Each term bears the characteristic stamp of its emotional history. [*Ethics and Language*, 82.]

In this instance, 'do so as well', while it succeeds in showing the kind of emotive meaning involved, is much more peremptory in tone than any ethical statement.

The descriptive meaning of the statement: 'This is good', appears in the working models as: 'I approve of this'. This also is not intended to be precise, but it does give us the essence of the statement's descriptive content and also serves to bring out the peculiar character of ethical argumentation. To offer reasons for a model judgement is not to provide a proof. If I say that x is good, and bring forward as reasons for my view the fact that it possesses the characteristics p, q, and r, then my interlocutor may admit that previously he had not been aware of these reasons, and that they have succeeded in convincing him that *x* really is good. But it is also possible that he may accept my reasons as true, but still deny that *x* is good. This shows that the reasons put forward are not intended as a *proof* of the moral judgement.

> The reasons which support or attack an ethical judgment ... are related to the judgment psychologically rather than logically. [*Ethics and Language*, 113.]

It is impossible, therefore, to speak of the validity of ethical arguments, except insofar as these arguments are designed to alter beliefs.

> The notion of validity retains its accustomed application to any aspect of an ethical argument that is concerned wholly with establishing beliefs. For the steps which go beyond these, questions about validity, in any helpful sense of the term, are irrelevant. [*Ethics and Language*, 155–6.]

The question which should normally be asked about ethical arguments, therefore, is not: Are they valid?', but: 'Are they successful?'.

3. The two patterns of analysis

To regard the descriptive meaning of ethical statements as concerned solely with attitudes would, however, be a distortion. Ethical judgements, as we have seen, often depend on certain beliefs concerning the object of the judgement. Thus I consider *x* to be good because I believe it to possess the characteristics *p*, *q*, and *r*. Sometimes these beliefs are only suggested by the statement they serve to support, but they may also form part of the very meaning of the statement.

> If we should suppose, as the working models very easily lead us to suppose, that important beliefs are *never* expressed by ethical judgments themselves, . . . that they are always expressed by the sentences that present supporting reasons for the judgments—we should ignore the flexibility of common language, and hence obscure the very factor which, throughout the whole body of ethics, is most urgently in need of attention. [*Ethics and Language*, 34.]

Thus when I say that X is a good man, part of my meaning is that I approve of X, but I may also mean that he is honest, kind, and truthful, that he possesses those characteristics on which the judgement of his goodness is based. Because of the vagueness of ethical terms, however, it may be very difficult to draw a line between what an ethical statement means and what it merely suggests.

> Ethical terms are more than ambiguous: They are *vague*. Although certain factors, at any one time, are definitely included among the designata of the terms, and certain others definitely excluded, there are many others which are neither included nor excluded. No decision has been made about these, either by the speaker or by the dictionary. The limits of the undecided region are so subject to fluctuation, with varying contexts and varying purposes,

that it becomes arbitrary, so far as common
usage is concerned, to specify where one sense
of the terms leaves off and another begins.
[*Ethics and Language*, 34–5.]

To offset this lack of precision Stevenson proposes
two 'patterns of analysis'. These are intended not
as strict definitions, but as models or patterns for
constructing definitions: their purpose is to outline
the common structure underlying different uses
of ethical terms. Because of the vagueness of
descriptive meaning, two patterns are required.

> The first pattern will be simply an extension
> of the working models. . . . The vagueness of
> the ethical terms will be removed, as an illustra-
> tion of one of the possibilities, by limiting their
> descriptive reference to the speaker's own
> attitudes. All other information they may con-
> vey will be taken as merely suggested. The
> second pattern will illustrate many other pos-
> sibilities, allowing the descriptive references of
> the ethical terms to become as complicated as
> any occasion or context may require. It will let
> descriptive suggestions, as the first pattern
> would classify them, acquire the more definite
> status of descriptive meanings. Emotive mean-
> ing will enter into both patterns. [*Ethics and
> Language*, 89.]

The two patterns, then, may be set out as follows.
The first pattern is this: 'This is good' means 'I
approve of this: do so as well'. By making suitable alterations we can fit the other types of
ethical statements into the same mould, as we

have already seen in the working models. Thus, 'He ought to do this' means 'I disapprove of his leaving this undone: do so as well', and so on.

The second pattern places emphasis on the flexibility of descriptive meaning. 'This is good' means 'This has the qualities or relations x, y, z...', and *good* has as well a laudatory emotive meaning which permits it to express the speaker's approval and tends to evoke the approval of the hearer.

> The distinguishing features of the second pattern, then, lie solely in the added descriptive meaning that it provides and the complications of methodology that arise as a consequence. [*Ethics and Language*, 206.]

Stevenson has some interesting things to say about the distinction in methodology—that is, in the methods used in arguing about ethical issues—entailed by the different patterns. When moral judgements are conceived as coming under the first pattern, disputes usually take the form of adducing beliefs as supporting reasons for these judgements. When this fails, recourse must be had to persuasion, to the use of language bearing a highly charged emotive meaning. The second pattern is chiefly dependent for its methodology on what Stevenson calls 'persuasive definition'. This involves an alteration in the descriptive meaning of a word while preserving its emotive meaning unchanged. Thus a political speaker might tell his audience that the countries under communist rule are the only true democracies. Here he is making use of the emotive meaning which attaches to the term *democracy* to win his audience's favour for communist forms of government. Similar tactics may be used with ethical terms such as *justice* and *charity*. When someone tells us that *true* charity begins at home, for instance, he may be endeavouring, by a skilful use of language, to extend the emotive aura of altruism to his own selfish actions.

4. Disagreement in attitude

Stevenson has been criticised on the grounds that, while presenting a subtle version of the emotive theory, he has offered no reasons for believing it to be true. Thus A. C. Ewing writes that his book 'is no doubt a very able exposition of subjectivism for those who are already convinced, but it does not, as far as I can see, bring any real argument for it'.[1] This is not an unfair criticism, but it overlooks one point—the book may itself be considered as a sustained argument for emotivism. If Stevenson has succeeded in showing that his theory offers a plausible explanation of how we use ethical terms, how we argue on ethical issues and so on, then he has provided an argument which, if not conclusive, is at least highly convincing. To evaluate his theory, therefore, we must measure it against the facts of ethical discourse.

The first question to be asked is: Has Stevenson answered effectively Moore's argument against subjectivism? Do ethical disagreements always involve disagreement in attitude? But first we must

[1] A. C. Ewing, *The Definition of Good*, New York 1947, 6.

be clear as to what in fact 'disagreement in attitude' means. The difficulty is that, while a difference in opinion has only to be articulated to cause disagreement in belief, a *difference* in attitude is not in itself sufficient to cause *disagreement* in attitude. When one man says 'I like sugar' and another says 'I dislike sugar', there is no disagreement between them, nor is there any cause for a dispute. Clearly disagreement in attitude must entail something more than mere difference.

In his various writings on the subject, Stevenson has, I find, offered four explanations of what it involves:

[1] Two men will be said to disagree in attitude where they have opposed attitudes to the same object—one approving of it, for instance, and the other disapproving of it—and when at least one has a motive for altering or calling into question the attitude of the other. [*Ethics and Language*, 25.]

[2] A and B will be said to disagree in attitude when they have opposed attitudes to something, and when at least one of them is trying to alter the attitude of the other.[1]

[3] Disagreement in attitude occurs when Mr A has a favourable attitude to something, when Mr B has an unfavourable attitude to it, and when neither is content to let the other's attitude remain unchanged.[2]

[1] C. L. Stevenson, 'Moore's Arguments against Certain Forms of Ethical Naturalism', *The Philosophy of G. E. Moore*, ed. P. Schilpp, Evanston 1942, 82.
[2] C. L. Stevenson, 'The Nature of Ethical Disagree-

[4] The difference between the two senses of disagreement is essentially this: the first involves an opposition of beliefs, both of which cannot be true, the second involves an opposition of attitudes, both of which cannot be satisfied. ['The Nature of Ethical Disagreement', 588.]

It is significant that no two of these definitions are equivalent. Stevenson is obviously in some doubt as to what must be added to a difference in attitude to cause disagreement. Moreover, in the first three definitions his description of this second element is inadequate. For it is not sufficient to say that a difference in attitude becomes a disagreement when one has a motive for altering, or is trying to alter, the attitude of the other, or when neither is content to let the other's attitude remain unchanged.

This does not tell us why they are not content to leave each other's attitudes unchanged. You do not explain the existence of a disagreement by saying simply that there is a motive for disagreement; you must go on to explain what that motive is. Furthermore, if difference becomes disagreement only whenever it happens that there is a motive present for altering the other's attitude, why is it that differences on ethical issues, when articulated, always involve disagreement? When one man says that an action is good and another that it is not good, it never makes sense to say that they are not in disagreement. To understand

ment', *Readings in Philosophical Analysis*, ed. H. Feigl and Y. Sellers, New York 1949, 587.

disagreement in attitude, therefore, one must know what the motive for altering the other's attitude is, and why it is always present with regard to moral attitudes but not with regard to other attitudes.

In his fourth definition, Stevenson has given us a more specific description of the second element in disagreement, but unfortunately it makes little sense. Disagreement in attitude 'involves an opposition of attitudes, both of which cannot be satisfied'. But we never speak of attitudes in this fashion, for to satisfy is to fulfil a want or desire, and an attitude as such does not imply a want of any kind. How, for example, could an attitude of disapproval be satisfied? It might be suggested that it is satisfied if what is disapproved of does not occur or goes out of existence. But then, what about disapproval of something which never has occurred—a flight to the moon, for example—or of something which has already gone out of existence, such as the Spanish inquisition?

Attitudes are, of course, often accompanied by desires, and clearly this is what Stevenson has in mind when he speaks of an attitude being satisfied. By a disagreement in attitude, therefore, he must mean a difference in attitude involving incompatible desires. This is in accordance with the other definitions, for when people have incompatible desires they each have a motive for altering the attitude of the other. Let us see if this interpretation fits the various examples which Stevenson puts forward of disagreement in attitude:

Suppose that two people have decided to dine together. One suggests a restaurant where there is music: another expresses his disinclination to hear music and suggests some other restaurant. It may then happen, as we commonly put it, that they 'cannot easily agree on which restaurant to choose'. . . . Further examples are easily found. Mrs A has social aspirations, and wants to move with the elite. Mr A is easy going and loyal to his old friends. They accordingly disagree about what guests they will invite to their party. The curator of the museum wants to buy pictures by contemporary artists; some of his advisers prefer the purchase of old masters; they disagree. John's mother is concerned about the dangers of playing football, and doesn't want him to play. John, even though he agrees [in belief] about the dangers, wants to play anyhow. Again they disagree. [*Ethics and Language*, 3.]

Clearly these are all cases involving incompatible desires. If there was any other way in which disagreement in attitude could arise, Stevenson would surely have given us an example of it.

We are now in a better position to assess Stevenson's reply to Moore. His answer is, in effect, that ethical disagreement results not from disagreement in belief, but from the presence of incompatible desires. But this reply is effective only if it can be shown that ethical disagreement always involves incompatible desires, and Stevenson has not even attempted to do this. He has pointed out merely a possible way of refuting

Moore: he has provided no evidence for believing that that possibility is a fact.

Could it be shown that ethical disagreement always involves incompatible desires? To do so one would have to prove that whenever A and B disagree on a moral issue A desires x and B desires not-x, or something incompatible with x. But what does x refer to here? It cannot be the doing of the action whose morality is at issue, for we can easily conceive of an ethical dispute in which neither protagonist desires to do the action in question. Thus A and B may dispute about the morality of euthanasia without either of them wishing to engage in mercy-killing. They might dispute as to whether the revolutionaries were right to execute Louis XVI, although neither has any propensity to regicide. Besides, many ethical disputes are not about actions, but about persons.

The only alternative, then, is that x should refer to the changing of the other's attitude to bring it into line with one's own; A must wish to change B's attitude, and B wish to change A's, or to preserve his own unchanged. This will not do, however, for it provides no reason why the expression of a moral attitude should always be accompanied by the desire that everyone else should share that attitude. The fact is that differences in attitudes ordinarily leave us unmoved. Most of us are sufficiently tolerant to regard another's attitude as his own concern. It is only when his attitude begins to interfere with our own interests that we try to change it. Now many ethical disputes have no practical bearing. Two people may disagree on the morality of capital punishment even though their practical outlook on the matter is identical—they both regard it as undesirable and wish to see it abolished. If their difference is merely one of attitude, there seems to be no reason why it should always provide cause for a dispute. The issue between them, then, is surely a speculative one, involving not disagreement in attitude, but disagreement in belief.

If this is so, then conflicting moral statements do contradict each other, and to say that a person is good or an action is right is to assert something about that action or person and not merely describe one's attitude towards them.

5. Emotive meaning

Emotive meaning has a central role in Stevenson's theory, so perhaps it is not out of place to begin our examination by repeating his definition of it:

> The emotive meaning of a word is the power that the word acquires, on account of its history in emotional situations, to evoke or directly express attitudes, as distinct from describing or designating them. [*Ethics and Language*, 33.]

There are then two elements to emotive meaning —the power to express attitudes and the power to evoke them. Stevenson places far too little emphasis on this distinction, however. Not that he ignores it, but rather he tends to assume that the two are inseparable—that, in other words, whenever a term has the power to express an attitude, it also has the power to evoke it. But this is far too simple a view of the matter for, in the first place, the attitude which an emotive term tends to evoke may be entirely different from the one it tends to express. Thus a judge who addresses a criminal in abusive terms to show his contempt is not trying to arouse similar feelings in the prisoner. His words may do so, of course, but they are more likely to arouse feelings of dismay, or perhaps of resentment.

Again, there are emotive terms which have little tendency to evoke feelings of any sort. Most expletive terms are of this type. These are not usually addressed to other persons—they can be used just as effectively when the speaker is alone—which goes to show, I think, that however good they are at expressing feeling, they are not intended to arouse it.

This blurring of the distinction between the two functions of emotive terms enables Stevenson to avoid certain difficulties in accounting for the origin of emotive meaning. Both of them, he explains, derive from the previous use of the term in emotional situations. Now it is certainly plausible to suggest that the power to express emotion is derived from the fact that the term is commonly used expressively. It is true, of course, that almost any utterance will serve to express an emotion if the speaker so wills it. Still, emotion can be expressed much more effectively if the terms chosen are commonly used in an emotive fashion.

But this is not true of the power to evoke emotion. Here the intention of the speaker is not enough. No matter how much you wish to evoke an emotion, unless you select terms which already have an evocative tendency, your utterance will be quite ineffective. And this proves, I think, that a term's evocative tendency cannot be derived from its evocative use in the past, since the evocative use presupposes the possession of the evocative tendency.

Perhaps what Stevenson means is that a term's evocative power derives from the fact that it was used to express emotion in the past. If this were the case, however, terms which are generally used to express emotion should also have the power to evoke it, and this, as we have seen, is simply not true. Most characteristically expressive terms have no evocative power, and even in the case of those which have an evocative power the emotion evoked is often different from the one expressed. In fact, the terms best suited to evoking emotion are usually both emotive and descriptive. Their evocative tendency is obviously linked to their descriptive meaning; they evoke emotion because they denote something towards which people normally feel that emotion. The descriptive meaning is certainly not the only factor involved. We have merely to compare *love* with *amatory feeling* to realise that the emotional associations which Stevenson mentions, and perhaps also the verbal structure of a word, are also important. But it is the descriptive meaning which is the primary factor. Unless the person addressed actually feels the appropriate emotion towards what the term denotes, then the term's emotional associations and verbal structure are of no avail. Suppose, for example, one should try to arouse contempt for an individual by describing him as a 'nigger'. If the person addressed respects negroes, then, no matter how often he has heard the term used contemptuously in the past, the only feeling it is likely to arouse in him is dislike for the person who used it.

Now ethical terms, according to Stevenson, have both descriptive and emotive meaning. The imperative character of *good*—its tendency to evoke an attitude of approval—should, therefore, be due to the fact that it denotes something of which people normally approve. But I cannot see how this is so on Stevenson's analysis.[1] We do not regard it as in any way abnormal if people do not share our attitudes. Less still, unless we are very egocentric or very powerful, do we regard our approval of something as anything approaching a conclusive reason why other people should approve of it. We don't try to persuade people to adopt our attitude by merely describing it. Rather, we describe the *object* of our attitude—in favourable or unfavourable terms, as the occasion demands. Our words may in fact be much more persuasive if our listener believes that we ourselves are uncommitted, that our attitude towards the object in question is detached.

This point is emphasised by the comment of an American critic of Stevenson, who may not, however, realise the full implications of his remark.

[1] This criticism applies only to the first pattern of analysis. The validity of the second pattern, as we shall see from my next section, may be questioned on other grounds.

I wonder if Stevenson has considered the probable emotive influence of his own doctrine. Would not a widespread acceptance of his analysis tend to destroy the present persuasive character of ethical utterances and so leave his theory without an object?[1]

But it hardly makes sense to say that people habitually use ethical terms without knowing what they mean. Is it not rather that, if Stevenson's analysis were correct, ethical utterances would have no *persuasive* character? Clearly something has gone wrong with his working models, for either their imperative element is non-existent, or their descriptive element is incorrect.

6. The second pattern of analysis

Stevenson, as we have seen, proposes two patterns of analysis for ethical terms. In the first pattern the descriptive meaning is purely subjective; the ethical statement asserts an attitude of approval or disapproval on the part of the person making the statement. In the second pattern, 'This is good' is analysed as 'This is *x*, *y*, and *z*', where *x*, *y*, and *z* are the characteristics of the object which induce one to call it good. This gives *good* a variable meaning, since 'good-making' characteristics may change completely from one class of objects to another.

At first glance, there is something odd about having two patterns of analysis. They are

[1] Max Black, *Language and Philosophy*, New York 1950, 220.

required, according to Stevenson, because of the vagueness of ethical terms. But if the two patterns are justified, then ethical terms are not merely vague—they are, in the second pattern at least, highly ambiguous. If *good*, when applied, say, to men and to motor-cars, is to be understood according to those characteristics of the objects which induce one to call them good, then the term is equivocal.

It should be noted, too, that the second pattern of analysis cannot be applied to such terms as *ought*, *duty*, *right*, and *wrong*. There are so many different reasons why an action is right, or wrong, or is a duty, or ought to be done, that the ascription of these terms rarely suggests the characteristics of the action which induced us to call it right or wrong, etc. In fact, it is difficult to think of any ethical term which could plausibly be analysed in terms of the second pattern. Expressions of the type 'X is a good man' seem the best suited. But even here, seeing the multiplicity of characteristics which might impel one to call a person good, the applicability of the second-pattern analysis seems doubtful. It is the non-ethical use of value terms, *good* and *bad* in particular, which gives most scope for the second pattern. If I call a car 'good', for instance, then it may be assumed that I believe it to be well-sprung, economical to run, mechanically reliable, and so on, and one could perhaps analyse *good* in this context in terms of these characteristics.

It seems to me, however, that this is an error, and that the meaning of *good* should never be confused with the criteria of goodness. Consider the sentence: 'I like that car'. This, when said by a person who is very set in his likes and dislikes, may suggest—just as strongly as his calling the car 'good'—that it possesses the characteristics noted above. But is it at all plausible to hold that *like* in this instance *means* 'possessing the characteristics *x*, *y*, and *z*'? *Like* is a reasonably precise term, and certainly not subject to the violent fluctuations of meaning which it would have on this analysis.

Again, compare the terms *good* and *small*. They are alike in this, that the criteria for calling something good or small vary greatly from one class of object to another, and when the criteria for a particular class are more or less determined, then to say that an object of that class is good or small suggests that it possesses this particular set of characteristics. But does *small* ever *mean* a particular set of dimensions? Surely not. It means simply a certain relation between the dimensions of an object and the standard dimensions of all objects of the same type. To think that it radically changes its *meaning* from one class of objects to another is to confuse one of the terms of the relation with the relation itself. It is as if a person who was told that Paris is to the east thought that 'being to the east' was a characteristic of Paris, and that it would still be to the east even if he was in Berlin.

Stevenson has made the same error with regard to *goodness*. What the second pattern deals with is not different meanings of the term, but instances of its application to different classes of objects— instances in which the terms between which the relation holds are different. It is not, as he suggests, because ethical terms are vague that he finds it necessary to put forward two patterns of analysis, but because he misunderstands the form of their signification.

4
A last look
at the
emotive theory

1. Prescriptive emotivism

We have been working, so far, on the hypothesis
that the problem with which the emotive theory is
concerned is the actual meaning of ethical statements, the meaning possessed by these statements
in ordinary usage. That this is the correct interpretation of the emotive theory of *Ethics and
Language* and of *Language, Truth and Logic*
seems to me unquestionable.[1] However, there is

[1] It is quite clear from *Ethics and Language* and the
part of *Language, Truth and Logic* which deals with
ethics that the purpose of their authors is to explain
how ethical terms are actually used. If their purpose
was merely to redefine ethical terms, then—quite apart
from the fact that they would surely have mentioned
this in the course of their writings—their work would
have had an entirely different character. Moreover,
several passages may be quoted in which Ayer and
Stevenson declare their intentions quite explicitly. Here
are two examples: *Language, Truth and Logic*, 105:
'We reject utilitarianism and subjectivism, not as pro-
posals to replace our existing ethical notions by new

evidence that emotivism is now looked on in a different light; it has come to be regarded as *prescriptive* rather than as *descriptive*, as laying down what ethical terms ought to mean rather than what they actually do mean.

This development is one which might have been anticipated. In ordinary discourse we often hear such remarks as 'I *believe* that suicide is wrong' and 'It is not *true* that lying is always wrong'. Any version of emotivism would find it difficult to explain the point of such remarks. On Ayer's version, they are entirely incomprehensible, since an expression of feeling is not something of which truth or falsity can be predicated, nor likewise can it be the object of belief. On Stevenson's theory, an explanation can be offered for the second remark: one might use it, for instance, to rebut the accusation that one would never approve of lying no matter what the circumstances. What Stevenson's theory cannot explain, however, is the fact that in ordinary discourse this remark is almost always used to counter the statement: 'Lying is always wrong'. For if, as he holds, the two remarks are not contradictory, then the second does not deny the truth of the first. As for the first remark, one has merely to translate it in

_____

ones, but as analyses of our existing ethical notions.' If Ayer's own purpose was to replace existing ethical notions by new ones, he could not have rejected utilitarianism and subjectivism on those grounds.

Ethics and Language, I: 'This book deals not with the whole of ethics, but with a narrowly specialised part of it. Its first object is to clarify the meaning of ethical terms.' One obviously does not clarify the meaning of ethical terms by simply redefining them.

accordance with Stevenson's pattern of analysis to recognise the difficulty. 'I believe that I believe in suicide' may not be an absurd remark, but it is certainly extremely odd, and this oddness would be unaccountable if Stevenson's account of moral judgement were correct.

It follows from all this that, if emotivism is descriptive as regards ethical terms, then it must be prescriptive as regards such terms as *belief* and *truth*. How much more straightforward to regard it as prescriptive from the beginning, as laying down not what ethical statements are intended to convey, but what they ought to be understood as conveying.

In a letter, part of which was published in *Mind* in 1961, we find Stevenson writing as follows:

> I think there is no doubt whatsoever that my two patterns of analysis in *Ethics and Language* do not give an account of what ordinary people *normally mean* when they use the ethical terms. The Arne Naess followers (who so often write in the little Swedish journal, *Theoria*) always talk as though analysis of meaning has as its proper aim just that—to reveal conventional meanings. And Moore used to talk that way too. But such an approach is a little foolish, in my opinion, in ignoring the fact (or at least, what appears to me to be a fact) that common usage is confused. I see no point in triangulating the current state of confusion. So what I was really attempting to do (my references to 'linguistic flexibility' being intended to point

out the need of doing it) was not to give just
what people have meant, but only to 'salvage'
from their meaning all that I, viewing the situation from an empirical viewpoint, could find
intelligible . . .

Thus, with some reservations, I am inclined
to think of *Ethics and Language* as a 'deliberately prescriptive proposal'.[1]

Unfortunately, this statement leaves several questions unanswered. It fails to make clear, in the
first place, the relation between Stevenson's
analysis and the actual meaning of ethical terms.
What he seems to be asserting is that his analysis
covers only part of what they mean. But this is
ambiguous, for it could be interpreted as saying
either that his analysis expresses an intelligible
core which is common to all uses of ethical terms,
or that it expresses one of the ways—the only one
which makes sense—in which these terms are
used.

Again, it is not clear in what sense he speaks of
common usage as 'confused'. Ordinarily, when
we speak of the use of a term as 'confused', we
mean that the speaker is unconsciously using the
term in two different senses. Here common usage
is the standard; a particular use of a term is regarded as confused if it combines two senses which
in common usage are kept distinct. But what
standard are you appealing to if you assert that
common usage is itself confused?

To answer these questions we must, I think,
interpret Stevenson's remarks in the light of an

[1] C. L. Stevenson, 'Letter', *Mind* LXX, 277 (1961), 95–6.

article on emotivism by Richard Robinson which was published in 1948.[1] Ethical judgements, according to Robinson, have a two-fold aspect: they are descriptive in that they attribute a certain quality to an action or object, and they are emotive in that they express the attitude of the speaker towards this object and evoke a similar attitude from the hearer. The descriptive meaning, however, is based on an error, since the quality which is attributed by ethical statements does not in fact exist.

> The descriptive function of ethical words is more or less as elucidated by Sir David Ross in *The Right and the Good*. That is to say, they name unanalysable qualities belonging to certain acts or objects in complete independence of all human feelings and thoughts. In this descriptive use the ethical words involve an error, because nothing has such an unanalysable independent attribute as they name. ['The Emotive Theory of Ethics', 83.]

Robinson's view is that the descriptive meaning of ethical statements should be discarded, but the emotive meaning retained. We should henceforth regard the statement '*x* is good' as expressing and evoking a favourable attitude towards *x*, but not as saying anything about it.

Stevenson seems to be saying something very like this in the remarks quoted above. Possibly he would not be so clear-cut in his explanation of

[1] Richard Robinson, 'The Emotive Theory of Ethics', *Proceedings of the Aristotelian Society*, supplementary volume XXII (1948), 79–101.

the actual meaning of ethical statements. He does, however, regard their actual meaning as in some way empirically unintelligible, and this suggests strongly the theory of the 'unanalysable independent attribute' of Sir David Ross.

To justify this version of emotivism would be an extremely complicated task. It would have to be shown: first, that ethical terms, in their ordinary use, name unanalysable, independent attributes; secondly, that no such attributes exist; and thirdly, that ethical terms should not be discarded completely, but should be regarded henceforth as purely emotive symbols.

Each step of the argument seems to me to be confronted with serious difficulties, and none has, in fact, been seriously attempted by the emotivists. It might be thought that for the first stage of the argument the emotivists could appeal to the writings of the intuitionists, since the theory in question has been borrowed from there. But this is not so. The intuitionist theory of moral judgement is based on Moore's refutation of naturalism, and according to the emotivists themselves this proves only that ethical terms have a meaning which is, in part at least, emotive.

Indeed the facts of ethical discourse seem to provide a conclusive argument against the theory that ethical terms denote unanalysable attributes. Ethical judgements are based upon reasons. We say that a man is good because he possesses certain qualities, that an action is right because it is of a certain type or because it will produce certain results. Now if ethical terms denote unanalysable attributes, the relation between these reasons and the judgement of goodness or rightness must be contingent. For if it is necessary, then—short of a theory of synthetic a-priori connections between judgements—it must be analytic, and the connection between 'X is *a*' and 'X is good' clearly cannot be analytic if *good* is unanalysable. Now if the connection between the reasons for holding that something is good, and the judgement that it is good, is contingent, we must be able to recognise the goodness of an object apart altogether from having any reasons for holding that it is good (just as the connection between heat and the expansion of mercury could never be discovered if we had no way of recognising the presence of heat without the use of a thermometer). But this is obviously not the case. The only way to decide whether a man is good or bad is to consider what sort of man he is. This holds true whether we are speaking in a moral or in a non-moral context. The goodness of an object, unlike a genuinely unanalysable attribute, cannot be judged independently of its other qualities. There is, therefore, a logical, and not merely a contingent, connection between a thing's goodness and its possession of certain other characteristics. And it is incorrect to say that goodness is a simple quality, or that ethical terms denote unanalysable attributes.

But even if we ignore this argument and assume, for the moment, that ethical terms do name unanalysable attributes, how could it be shown that such attributes do not exist? The most that one could say is that there is no evidence for their existence. This might be sufficient were it not for the universal belief in their existence. Everyman may be unaware of the intuitionist theory of ethics, but he does believe that things really are good and bad in the ordinary sense of these terms. If the newer version of emotivism is correct, then this belief is mistaken. To hold that *good* and *right* denote certain qualities which do not in fact exist, is to hold that nothing is ever really good or bad, no action ever really right or wrong. No reasonable person could, I think, seriously propose such views, and the emotivists would certainly declare that they are not denying these tenets of common sense but merely reinterpreting them. I do not see, however, how this clears them of the charge of absurdity. Any statement can be made to be true by redefining its terms. The absurdity here arises from the denial that anything is ever good or bad, any action ever right or wrong, as these terms are understood in ordinary speech—which is what the newer emotivism is in fact doing.

The final stage in the argument—the attempt to show that ethical terms, despite their misleading character, ought to be retained—though less important, seems to me to be no less difficult than the others. If ethical terms are essentially misleading, why should they not be discarded? Would not that be the obvious way of dispelling the idea that there are objective ethical properties? The task of expressing our feelings and attitudes could be safely left to non-ethical language.

2. The emotive theory and the status of ethics
This insistence on the retention of ethical language

is obviously associated with the emotivists' contention that their theory does not destroy ethics or lower its status in any way. Emotivism, they claim, is morally neutral. It has no bearing on traditional moral standards. The questions it discusses are those of meta-ethics, not of ethics proper. The emotive theory, according to Ayer,

> ... is entirely on the level of analysis; it is an attempt to show what people are doing when they make moral judgements; it is not a set of suggestions as to what moral judgements they ought to make. ['On the Analysis of Moral Judgements', 245–6.]

Stevenson, in his Preface to *Ethics and Language*, expresses the hope that his theory has shown that

> empiricism, so often criticized as distorting ethics, can in fact give it a place whose importance is beyond question. [*Ethics and Language*, vii.]

I am not at all clear, however, how his theory could be said to show this. Ethics, on his view, refers simply to certain terms which we use for expressing our feelings and attitudes and for persuading others to adopt similar attitudes. It is no doubt an important question as to what attitudes we adopt or persuade others to adopt, but is it an ethical one? We can also express our attitudes or persuade others by means of non-ethical terms. Ethics seems to refer merely to a special, and indeed misleading, terminology, and I do not see why particular importance should be attached to it.

Stevenson might perhaps claim, though he does not do so in his writings, that there are specifically *moral* attitudes which are distinct from non-moral ones. But even if we grant their existence, how could it be shown that such attitudes are of special importance? On his theory there does not seem to be any foundation for the idea that they take precedence over non-moral ones.

Ayer is more concerned with showing that the adoption of emotivism is unlikely to have a detrimental effect on people's morals.

> Does not the promulgation of such a theory encourage moral laxity? Has not its effect been to destroy people's confidence in accepted moral standards? And will not the result be that something mischievous will take their place? Such charges have indeed been made, but I do not know upon what evidence. The question how people's conduct is actually affected by their acceptance of a meta-ethical theory is one for empirical investigation; and in this case, so far as I am aware, no serious investigation has yet been carried out. ['On the Analysis of Moral Judgements', 248–9.]

This seems to me to be peculiarly naïve. It hardly requires empirical investigation to realise that people who adopt the view that moral judgements are merely expressions of feeling will not be greatly influenced by ethical considerations in their daily life. In fact it is not even clear what it would mean for them to be influenced by ethical considerations. It can hardly mean being influenced by their feelings simply, and the only alternative seems to be that it would mean being influenced by the persuasive character of moral language. But this is an unlikely occurrence, for in the case of one's own moral judgements one already possesses the feelings which they allegedly express, and another's moral judgements would have little impact on one who regards them as mere expressions of feeling.

The charges against which Ayer defends the emotive theory are ones which could have no real meaning for the emotivist. 'Moral laxity' refers, in ordinary usage, to the habit of allowing one's feelings and desires to overrule one's moral judgements when one is choosing a course of action. But if moral judgements are themselves expressions of feeling, then it is impossible to see how this could ever occur. Again, what could it mean to say that emotivism had destroyed people's confidence in accepted moral standards? Such standards are, in emotivist terms, mere expressions of feeling. One may share these feelings or not, but in neither case is there question of having confidence in them. This terminology is clearly a relic of objectivism in ethics, according to which to have confidence in a moral standard is to hold that what it lays down as right really is right. The emotive theory would no doubt destroy that sort of confidence, but that is not one of the things which a convinced emotivist like Ayer would lay to its charge.

3. The emotive character of ethical terms

To reject the emotive theory is not, of course, to answer the question: Do ethical terms have an emotive content? We have found, I believe, conclusive reasons for believing that they are not entirely, nor even primarily, emotive, but the question remains: Are ethical statements partially emotive, or are they rather exclusively factual, in character?

The main argument for the partially emotive character of ethical terms is an adaptation by Stevenson of Moore's refutation of naturalism:

> The central contention of Moore's ethics can be presented in a sentence: 'Propositions about the good are all of them synthetic'. In other words, given *any* ethical judgement of the form 'N is good', where 'N' stands for a naturalistic term and 'good' is used in any typical sense, the judgement will never be analytic ... Although the present account permits 'N is good' to be analytic, it does not therefore declare it trivial, or urge that it should provoke no opposition. An ethical predicate (as we have repeatedly seen) does not merely reiterate the subject, but adds an emotive meaning. Moore has intellectualized this emotive meaning into an indefinable quality; but at least he recognizes an added factor which the purely scientific analyses of ethics are accustomed to ignore. [*Ethics and Language*, 271–2.]

This transforms Moore's refutation of naturalism into an argument for emotivism, for if *good* is descriptive but does not denote something simple, then it seems that its indefinability must be due to the fact that it also has a non-descriptive function. The argument loses much of its appeal, however, when we apply it to particular cases. In English, *papist* and *nigger* are almost invariably terms of opprobrium, that is to say, while having the same descriptive content as *Roman catholic* and *negro* respectively, they are distinguished from these by the fact that they also express the disapproval of the speaker. Despite this, however, the statements: 'A papist is a Roman catholic', or: 'A nigger is a dark-skinned person', are undeniably trivial; they convey no information to anyone who understands English. To put this in Moore's terminology, it cannot be asked with significance whether a papist is a Roman catholic or a nigger is a dark-skinned individual. This test may be made for any emotive term which possesses a non-emotive synonym, and the result will, I believe, in all cases be the same. The refutation of naturalism, therefore, whatever its real significance, cannot be adduced as proof for the emotive character of ethical terms.

A second argument for the emotive character of ethical terms has been based on the fact that it makes no sense to say: 'This is good, but I disapprove of it', or: 'This is wrong, but I approve of it'. This, it has been claimed, shows that *good* and *wrong* express approval and disapproval respectively, and so have an emotive content. This argument would be valid if 'I approve' or 'I disapprove' were invariably expressions of feeling, but this, so far as I can see, is false. When a minister of state affixes his stamp of approval to a written proposal, we would not normally say that he is thereby expressing his feelings or asserting that he had a particular feeling. To approve is sometimes equivalent to making a choice, sometimes to adopting an attitude. No doubt certain feelings could accompany these actions, but there seems to be no necessary connection between the two. 'I play golf on Saturdays, though I don't approve of it' is about as nonsensical as 'This is good though I don't approve of it', yet no one is likely to suggest that 'I play golf on Saturdays' involves an expression of feeling.

These two arguments are obviously inconclusive, but this would not lead us to conclude that ethical terms are devoid of all emotive content. Some non-ethical uses of *good*, such as: 'Good!', or: 'That's good!', when said as an exclamation, are simply expressions of feeling, and it would be odd if this emotive character were to disappear completely in other uses of the term. What I wish to argue, however, is that, if moral judgements are principally descriptive, then their emotive character is of little or no importance for moral philosophy. For, in the first place, our understanding of moral terms will depend entirely on our grasp of their descriptive meaning. This is clear from an example. The term *God* would normally be regarded as having a certain emotive character since it expresses, on the part of the believer at least, feelings of respect and reverence. Yet to understand the term one must concentrate on its descriptive content; once this is grasped, the reason why it possesses certain emotive overtones is also evident. The same is true of similar terms, including ethical ones. Once we understand their descriptive content, it should be immediately obvious why this emotive character attaches to them, and further enquiry into the latter becomes superfluous.

Secondly, the emotive content of ethical terms can have no bearing on the truth or falsity of moral judgements. Purely emotive expressions are neither true nor false, and one need take no account of the emotive character of factual statements when their truth or falsity is being considered.

Thirdly, emotive content cannot, as we have seen in the chapter on Stevenson, explain the peculiar practical character of moral judgements. The chief difficulty in the moral life is the frequency with which our moral judgements conflict with our feelings. This would not be the case if their practical character was based on their emotive content.

The emotive theory rightly underlines the practical nature of moral judgement. This is something which had been overlooked by the intuitionist theories, and the emotivists did well to emphasise it. Where they went wrong was in drawing an absolute distinction between factual judgements and practical ones. Practical judgements are practical *because* of what they assert, and not because they do not assert anything.

5
Interlude:
A new approach
to meaning and
language

In 1955 Geoffrey Warnock, a leading Oxford philosopher, wrote: 'I am not, nor is any philosopher of my acquaintance, a logical positivist'.[1] But if Warnock and his colleagues were no longer positivists, neither were they, in the traditional sense of the term, metaphysicians. The aspect of logical positivism which had come to be rejected was not so much its positivism as its views on language. Logical positivism had inherited from logical atomism the theory that, the function of language being to describe reality, all meaningful utterances can be broken down into atomic statements whose terms denote simple elements of reality. This is the view which was put forward by Wittgenstein in the *Tractatus*. Its subsequent disappearance was due mainly to the work of Wittgenstein himself. His later thought was not published until after his death in 1951, but it had exercised a growing influence since the nineteen-

[1] G. Warnock, 'Analysis and Imagination', *The Revolution in Philosophy*, ed. G. Ryle, 124.

thirties through his lectures at Cambridge and the circulation of private manuscripts.

Wittgenstein did not reject his old ideas completely. They were unsatisfactory, he held, not because they were false, but because they were one-sided and incomplete. Language *does* have the function of describing, but it has many other functions as well; words *do* sometimes acquire their meaning from what they denote, but there are numerous other forms of meaning. What Wittgenstein is above all concerned to show is the *complexity* of language. He is not concerned with laying down what language is: rather, he shows us language at work. Philosophers have been obsessed with the idea that, because everything which comes under the heading of language has a common name, it must also have a common nature. Wittgenstein's advice is: 'Don't think, but look'.

> Consider for example the proceedings that we call 'games'. I mean board-games, card-games, Olympic games, and so on. What is common to all?—Don't say: 'There *must* be something common, or they would not be called "games"' —but *look and see* whether there is anything common to all.—For if you look at them you will not see something that is common to all, but similarities, relationships, and a whole series of them at that . . . I can think of no better expression to characterize these similarities than 'family resemblances'; for the various resemblances between members of a family: build, features, colour of eyes, gait, tempera-

ment, etc. etc. overlap and criss-cross in the same way.—And I shall say: 'games' form a family.[1]

The various activities which are called language cannot be brought under any one definition. To say that language is descriptive would be equivalent to saying that games are played between two sets of teams using a ball. Language is an activity, but it has as many different purposes and methods as any basic human activity. To understand it, we must simply recognise its complexity.

At one point Wittgenstein makes a list—not, of course, intended as complete—of different kinds of uses to which language is put. (*Philosophical Investigations*, para. 23.) Here are some sample entries:

Giving orders and obeying them—
Reporting an event—
Making up a story: and reading it—
Play-acting—
Translating from one language into another—

These differing forms of linguistic activity Wittgenstein styles 'language games'. Like games, they have the same sort of criss-cross relationship to each other as have the members of a family. Like games, each also has its own peculiar set of rules. To understand a particular utterance we must look on it as a move in a language game. A move in language, like a move in chess, is incomprehensible to one who is ignorant of the

[1] L. Wittgenstein, *Philosophical Investigations*, Oxford 1953, para. 66.

purpose of the game or the rules according to which it is played.

Philosophers, according to Wittgenstein, have failed to appreciate the multiplicity of language games contained in ordinary speech. They have tended to apply the one set of rules to every type of utterance. Thus the logical positivists, in setting up the principle of verification as a general criterion of meaning, tried to give universal validity to rules which apply only to scientific language. The logical atomists, including Wittgenstein himself in his earlier writings, took mathematics as their model. They assumed that mathematics, because it has perfectly clear concepts and forms of reasoning, is the ideal language; ordinary language fulfils its function properly only in so far as it acquires the form of a precise calculus. But this is to overlook the different functions of language.

> In philosophy we often *compare* the use of words with games and calculi which have fixed rules but cannot say that someone who is using language must be playing such a game.—But if you say that our languages only approximate to such calculi you are on the brink of a misunderstanding. For then it may look as if what we were talking about were an *ideal* language. As if our logic were, so to speak, a logic for a vacuum.—Whereas logic does not treat of language—or of thought—in the sense in which a natural science treats of a natural phenomenon, and the most that can be said is that we *construct* ideal languages. . .

Every sentence in our language 'is in order as it is'. That is to say, we are not *striving after* an ideal, as if our ordinary vague sentences had not yet got a quite unexceptionable sense, and a perfect language awaited construction by us. [*Philosophical Investigations*, paras. 81 and 98.]

Our everyday language 'is in order as it is'. It is only when philosophers misinterpret the forms of language that difficulties arise. This is particularly true of the language which describes our mental activities and inner experience. The language itself is unexceptionable; it is philosophers' interpretations of it which have caused trouble. Thus the terms *knowing* and *understanding* have been interpreted as referring either to mental acts or to states of mind. But this is not how the terms are used in ordinary language. When we say that an individual knows or understands something, we do not mean that he is engaged in a certain mental process or having a particular mental experience. The statement is no less true when his mind is on something completely different: it remains true when he is asleep. Getting to know or understand something is more like acquiring a skill than performing a mental activity or having an experience.

The grammar of the word 'knows' is closely related to that of 'can', 'is able to'. But also closely related to that of 'understands' ('Mastery' of a technique). [*Philosophical Investigations*, para. 150.]

And this throws considerable light on the concept of meaning. Because we say in ordinary language that an expression or word *has* a meaning, we come to think of the meaning as a thing of the same kind as the word, though also different from the word. 'Here the word, there the meaning. The money and the cow that you can buy with it.' (*Philosophical Investigations*, para. 120.) But, then, what is the meaning? Is it what the word names? But what do universal terms name? Platonic idealists thought that they name universal ideas, while logical atomists believed that they are complex terms which can be analysed completely into singular terms. The most popular answer, however, was that they name mental concepts. Meaning is, therefore, the inner process which accompanies the utterance of words.

Against this Wittgenstein points out that the criterion whether one knows the meaning of a word is not whether one has a particular inner experience when the word is uttered, but simply whether one is able to use the word correctly. In ruling out inner experience here, as elsewhere, Wittgenstein is not advocating behaviourism. He does not deny the occurrence of inner experiences which are inaccessible to others. The use of a particular term may, in fact, be always accompanied by a certain visual image; when we learn to understand something we may have some kind of 'inner feeling' of comprehension. What he does deny is the *relevance* of these experiences. The feeling of comprehension can occur, and yet it may turn out later that we have not really understood after all. When a person uses a word correctly, we know at once that he understands what it means; we do not need to enquire whether he had a particular experience which accompanied the use of the term. This shows that word and meaning are not two distinct entities, as we are inclined to suppose. A word is like a tool. To know what it means is to know how to use it: to learn its meaning is to acquire a skill, not to acquire an item of knowledge.

> For a large class of cases—though not for all—in which we employ the word 'meaning' it can be defined thus: the meaning of a term is its use in language. [*Philosophical Investigations*, para. 43.]

Philosophy, for Wittgenstein, consists in showing how certain terms—the terms which are at the centre of philosophical discussions—are used in the language game which is their original home. 'A philosophical problem has the form "I don't know my way about".' (*Philosophical Investigations*, para. 123.) You can conceive of someone saying this in a town where all the streets are known to him. What he wants is not a new item of knowledge, but a means of getting the knowledge he already possesses in proper perspective. The same is true of philosophy. We already possess all the knowledge we require to solve its problems. The difficulty is that 'we do not *command a clear view* of the use of our words.—Our grammar is lacking in this sort of perspicuity' (*Philosophical Investigations*, para. 122).

There is, then, no knowledge peculiar to philosophy; there are no philosophical facts. The function of philosophy is not to offer anything in the way of explanation or deduction, but merely to describe the manner in which philosophical terms are used in ordinary speech.

We may not advance any kind of theory. There must not be anything hypothetical in our considerations. We must do away with all *explanation*, and description alone must take its place. And this description gets its light, that is to say its purpose, from the philosophical problems. These are, of course, not empirical problems; they are solved, rather, by looking into the workings of our language, and in such a way as to make us recognize those workings: *in despite of* an urge to misunderstand them. The problems are solved, not by giving new information, but by arranging what we have always known. Philosophy is a battle against the bewitchment of our intelligence by means of language. [*Philosophical Investigations*, para. 109.]

It is not difficult to visualise the effect of this doctrine on moral philosophy. If everyday language is in order as it is, there is no point in asking whether moral language is meaningful, or whether it is based on a confusion and needs to be redefined. The task of moral philosophy is to *investigate* everyday moral discourse, rather than to cast doubt on its validity. Moral philosophers are henceforth far more sensitive to the charge that their theories are incompatible with ordinary language. Traditional moral theories are no longer rejected out of hand. They are held to be, not so much inaccurate, as radically incomplete. In defining moral terms, they have concentrated on one aspect of moral language to the detriment of others. What we must ask is, not how moral terms are to be defined, but how the part which they play in human discourse is to be characterised. The character of moral language is much too complex to be encompassed within the bounds of simple definitions. Instead we must try to describe the way in which moral terms function in the language game to which they belong.

As it happens, the theories of moral judgement which were evolved under the influence of the later philosophy of Wittgenstein may conveniently be divided into two classes. The first is characterised by the belief that moral judgements, in their primary function at least, do not assert anything, do not express genuine propositions. The only way to explain moral judgements, therefore, is by describing their function in ordinary language. This line of thought is represented by three Oxford moralists: J. O. Urmson, R. M. Hare, and P. H. Nowell-Smith. The second class differs from the first in holding that moral judgements *do* express genuine propositions. To say that something is good, or that one ought to do a certain action, is not, however, according to this view, to attribute a property, in any sense of the term, to that object or action. What we are saying rather is that we have good reasons for approving of that object or doing that action. This 'good reason' approach is here represented by Stephen Toulmin and Kurt Baier.

I do not wish to place too much emphasis on this classification. It would be wrong to suppose that both classes do not have a great deal in common, or that within each class there are not considerable differences of opinion. The classification is useful, however, from the point of view of exposition and criticism, and is unlikely, provided these reservations are kept in mind, to produce any misunderstanding.

Part 2

The function of ethical statements

6
J. O. Urmson

1. Grading

In this second part of my book I propose to examine the three most notable attempts to explain ethical statements in terms of what they do rather than in terms of what they say or express. The first of these is contained in an article by J. O. Urmson which was first published in 1950.[1] Urmson excludes such terms as *right* and *wrong* from the scope of his article. ('On Grading', 186.) He is concerned only with what are known as 'value terms'. The key to an understanding of these, he claims, is to be found in the process of grading. Consider, for example, the manner in which apples are graded. Apples being prepared for the market are normally arranged in different classes according to quality. In England, under Ministry of Agriculture regulations, marketable apples are divided into three classes, named, in

[1] J. O. Urmson, 'On Grading', *Mind* LIX (1950); reprinted in *Logic and Language* II, ed. Antony Flew, Oxford 1953, 159–86.

descending order of merit, 'Super', 'Extra Fancy', and 'Fancy'. For each of these classes there are detailed and rather specific criteria of shape, size, maturity, etc.

Value terms, according to Urmson, have essentially the same function as *Super, Extra Fancy,* and *Fancy,* that is to say, they are grading labels. Of course, almost any term may be used as a grading label if one so wishes. Thus essays or answer papers are often marked 'A', 'B', 'C', or 'X', 'Y', 'Z', and they could as easily be marked 'red', 'white', and 'green' if the order of these terms had been decided beforehand. However, one must distinguish between 'professional grading terms' and terms which may be used occasionally for grading but are normally used otherwise. Professional grading terms are used exclusively, or almost exclusively, for grading. And it is to this class that value terms belong. When we call something 'good', we place it in the class which comes between the classes labelled 'excellent' and 'very good' on the one hand, and those labelled 'indifferent' and 'bad' on the other. When we call someone 'brave', we place him in the class which comes between the class labelled 'rash' and 'cowardly'.[1]

Now the first thing to be noted about grading labels is that they are not descriptive terms. The statement: 'This is an Extra Fancy apple', is not intended to supply information. Its purpose is rather to place the apple, mentally at least, in the

[1] Urmson seems to have overlooked the fact that bravery does not come between rashness and cowardice when these qualities are arranged in order of merit.

class entitled 'Extra Fancy'. To be labelled 'Extra Fancy' an apple must, of course, be of a certain shape, size, maturity, etc., but the term *Extra Fancy* does not mean 'possessing these characteristics'. This is clear from the fact that one may learn to carry out the physical process of grading successfully, yet remain unaware of the significance of what one is doing. There is an obvious distinction between this purely physical grading and the activity of one who knowingly grades the apples in order of merit. But if we were to identify the meaning of a grading label with the criteria for its application, this distinction would be non-existent. And this is evidently false.

This means that we must reject any form of ethical naturalism. The term *good* does not mean the qualities which an object must possess in order to be called good any more than *Super* means the qualities of shape, size, etc., which an apple must possess to be called 'Super'. Non-naturalist or intuitionist ethical theories can be deflated in a similar manner. For while it may be plausible to suggest that goodness is a non-naturalist attribute distinct from the natural criteria for calling something 'good', it obviously makes no sense to suggest that there is present in apples of a certain type a non-natural attribute of superness or extra-fanciness. The emotive theory does indeed underline the non-descriptive character of grading labels, but it has nothing to add on the positive side, for, clearly, it will not do to regard 'This is an Extra Fancy consignment of apples' as a squeal of delight.

But all these three views, naturalism, intuition-ism and the emotive theory, have seized on some points of importance ... Naturalism rightly emphasizes the close connection between the grading label and the set of natural characters which justify its use; intuitionism rightly empha-sizes that this close connection is not identity of meaning and insists on the different character of grading labels and natural descriptions. Both rightly stress the objective character of grading. The emotive theory, agreeing with intuitionism about the fault of naturalism, rightly stresses that the intuitionist cure of suggesting that grading labels are a special kind of non-natural descriptive adjectives will not do. ['On Grad-ing', 171.]

What Urmson wishes especially to emphasise is that grading is, in the terminology of Wittgenstein, a separate language game. It can be illuminatingly compared to other language games, but to forget that these are merely comparisons, to define grad-ing in terms of other language games, is inevitably to distort it.

We must say firmly ... that to describe is to describe, to grade is to grade, and to express one's feelings is to express one's feelings, and that none of these is reducible to either of the others; nor can any of them be reduced to, defined in terms of, anything else. We can merely bring out similarities and differences by examples and comparisons. ['On Grading', 171.]

But if grading terms are not descriptive and their meaning and criteria of application are distinct, how are these criteria arrived at in the first place? Urmson's reply is that the problem of what are the accepted criteria for any particular grading label is quite different from the problem of why we accept these criteria. This point has hitherto often been overlooked, with the result that many ethical theories begin to make sense only when we stop looking at them as explanations of grading criteria and regard them instead as explanations of why we accept and employ such criteria. Thus subjectivism makes no sense when taken to mean that there are no objective grading criteria: but as an explanation of how grading criteria are arrived at for certain types of objects, it is a very formidable theory indeed. Cheese, for instance, accords with the tastes of the majority when it has the characteristics a, b, and c; these, as a result, have become the accepted criteria for grading cheese, even for those who do not share the majority's tastes. A similar case can be made—over a more limited range of objects—for the utilitarian and social theories of goodness. There are, in fact, all sorts of different reasons why grading criteria come to be accepted: no catalogue of them could hope to be complete. The main thing is that there is usually general agreement on criteria, though the means of reaching it are often diverse, and without such agreement reasoned discussion on values would be impossible.

2. Are grading labels non-descriptive?
How are we to look on this attempt to explain value judgements in terms of grading? It may perhaps be worth noting, first of all, that through-

out the essay Urmson uses the term *grading* in a somewhat restricted sense. By *grading* we often mean simply *classifying*. In this sense, we can grade objects in all sorts of ways—according to size, shape, colour, and so on. Indeed, any predicate can be looked on as a professional grading label. For to call something x is to place it in the class of objects which are x, as opposed to the class of objects which are not-x. But to characterise evaluation in this wide sense obviously throws no light on the nature of value judgement, and if every predicate is a professional grading label, it is absurd to suggest that professional grading labels are non-descriptive. What Urmson does is to see *grading* in the narrower, but legitimate, sense of 'classifying according to merit'. This is clear from such incidental remarks as: 'I use "grade" rather than "evaluate", for example, largely because "evaluate" tends to be associated with a special kind of theory' ('On Grading', 185); and 'They [i.e, certain value terms] can be recognised as grading labels in that they show order of merit' ('On Grading', 164); and also from his denial that one who arranges apples without being aware that he is arranging in order of merit can properly be said to be grading.

Urmson's theory, then, is composed of two elements:

1. The function of value judgements is to grade or arrange in order of merit.
2. Value terms (i.e, grading labels) are non-descriptive.

The second element is not merely an addendum.

If value terms *are* descriptive, to say that their function is to grade no more provides an explanation of value than the statement: '*Red*, *green*, and *blue* are labels used for classifying surfaces', provides an explanation of colour.

The case for the non-descriptive character of grading labels is based primarily on the distinction which Urmson draws between grading and mere classifying. Ordinary class labels are descriptive. Grading must therefore differ radically from mere classifying for grading labels to be non-descriptive.

To substantiate this distinction Urmson considers the possibility of a person learning to grade correctly by watching others at work, yet remaining unaware of the full significance of what he is doing.

Without further information our intelligent apprentice, although he would have learnt to grade the apples, or sleepers, in the sense in which a parrot can learn to speak English, might realize no more than the parrot that he was grading. He might not guess but that he was playing some rather tedious game or tidying up or assisting in some scientific classification ...

One moral of this is quite obvious; grading, like speaking English in the sense in which parrots cannot speak English, or lying or committing murder, is something which you cannot in the full sense do without understanding what you are doing. The other moral, equally obvious, is that grading is quite different from tidying up or scientific classification, but the difference lies in the purpose of the grader, not in its external form. ['On Grading', 160–1.]

This sounds plausible at first sight. When we classify objects according to, say, colour, there appears to be no difference between the meaning of the class labels and the criteria of their application: hence, there is no possibility of learning to classify the objects correctly while remaining unaware of the full significance of the task.

A moment's thought, however, shows that this whole distinction between classification and evaluation is quite bogus. There are innumerable non-value terms whose criteria of application are distinct from the meaning of the terms themselves. For example: a person who does not understand English, and who has learned to use a thermometer correctly without realising its precise function, might succeed in correctly classifying liquids into 'hot', 'lukewarm', and 'cold' while remaining unaware of the meaning of these terms. A colour-blind individual, by measuring light-wave frequencies, could classify objects according to colour, yet might, conceivably, be unaware of the significance of what he is doing. These examples could obviously be indefinitely multiplied. Admittedly, they are highly unlikely occurrences in real life; but in this they do not differ from Urmson's example of the intelligent apprentice. That they are theoretically conceivable is sufficient to show that the distinction between grading and classification is untenable.

This is a conclusion of some importance. Terms

such as *red, green,* and *blue,* or *cold, lukewarm,* and *hot,* are clearly descriptive, and if their meaning differs from the criteria of their application, there is no reason for supposing that value terms have no descriptive meaning because their meaning and criteria of application are distinct.

The distinction between grading and classifying is not the sole basis for Urmson's view that value terms are non-descriptive. He also argues from the peculiar relation between the grading label and the grading criteria:

> Let us go back to the problem of the relation between the natural criteria A B C and the grading label X which they justify. Is the sentence 'Anything which is A B C is X' analytic or synthetic? We have already noticed the naturalistic difficulties involved in answering 'analytic', but yet the pointlessness, the impossibility, of maintaining that a thing is X if it is not A B C or denying that it is X if it is A B C makes the answer 'synthetic' equally implausible. But if we see that grading is different from ordinary description we can understand why this dilemma is insoluble; for the question whether the connection between two sets of characteristics is analytic or synthetic is a question which is designed to be asked where the related characters are descriptive. ['On Grading', 171–2.]

This is not the place to discuss the validity of classifying all descriptive statements as either analytic or synthetic. To counter Urmson's argument it is necessary only to point out that there are numerous non-value predicates which are certainly descriptive and concerning which exactly the same problem arises. For example, is the statement: 'Any man who weighs more than one hundred and eighty pounds is heavy', analytic or synthetic? The term *heavy* does not mean 'exceeding one hundred and eighty pounds', as is clear when it is applied to, say, a ship. But neither can the statement be synthetic, since if anyone denied it, we would assume, not that he had made an error of fact, but that he did not understand the meaning of the word. Now *heavy* is admittedly a descriptive term. Clearly, then, there is no reason for supposing, because the same problem arises with regard to value terms, that they are non-descriptive.

Urmson's final argument is that, if grading labels are descriptive, they must designate either the criteria of their application or some further property whose presence is revealed by the presence of the criteria, just as the presence of a disease is revealed by the symptoms. Grading labels, as he has already shown, do not designate the criteria of their application; and the theory that they designate distinct properties hardly warrants examination.

Though I clearly do not accept this theory, I shall not attack it; probably even those who support it in the case of 'goodness' would not wish to support it in the case of 'Extra Fanciness' or 'Full Fruit Standardness'. The reason for mentioning it as a theoretical possibility is that all the arguments of Moore and Ross can be converted to apply to all cases of grading labels. It is hard to see why it should be true of 'goodness' but not of 'Extra Fanciness'. ['On Grading', 170.]

This seems to me to be simply a misunderstanding. For those who regard *good* as designating a property distinct from the criteria of goodness, the terms *Fancy*, *Extra Fancy*, and *Super* denote, not three distinct properties, but three different degrees of goodness. In applying grading labels, therefore, we are not attributing different properties, but different degrees of an already specified property. And if you understand grading in the narrow sense, as Urmson does, the property in question is value. All this, in my opinion, is not merely not implausible—it is so obvious as to be hardly worth stating. It might also be added that the term *property* can have a much wider connotation than that given it by Moore and Ross, so that in attacking Urmson's argument we are not necessarily defending ethical intuitionism.

3. Grading criteria

So far we have been concerned with arguments. But the theory to which these are adduced in support has also a major difficulty to contend with: How are grading criteria arrived at? The problem arises only because grading labels are held to be non-descriptive. Criteria can easily be obtained for descriptive terms, either through logical analysis—e.g, a triangle's equiangularity is a criterion of its equilaterality—or through experience—e.g, the expansion of mercury is a criterion of temperature. But obviously neither of these ways is open to non-descriptive terms. Urmson's solution is that criteria of goodness—indeed, of all grading labels—are arrived at in numerous different ways which apparently are not interconnected.

> We cannot aim at a complete catalogue; in no circumstances could we have a right to regard any catalogue as complete. No doubt some criteria for some things are retained for all kinds of odd reasons. ['On Grading', 181.]

There are two comments one can make on this:

1. If both the criteria of goodness and the method of arriving at these criteria vary from one type of object to another, one must conclude that the meaning of *good* varies also. Now no-one, I believe, would want to say that *good*, when applied to cabbages and kings, is an equivocal term. Urmson himself says:

> If the grading label 'good' were, in each of these and all other cases, merely shorthand for the sum of the criteria (naturalism) we should have the absurd situation that 'good' was a homonym with as many punning meanings as the situations it applied to: it could not significantly be used of a theatrical performance in the sense in which it is used of an apple. This, granted our present assumptions, constitutes a most graphic refutation of naturalism. ['On Grading', 175–6.]

To my mind, it constitutes an equally graphic refutation of his own theory. For on his view, when *good* is applied both to apples and to theatrical performances, all that the two uses have in common, apart from the term itself, is that in both instances *good* is used as a grading label. But if this in itself enabled us to say that *good* has the same meaning in each instance, then we should also say that all grading labels had the same meaning. And this is clearly absurd.

2. If Urmson's account of how grading criteria are acquired is correct, it is not clear why grading terms do not have a descriptive meaning. The criteria of goodness in cheese, according to this, derive from the tastes of the majority. But would not 'a good cheese' then mean 'the cheese which accords with the tastes of the majority'? Admittedly there are accepted criteria of use and accepted means of arriving at these criteria for certain non-descriptive terms, such as *hurrah!* But there is an important difference. The criteria here are not criteria of application, for *hurrah!* is not *applied* to anything; one cannot use *hurrah!* as the predicate of an indicative sentence, as one does with grading labels. If in fact it were permissible to make the remark: 'This is an *hurrah!* situation', then quite clearly *hurrah!* really would be a descriptive term. Urmson might indeed claim that, while grading labels as such are non-descriptive, they *acquire* a descriptive meaning only because there is an accepted method of developing the criteria of their application. But the point is that without an accepted method of developing such criteria, grading labels could not be used for communication; since they could mean anything, in practice

they would mean nothing. In other words, grading labels must, if they are to communicate at all, have a descriptive meaning.

Value terms are, of course, used for grading. No one could possibly deny this. Urmson's theory becomes controversial only when he identifies the meaning of value terms with their use as grading labels. That this identification is invalid can, I think, be shown as follows. *Good*, *very good*, and *excellent*, when used as grading labels, are mutually exclusive. An answer paper, for instance, cannot be both *excellent* and *good*. But this is not at all true of *good* as it is normally used. If you remark that a certain film is good, and someone asks, 'How good?', you are quite free to say, 'It was excellent'. Here *excellent* is used not in opposition to *good*, but as a particular grade of goodness. This shows, I believe, that *good*, in its normal use, is not a grading label. One may of course, if one wishes, regard it as classifying objects into either good or bad. But in this sense, as we have seen, every descriptive term is a grading label.

7
R. M. Hare

1. Moral judgements and imperatives

The functionalist theory of meaning encouraged
the view that the problem of the nature of moral
judgement may be reformulated as 'What are
moral judgements for?' When stated like this,
there is only one possible answer—the purpose of
moral judgement is to guide human conduct.
This does not seem to get us very far, however,
for presumably all sides, emotivists and intuitionists alike, would agree on this point. The
crucial question is rather: How do moral judgements guide human conduct? And this seems to
rule out both emotivism and intuitionism, for
while both emotive utterances and statements
may be used to guide human conduct, that is not
their specific function. The specific function of
emotive utterances is to express one's feelings,
of factual remarks to state what is the case. What
sort of expression has the specific function of
guiding human conduct?

According to R. M. Hare the answer is:

'prescriptive utterances'.[1] This in itself is not very informative, for one could hardly define a prescriptive utterance except as one whose specific function is to guide conduct. Hare makes clear, however, that for him the basic type of prescriptive utterance is the imperative. This does not mean that he regards moral judgements as merely disguised imperatives, as did Carnap. Moral judgements, though not imperatives, share many of the features of imperatives, and both may be regarded as sub-classes of the general class of prescriptive utterances.

But if moral judgements are not imperatives, how can they guide conduct, how can they tell us what to do? The answer is that they *entail* imperatives. And this is something which is true of all value judgements. 'Stealing is wrong,' for example, entails 'Do not steal'. '*a* is better than *b*' entails 'If choosing between *a* and *b*, choose *a*'. Value terms, however, are not always used to evaluate. When I say that something is good, I may not, for a variety of reasons, be expressing a value judgement. The infallible test is: Does my statement entail an imperative? If it does not, then my statement is not genuinely evaluative.

Value judgements, then, though they entail imperatives, are not just imperatives under another form of words. What is it which distinguishes them from the latter? The answer, according to Hare, is two-fold. Value judgements (Hare includes all moral judgements under this heading)

[1] Hare's ethical theories are contained in two books: *The Language of Morals*, Oxford 1952; and *Freedom and Reason*, Oxford 1963.

are primarily prescriptive, but they may also have a certain descriptive meaning. This results from the fact that the standards used in evaluation are usually constant. A motor-car, for example, is not normally termed good unless it possesses certain characteristics—it must be economical, reliable, comfortable, etc. Hence, when I say that a particular car is good, part of what I convey is that the car possesses those qualities without which it would not be called good. In other words, the distinction which Urmson draws between the meaning and criteria of value terms sometimes breaks down. Certain criteria become so closely associated with the application of a value term as to become part of the meaning of that term when it is applied to a particular type of object.

The second distinguishing feature of value judgements is what Hare calls their 'universalisability'. Imperatives are not normally universalisable. One may issue the command: 'Close the window', without at all wishing to accept the principle 'Let all windows be closed'. To issue a moral judgement, however, is *eo ipso* to signify one's acceptance of a universal moral principle. One cannot hold that it was wrong of someone to tell a lie without thereby accepting a universal moral principle of the form 'Do not lie'.

This covertly universal character of moral judgements is due to the fact that they are partially descriptive.

In so far as moral judgements do have descriptive meaning, in addition to the other kind of meaning which they have, they share this characteristic, which is common to all judgements which carry descriptive meaning. [*Freedom and Reason*, 10.]

Every singular descriptive judgement is universalisable. Thus, if we say that something is red, we commit ourselves to the view that anything which is like it in the relevant respects (i.e, those respects which entitle us to call it red) is also red. For every descriptive term, then, there is a meaning-rule which governs its application. This meaning-rule is a purely logical thesis for terms which are entirely descriptive. But value terms, as we have seen, are primarily prescriptive. Consequently, the meaning-rules which govern their application are really substantial moral principles. The statement: 'You ought not to do this', entails 'You ought not do anything which is like this in the relevant respects'. And this is obviously more than a purely logical thesis, since it entails the moral rule: 'Do not do actions of this particular type'.

2. The logic of imperatives and of moral principles

Hare's theory then gives moral rules (i.e, imperatives) logical precedence over moral judgements. We can judge that a particular action is wrong or ought not to be done only if we have committed ourselves to the rule which forbids the doing of any similar action. This reversal of the usual relationship in moral theory between judgements and rules gives rise to a particularly formidable problem. If moral rules are more fundamental than moral judgements, can there be any such thing as a rational ethic? A descriptive judgement must be in accordance with the facts; an imperative seems to depend entirely on the decision of the individual who issues it. If morality is based ultimately on imperatives, then may not any action be morally justified?

Hare's answer to this problem has two aspects. In the first place, he points out, it is a mistake to draw too great a distinction between imperatives and indicatives. They have far more in common than may at first appear. To emphasise this point he suggests a recasting of imperatives and indicatives as follows:

> Your shutting the door in the immediate future, please. Your shutting the door in the immediate future, yes. [*Language of Morals*, 17.]

These two sentences correspond to the normal English sentences, 'Shut the door' and 'You are going to shut the door'. What the reformulation brings out is that both expressions refer to the same state of affairs—that described in the first part of each formulation—, but while indicatives assert that that state of affairs is the case, an imperative demands that it be brought about.

Moreover, imperatives, like indicatives, are subject to logical rules: imperatives can contradict each other, for example, 'Shut the door' is contradicted by 'Don't shut the door'. More important still, relations of entailment can occur between imperatives. This is clear from the occurrence in imperatives of the logical constant *all*. To know the meaning of *all* is to know that one cannot, without self-contradiction, say certain things—'All men are mortal, and Socrates is a man, but Socrates is not mortal', for example. We could not attach any significance to *all* without knowing certain rules of entailment. Hence, the fact that *all* occurs in imperatives is a clear indication that imperatives are governed by relations of entailment. From 'Take all the boxes to the station' and 'This is one of the boxes', we may infer 'Take this to the station'. There is a difficulty here, however. One of the premisses is an imperative; the other is a statement of fact. Why then does the conclusion take one form rather than the other? To meet this issue Hare formulates two rules:

1. No indicative conclusion can be validly drawn from a set of premisses which cannot be validly drawn from the indicatives among them alone.
2. No imperative conclusion can be validly drawn from a set of premisses which does not contain at least one imperative.

[*The Language of Morals*, 28.]

The second rule, he claims, is of the first importance for ethics. It forms the basis of several well-known ethical theories—among others, Kant's insistence on the autonomy of the will, Moore's refutation of naturalism, and Hume's declaration that *ought* cannot be derived from *is*.

It also seems to involve something else. If an imperative can be derived only from premisses containing at least one imperative, it appears that any chain of reasoning of this type must, if it is to

114

avoid an infinite regress, eventually end in an imperative which does not need to be derived, which is somehow self-evident. But Hare denies this. An imperative, he argues, can be self-evident only by being devoid of content. If it tells us to do one thing rather than another, it must be 'contingent'. A self-evident principle would have no practical bearing, and therefore no relevance to morals.

Where then do we get our fundamental moral principles? Like the rules of any human activity, we are taught them initially by our elders. But as we become adult we learn to make our moral decisions for ourselves. The principles which we were taught grow more complex as we adapt them to the circumstances in which we find ourselves. Some will probably be rejected entirely. Ultimately, then, the principles which guide our conduct are based on our own personal decisions.

> To become morally adult . . . is to learn to use 'ought'-sentences in the realisation that they can only be verified by reference to a standard or set of principles which we have by our own decision accepted and made our own. [*Language of Morals*, 77–8.]

It will be seen that Hare has, as yet, given only a partial answer to the problem of the rational character of morals. He has shown how singular imperatives may be derived from universal rules by a strictly logical process, but the question remains: How are these universal rules arrived at? To say that they are based on one's personal decision is no answer, for this decision may be entirely arbitrary.

In *The Language of Morals* Hare did not provide any real answer to this problem, and was forced to admit that

> if an enquirer still goes on asking 'But why should I live like that?' then there is no further answer to give him ... We can only ask him to make up his mind which way he ought to live; for in the end everything rests on such a decision of principle. [*Language of Morals*, 69.]

But in *Freedom and Reason* he offers a new approach to the problem. This is based on the two-fold character of moral judgements—their prescriptivity and their universalisability. Since moral judgements are prescriptive, we can choose as universal principles only those moral rules which we are prepared to subscribe to ourselves. And since moral judgements are universalisable, we cannot lay down as a rule of action for ourselves one which is not binding equally on everyone.

> When we are trying, in a concrete case, to decide what we ought to do, what we are looking for ... is an action to which we can commit ourselves (prescriptivity) but which we are at the same time prepared to accept as exemplifying a principle of action to be prescribed for others in like circumstances (universalizability). If, when we consider some proposed action, we find that when universalized, it yields prescrip-

tions which we cannot accept, we reject this action as a solution to our moral problem—if we cannot universalize the prescription, it cannot become an 'ought'. [*Freedom and Reason*, 89–90.]

Hare seems here to be offering a variant of the Golden Rule, or of Kant's famous dictum that 'I ought never to act except in such a way that I can also will that my Maxim should become a universal law'.[1] However, he insists on one fundamental difference. The Golden Rule and the Categorical Imperative are both moral rules. The universalisability of moral judgements is a purely logical thesis which derives from the special character of moral judgements. His insistence on this point is easily understood, for it would be begging the question to base the rationality of morals on something which is itself a moral judgement.

3. The function of value terms
To explain the function of value terms, Hare calls our attention to the *Oxford English Dictionary*'s explanation of *good*:

> The most general adjective of commendation, implying the existence in a high, or at least satisfactory, degree of characteristic qualities which are either admirable in themselves or useful for some purpose.[2]

This provides the substance of an answer to the

[1] I. Kant, *Groundwork of the Metaphysic of Morals*, trans. H. J. Paton, London 1956, 17.
[2] Quoted in *The Language of Morals*, 79.

problem. The primary function of value terms is to commend, and that is why they cannot be defined in a purely descriptive manner. Moore's rejection of naturalism was justified, therefore, but it should have been based, not on the peculiar character of the property which *good* denotes, but on the fact that

> value terms have a special function in language, that of commending, and so they plainly cannot be defined in terms of other words which cannot perform this function. [*Language of Morals*, 91.]

What does commending involve? In answer Hare points to the connections between value terms and choice. We never evaluate objects unless there is a question of someone choosing them. Thus, we never speak of a good wireworm because we never find occasion to choose one. Secondly, a person's value judgements are manifested by his choices. When an individual chooses between two things we can be sure that he chooses the one which he regards as best. And if a person speaks of something as bad, yet continues to choose it, we can be sure that he is insincere. The primary purpose of value judgements, then, is to guide choices.

> When we commend or condemn anything, it is always in order, at least indirectly, to guide choices, our own or other peoples', now or in the future. [*Language of Morals*, 91.]

But value terms are not merely commendatory:

> Value expressions sometimes acquire—by

118

reason of the constancy of the standards by which they are applied—a certain descriptive force. [*Language of Morals*, 7.]

The descriptive function of value terms is, however, subordinate to their commendatory function. The evaluative meaning is constant for every class of object: the descriptive varies from one class to the next—the qualities required in a good motor-car are entirely different from those required in, say, a good novel. Moreover, the evaluative meaning may be used to alter the descriptive meaning. If tastes in novels or in motor-cars were to change, the descriptive meaning of *good* as applied to them would also change, but its evaluative meaning would remain the same. The descriptive meaning is clearly dependent on the evaluative meaning and subordinate to it. In fact, it can be misleading to speak of the descriptive content of value terms as forming part of their meaning. For we would not want to say that someone does not know the meaning of 'a good *x*' simply because he doesn't know what qualities are required in an *x* for it to be called good.

The meaning of a good motor-car (in another sense of meaning) is something that might be known by someone who did not know the criteria of its application; he would know, if someone said that a motor-car was a good one, that he was commending it, and to know that would be to know the meaning of the expression. [*Language of Morals*, 117.]

But value terms such as *good* may also be used

119

in a purely descriptive sense. This occurs when the speaker is not making a value judgement himself, but is referring to the value judgements of others. Thus someone may be referred to as 'a good man' when it is clear from the context that he is good only according to certain conventional standards to which the speaker does not himself subscribe. Sometimes it is difficult to decide whether a particular statement is genuinely evaluative or merely descriptive. The infallible test is: Does the statement entail an imperative? If, for example, someone terms bad an action which he has the habit of doing himself, we can be quite sure that he is not making a genuine value judgement.

Moral judgements are merely a sub-class of value judgements. They have no special characteristics of their own. The criteria for applying value terms are, of course, different in moral contexts. The characteristics which one must possess to be a good man are different from those we expect in a good carpenter or a good singer. This does not affect the evaluative function of these terms, which remains the same whether they are applied morally or otherwise. It has indeed been held that *good* has a totally different meaning in moral contexts, and we can see a reason for this view even though it is erroneous. Our assent to a non-moral value judgement may be purely theoretical, since we may never be forced with a choice on which it would have a bearing. But assent to a moral judgement always involves the effort to conform to it. We cannot judge that one ought always tell the truth and at the same time tell lies whenever convenience demands it.

> If we add to this the logical point, already mentioned, that moral judgements always have a possible bearing on our own conduct, in that we cannot in the fullest sense accept them without conforming to them ... then no further explanation is needed of the special status of morals. This special status does not require a special logic to back it up; it results from the fact that we are using the ordinary apparatus of value-language in order to commend or condemn the most intimate actions of ourselves and those like us. [*Language of Morals*, 143.]

I propose to examine Hare's theory under three headings—his arguments for the theory, the theory itself, and a consequence of the theory. I will then say something on Hare's attempt to provide a rational basis for ethics, and will end with some remarks on prescriptivism as a theory of moral judgement.

4. The arguments

Hare's theory in brief, as we have seen, is that moral judgements are prescriptive, their primary function being to commend or guide choices; any descriptive meaning they may possess is subordinate to their prescriptive character.

He has two arguments in support of this. The first is from *The Language of Morals*. Here he points out that *good*, or any similar word, cannot be defined in non-value terms. If, for example, we regard the statement '*p* is a good picture' as meaning, say, '*p* has a tendency to arouse a feeling of admiration in members of the Royal Academy', then we can no longer say meaningfully something we do sometimes want to say, that is, that members of the Royal Academy have a good taste in pictures.

What we wanted to do was to *commend* the pictures which the members of the Royal Academy admired. Something about our definition prevented our doing this. We could no longer commend the pictures which they admired, we could only say that they admired those pictures which they admired. Thus our definition has prevented us, in one crucial case, from commending something which we want to commend. That is what is wrong with it.

Let us illustrate this by another example . . . Let us consider the sentence 'S is a good strawberry'. We might naturally suppose that this means nothing more than 'S is a strawberry and S is sweet, juicy, firm, red, and large'. But it then becomes impossible for us to say certain things which in our ordinary talk we do say. We sometimes want to say that a strawberry is a good strawberry because it is sweet, etc. This —as we can at once see if we think of ourselves saying it—does not mean the same as saying a strawberry is a sweet, etc. strawberry because it is sweet, etc. But according to the proposed definition this is what it would mean. Thus here again the proposed definition would prevent us saying something that we do succeed in saying meaningfully in our ordinary talk. [*Language of Morals*, 85–6.]

Good clearly cannot be defined in descriptive terms. This means that it does not designate a complex property. And there are equally good reasons for believing that it does not designate a simple property. It follows that *good* has a function other than that of designating or denoting.

Value-terms have a special function in language, that of commending; and so they plainly cannot be defined in terms of other words which do not perform this function: for if this is done, we are deprived of a means of performing the function. [*Language of Morals*, 91.]

This argument is badly set out. The theory that the function of *good* is to commend should properly be included in the conclusion and not form part of the argument itself. By including it earlier Hare has, I believe, confused the structure of the argument and weakened its force. For he is obviously mistaken in asserting that a definition of *good* hampers our ability to commend. To say of a strawberry that it is sweet, juicy, firm, etc., *is* to commend it; that 'good strawberry' has been defined in those terms only emphasises this fact. The same is true of the other example. To say that a picture is admired by members of the Royal Academy is to commend it—unless, of course, one has little regard for the taste of that body, but in that case 'good picture' would not have been defined in those terms.

The argument then amounts to this. *Good* cannot be defined in descriptive terms, because to say that it is equivalent to '*a, b,* and *c*' is to render meaningless something which we do sometimes want to say, that is, that S is good because it is *a, b,* and *c*. The weakness of this argument can be exposed by reproducing Hare's statement with a few significant alterations:

> Let us consider the sentence 'S is a tall man'. We might naturally suppose that this means nothing more than 'S is a man and S is more than six feet in height'. But it then becomes impossible for us to say certain things which in our ordinary talk we do say. We sometimes want to say that a man is a tall man because he is six feet in height. This—as we can at once see if we think of ourselves saying it—does not mean the same as saying that a man is six feet in height because he is six feet in height. But according to the proposed definition this is what it would mean. Thus here again the proposed definition would prevent us saying something that we do succeed in saying meaningfully in our ordinary talk.

This argument, which has exactly the same force as Hare's argument about *good*, proves not that *tall* is indefinable—it is manifestly a definable term—but that its meaning and the criteria of its application are distinct. Hare's argument, therefore, serves only to rule out the hypothesis that *good* is definable in terms of the criteria of its application, and this, so far as I am aware, is a view which has never been seriously put forward, since it has the absurd consequence of implying that *good* has as many different meanings as there are kinds of object to which it may be applied.

But could Hare's argument be adapted to counter any attempt to define *good* in descriptive terms? The answer, I believe, must be: No. The argument is based on the fact that we say such things as 'S is good because it is *a*, *b*, and *c*', and this is true only when '*a*, *b*, and *c*' refer to the criteria of goodness. This is clear from a comparison with *tall*, for while we do say such things as 'S is tall because he is six feet high', we do not say 'S is tall because he is of a height notably exceeding the height of the average member of the class to which he belongs'. This merely explains the meaning of the original statement, when what is required is evidence of its truth. It would be used, therefore, only when there is question of explaining the meaning of *tall* to one who did not understand the term.

Hare's second argument concerns *ought* rather than *good*, but the conclusion, as before, is intended to apply to all moral terms.

> It is because I *can* act in this way or that, that I ask, 'Shall I act in this way or that?'; and it is, typically, in my deliberations about this 'Shall I?' question that I ask the further, but related, question, 'Ought I to do this or that?' Thus it is because they are prescriptive that moral words possess that property which is summed up, perhaps over-crudely, in the slogan '"Ought" implies "can"'. If descriptivism were a complete account of evaluative language, this slogan would never have arisen. We shall

see that imperatives also imply 'can', in the same sense of 'imply', and for the same reasons, as does 'ought'. [*Freedom and Reason*, 51.]

There is one preliminary point to be made about the scope of this argument. It might seem that it could at best prove merely that *ought* statements are not purely descriptive—that, in other words, it does not show that their *primary* function is prescriptive. Against this, however, there is the fact that where *ought* does not imply *can*, we do not regard the judgement as a genuine moral one. Hence if the property of implying *can* derives from the prescriptive character of moral judgements, it seems to follow that this prescriptive character is primary.

The argument may be set out as follows. Descriptive statements do not imply *can*. Prescriptive statements do. Assuming that these are the only possibilities, *ought* statements, since they imply *can*, must be prescriptive rather than descriptive.

The first premiss will certainly surprise anyone who is acquainted with the scholastic axiom: *ab esse ad posse valet illatio*. Any statement which asserts that someone *is* doing something implies that he *can* do it. If I say that John is swimming or playing cricket, it follows that he can do these things, even though such statements are purely factual.

The second premiss of the argument seems to me to be equally unfounded. The basic type of prescriptive utterance, the command or imperative, does not imply that the person to whom it is issued is capable of fulfilling it. Some commands are issued, as in an examination of physical fitness for example, with the purpose of finding out whether the person to whom they are addressed can carry them out or not. I do not see that, in these cases, the command is rendered any the less valid by the discovery that the person is incapable of carrying it out. Hare does not leave this premiss undefended, however.

> The sense of 'imply' in which 'ought' implies 'can' is not that of logical entailment. It is a weaker relation, analogous to that which Mr. Strawson has claimed to exist between the statement that the King of France is wise, and the statement that there is a King of France. If there is no King of France, then the question whether the King of France is wise does not arise. And so, by saying that the King of France is wise, we give our hearers to understand that we think, at least, that the question arises to which this is one possible answer, and that, accordingly, there is a King of France. And similarly, if we say that somebody ought to do a certain thing, and 'ought' has its full (i.e. universally prescriptive) force, then we give our hearers to understand that we think that the question arises to which this is a possible answer, which it would not unless the person in question were able to do the acts referred to.
> Now it must be noticed that imperatives also imply 'can' in the same way as 'ought' does when used with its full force. If I tell or ask someone to do something . . . I give him to

understand that I think that the question to which I have given him an answer arises—i.e. that a decision is open to him. It would not do to tell a soldier to pick up his rifle if it were fixed to the ground. [*Freedom and Reason*, 53–4.]

I want, first of all, to question Hare's view that the sense in which *ought* implies *can* is not that of logical entailment. To do so we must go back to Strawson. Here is the relevant passage:

> To say 'The king of France is wise' is, in some sense of 'imply', to *imply* that there is a king of France. But this is a very special and odd sense of 'imply'. 'Implies' in this sense is certainly not equivalent to 'entails' (or 'logically implies'). And this comes out from the fact that when, in response to his statement, we say (as we should) 'There is no king of France', we should certainly *not* say we were *contradicting* the statement that the king of France is wise. We are certainly not saying that it is false. We are, rather, giving a reason for saying that the question of whether it is true or false simply does not arise.[1]

There is a good deal one could say about this passage, but I will have to confine myself to what is essential for our purpose. The assertion that ' "The King of France is wise" implies "There is a king of France" ' only in a very special and

[1] P. F. Strawson, 'On Referring', *Mind* LIX (1950); reprinted in *Essays in Conceptual Analysis*, ed. A. Flew, London, 34.

odd sense of *imply*' is demonstrably incorrect. In his book *Introduction to Logical Theory*, Strawson defines entailment as follows:

> To say that one statement entails another is to say that it would be inconsistent to make the first and deny the second.[1]

Now it would indeed be inconsistent to assert 'The King of France is wise' and deny 'There is a king of France', for it is logically impossible that the first of these statements and the negation of the second should both be true. It follows that the first statement entails the second, on Strawson's definition of the term *entail*. And since this is, I believe, a generally accepted definition, there is no justification for saying that '"The King of France is wise" implies that "There is a king of France" only in a very special and odd sense of *imply*'.

What is important from our point of view, however, is that *ought* implies *can* in the same strict sense of logical entailment, for it is logically impossible that 'I ought to do this' and 'I cannot do it' should both be true if we are using *ought* to make a moral judgement.

Consider now the rule which Hare has previously laid down on the logical relationship between imperatives and indicatives.

> No indicative conclusion can be validly drawn from a set of premisses which cannot be validly drawn from the indicatives among them alone. [*Language of Morals*, 28.]

[1] P. F. Strawson, *Introduction to Logical Theory*, London 1952, 19.

This means that imperatives do not imply *can* in the strict sense. It follows that imperatives do not imply *can* in the same way as *ought*. Moreover, it also follows that *ought* implies *can* qua descriptive statement. And since, as we have seen in a preliminary to this argument, it is with respect to its primary function that *ought* implies *can*, the primary function of *ought* statements in a moral context must be the giving of information.

The only possible way for Hare to avoid these consequences is to renounce the rule which we have just quoted. But I do not see how he can do this, for it seems indisputable that if an imperative says nothing which is either true or false, it cannot strictly imply something which is either true or false. In any case, it seems clear that his view that imperatives imply 'thinks he can' is due to a misunderstanding. For 'thinks he can' follows not from the imperative itself, but from the *fact* that it has been issued by somebody. And it is more correctly described as an assumption than as an implication, since it is not always verified.

5. The theory
The theory is that 'the primary function of the word "good" is to commend ... When we commend or condemn anything it is always in order, at least indirectly, to guide choices, our own or other people's, now or in the future.' (*The Language of Morals*, 127.) The theory then rests on two assumptions.

1. We commend or condemn only those things which are possible objects of choice.

2. Value judgements guide choices, not by providing information about the objects of choice —if this were so, commending would be a form of describing—but through their prescriptive character, that is, the fact that they entail imperatives.

Both these assumptions appear to me to be false. To refute the first we have merely to point to the fact that we make use of such expressions as 'a good father' and 'good luck'. These are not used to guide choices since these are things which cannot be chosen. Possibly Hare would say that the choice here is hypothetical. But this means that these expressions would be used only on the occasion of an extravagant, if not ridiculous, hypothesis, whereas in fact they occur in the most serious and sober discourses. The conclusion is that either these are not typical uses of the term *good* or else Hare's theory is defective. But only one who is looking at the world through the coloured spectacles of a philosophical theory would seriously suppose that *good* is being used here in a sense which is not truly evaluative.

All this is borne out by an examination of the relations between value and choice in practice. In evaluating we consider only the object itself. But in choosing or in guiding someone else's choice many extraneous factors have to be considered. In choosing a car, for instance, there are the questions of how much money I can afford to pay and the purpose for which I require it. An evaluation does not, therefore, imply any sort of imperative about choosing. This would be to leave these other factors out of account. Thus the statement: '*a* is better than *b*', cannot imply, as it does on Hare's theory,[1] 'If choosing between *a* and *b*, choose *a*', for one may be well aware of *a*'s superiority yet be unwilling to choose it for other reasons.

The second assumption is that value judgements guide choices through their imperative character. There is, of course, no doubt that value judgements do guide choices (though this is not their specific function for, as we have seen, some perfectly respectable value judgements do not do so). This, however, is not a conclusive proof of their prescriptive character, for one may guide choices by means of factual statements. A guide-book, for instance, could be entirely composed of purely descriptive remarks.

In what way, then, do value judgements guide choices? Is it because they entail imperatives, or because of the information which they provide about the objects of choice? If these are the only possibilities, then the answer may be given immediately. Imperatives do not in fact guide choices: rather, they remove the necessity of choice. Once we have been told what to do, we no longer have to choose our course of action. A soldier on the barrack-square, for example, is not having his choices continually guided by the orders from the sergeant-major. Imperatives guide conduct, but not choices. Once we set ourselves to obey the commands of a certain authority, we no longer have to choose; we simply do what we are told.

[1] See *Language of Morals*, 184.

It might be objected, on Hare's behalf, that we would not obey a command unless we had already chosen to obey it. As free agents we do not automatically do as we are ordered. A free choice must intervene between the issuing of the command and the doing of the action, and this choice is obviously guided by the command.

It is true, of course, that we would not obey unless we had previously chosen to do so. But it would be a mistake to suppose that such a choice is made each time a command is obeyed. The soldier on the barrack-square has chosen to obey his sergeant-major, but he does not make this choice each time the sergeant-major issues a command. Rather he obeys all the commands under the influence of the initial choice. And this initial choice was not itself guided by the commands, since it is the condition rather than the effect of their influence.

The choice to obey may indeed be influenced by the thought of what will happen if the command is not obeyed. But this influence derives, not from the command itself, but from the sanctions which support it. Clearly one cannot be guided by a command which one has not already decided to obey.

6. A consequence of the theory

Hare's theory of moral judgement has the extraordinary characteristic of implying that we never do anything which we think we ought not to do. If 'I ought to do x' entails 'Do x', one cannot apparently say that someone did not do x although he thought he ought to do so, for this implies that he told himself to do x and decided not to do it at one and the same time.

> Moral judgments always have a possible bearing on our conduct in that we cannot in the fullest sense accept them without conforming to them. [*Lauguage of Morals*, 143.]

Moral weakness is such a commonplace of human experience that we would have expected Hare to go to almost any lengths to avoid this consequence. But he is faced with Hobson's choice; to argue that his theory leaves room for genuine moral weakness would be at least as difficult as justifying the 'Socratic paradox'. The crucial point is not so much his conception of moral judgements as primarily prescriptive as his view that one's moral principles derive from one's personal decisions. One cannot decide to adopt a certain rule and, at the same time, decide not to act in accordance with it. The two decisions are incompatible; in deciding to act contrary to the principle one is *eo ipso* rejecting it as one's rule of action.

Hare then takes on what may seem the hopeless task of defending the view that we never act in a manner contrary to that which we think to be right. In his first book, *The Language of Morals*, he argues from the vagueness of the expression 'thinks he ought':

> If we interpret my definition strictly, and take it in conjunction with what was said earlier about the criteria for sincerely assenting to a command, the familiar 'Socratic paradox' arises, in that it becomes analytic to say that everyone

134

always does what he thinks he ought to (in the evaluative sense). And this, to put Aristotle's objection in modern dress, is not how we use the word 'think'. The trouble arises because our criteria, in ordinary speech, for saying 'He thinks he ought' are exceeding elastic. If a person does not do something but the omission is accompanied by feelings of guilt etc., we normally say that he has not done what he thinks he ought. It is therefore necessary to qualify the criterion given above for 'sincerely assenting to a command' and to admit that there are degrees of real assent, not all of which involve actually obeying the command. But the detailed analysis of this problem . . . must wait for another occasion. [*Language of Morals*, 169–70.]

The trouble with this, however, is that the Socratic paradox also renders meaningless many commonplace expressions in which the word *think* does not occur, as, for example, 'I am going to take the day off, although I ought to be working'.

Hare concedes this point in his promised detailed analysis of the problem. (*Freedom and Reason*, 67f.) But he denies that *ought* is being used here in its typical sense. He points out that we can also say 'I ought to do such-and-such, but I can't'. Here *ought* is being used in an 'off-colour' manner, for *ought* in its typical sense implies *can*. 'I ought, but I won't' is, in his view, a similar 'off-colour' use of the word.

I believe it can be shown, however, that the two cases are not parallel. When the statement:

'I ought to do this', is intended to express a moral judgement, it implies that it would be immoral for me not to do this action. Now it makes no sense to say: 'It would be immoral for me not to do this thing even though I cannot do it', if the last part of the statement is strictly true. It cannot be immoral for me not to do something which it is not within my power to do. But the same cannot be said of: 'I don't intend doing this even though it is immoral of me not to do it'. This, it is true, is not the sort of statement one would expect to hear. People do not normally avow their moral weakness so explicitly. The statement is psychologically odd, but it is not logically defective. It makes perfectly good sense, and few of us would care to deny that there have been occasions when we could truthfully have made this remark about ourselves.

Hare argues, however, that whenever we make a remark of the form: 'He did not do what he thought he ought', the person referred to was either incapable of doing the action or else did not, in the strict sense, think that he ought to do it.

It will not do to quote cases in which people *cannot* bring themselves to do what they think they ought to do ... It cannot be said, it is objected, that the morally weak person *cannot* do what he thinks he ought, because he is obviously as able as the rest of us. But 'able' here refers only to physical ability. In a deeper sense the man cannot do the act. This is clearest in cases of compulsive neuroses in which 'psychological' impossibility comes close to 'physical'; but it also holds in more normal cases of weakness of will, as the word 'weakness' indicates.

Nor will it do to quote cases in which a man goes on saying that he ought, but fails to act, even though he can act, in every sense of 'can'. For this is the case of what I called purposive backsliding, or hypocrisy; and these are allowed for. If a man does what he says he ought not to, though perfectly able to resist the temptation to do it, then there is something wrong with what he says, as well as with what he does. In the simplest case it is insincerity; he is not saying what he really thinks. In other cases it is self-deception. [*Freedom and Reason*, 82–3.]

Hare rules out the possibility of a counter-example by claiming that whenever we say: 'I did not do what I thought I ought', either we do not mean what we say or *ought* is being used in a secondary sense. Now the sole reason for thinking that such is always the case is his theory of moral judgement. In other words, he is arguing from the truth of his own theory to the impossibility of a counter-example. But any theory implies the impossibility of a counter-example, since a counter-example would show the theory to be false. This is merely an exemplification of a rule of logic; it tells us nothing about the actual truth of the theory.

What Hare *has* succeeded in showing is that from the fact that we commonly say such things as 'I did not do what I thought I ought', we cannot conclude *immediately* to the falsity of his theory. We must show that there are occasions when such statements are true, even though they express genuine moral judgements. The obvious way to do this is to appeal to our own experience. Most people would, I feel sure, regard as nonsense the suggestion that one cannot freely tell a lie and at the same time sincerely assent to the principle that lying is immoral.

As a philosophical refutation, however, this leaves something to be desired. Each person, after all, can speak only for himself. What is needed is an argument on the general level. This can, I believe, be supplied from a consideration of the fact that, as Hare himself emphasises, moral judgements guide conduct.[1] This they cannot do if we never act contrary to our moral principles, for if we never do what we think we ought not to, then, from the moral point of view, everything is permitted. No matter what action we decide on, we can be sure that it will not be something which we ought not to have done.

Hare might perhaps protest that our moral principles guide us before we actually decide what to do, in the process of making the decision. In other words, the fact that we accept a certain principle will influence us to act in accordance with it, even though we can no longer be said to

[1] See, for example, *Freedom and Reason*, 67: 'The ethical theory which has been briefly set out in the preceding chapters is a type of prescriptivism in that it maintains that it is one of the characteristics of moral terms ... that judgements concerning them are, as typically used, intended to guide conduct.'

accept this principle if we decide to act in a contrary manner. I do not think that this is a genuine loop-hole. On Hare's theory, to accept a moral principle is, in effect, to decide to act in accordance with it; if this were not so, it would be possible for us to act contrary to our principles. Now this means that, so long as we accept a particular principle, we cannot be undecided as to whether we will act in accordance with it or not. If we *are* undecided, then we do not really accept the principle. And certainly one cannot be guided by principles which one does not accept.

7. A rational basis of ethics

Since, on Hare's view, our moral judgements depend on our moral principles, the question arises: How are our moral principles arrived at? If we choose them ourselves, then it seems that we may choose whatever moral principles we please, and adapt them as we wish. This deprives ethics of all value as a rational guide to conduct. To avoid this consequence, Hare pointed out that imperatives need not be based on our personal whims: they can be derived by a strictly logical process from universal imperatives. But this merely places the problem one step further back. Whence do our ultimate principles derive?

In his first book, *The Language of Morals*, Hare says simply that they are based on our personal decision.

To become morally adult ... is to learn to use 'ought'-sentences in the realisation that they can only be verified by reference to a standard or set of principles which we have by our own decisions accepted and made our own. [*Language of Morals*, 77–8.]

Unless this decision is justified in some way, however, we are as badly off as before, for no amount of reasoning will produce a rational conclusion if the ultimate premisses do not have a rational basis.

Hare's reply is as follows:

If asked to justify as completely as possible any decision, we have to bring both effects—to give content to the decision—and principles, and the effects in general of observing those principles, and so on, until we have satisfied our inquirer. Thus a complete justification of a decision would consist of a complete account of its effects, together with a complete account of the principles which it observed, and the effects of observing those principles. [*Language of Morals*, 68–9.]

Since we cannot, ex hypothesi, bring in principles to justify a decision to adopt ultimate principles, this means that ultimate principles are justified solely by their effects. But Hare himself has ruled out this kind of justification, for to describe the effects is to make a series of factual remarks and, according to his own rule, an imperative cannot be validly deduced from premisses which are merely factual. The individual is free to choose whatever effects, and therefore whatever principles, he wishes, and this leaves us precisely where we were before.

140

Hare makes one final effort to extricate himself from the difficulty.

> If the inquirer still goes on asking 'But why *should* I live like that?' then there is no further answer. We can only ask him to make up his own mind which way he ought to live; for in the end everything rests upon such a decision of principle. He has to decide whether to accept that way of life or not; if he accepts it, then we can proceed to justify the decisions that are based upon it; if he does not accept it, then let him accept some other, and try to live by it. The sting is in the last clause. To describe such ultimate decisions as arbitrary because *ex hypothesi* everything which could be used to justify them has already been included in the decision, would be like saying that a complete description of the universe was utterly unfounded, because no further fact could be called upon in corroboration of it. [*Language of Morals,* 69.]

The reference to a complete description of the universe is misleading, since descriptions are condemned, not for being unfounded—'an unfounded description' has a very odd ring about it—but for being inaccurate, and the accuracy of a description does not depend on any further fact being called in corroboration of it. Hare's ultimate decision, on the other hand, might be entirely arbitrary. To say that such a decision ought to be well-considered is to make a moral judgement —one for which there is no room at this stage, since ex hypothesi we are considering the adoption of ultimate moral principles. If the decision to adopt is governed by a moral principle, then clearly the principles we are adopting are not ultimate. Hare's remark: 'If he does not accept it, then let him accept some other and try to live by it', must also be ruled out. This is simply another moral principle. To impose it on others would be to deny that they are free to choose their principles for themselves. There seems no reason, then, why the choice of ultimate principles should not be revised as often as one sees fit. This being so, can one have any further faith in a rational basis of ethics?

As a criticism of Hare's position, however, this is incomplete, for in his second book, *Freedom and Reason*, he develops a different solution to the problem. This is based on the universalisability of moral judgements. One cannot judge that a particular action ought not to be done without— since moral judgements are covertly universal— committing oneself to the position that all actions similar to the first in the relevant respects ought not to be done likewise. This restricts our choice of moral principles enormously, for it means that we can not prescribe an action for ourselves without prescribing it for all in similar circumstances, nor can we prescribe an action for others without prescribing it, in similar circumstances, for ourselves. Moral principles cannot, therefore, be chosen or adapted at the whim of the individual; they constitute a genuine guide to conduct.

This theory owes a good deal to Kant. But it has some original features and, as an attempt to provide an objective basis for moral judgements, it merits serious consideration.

The first thing we must investigate is the reason why moral judgements are covertly universal:

> We must now notice the connexion between the fact that some judgements are descriptive and another feature which it has become the custom to call, when we are speaking of moral judgements, *universalizability*. It is important to emphasize that moral judgements *share* this feature with descriptive judgements, although the differences between them in other respects are, as we shall see, sufficient to make it misleading to say that moral judgements are descriptive. Nevertheless, insofar as moral judgements do have descriptive meaning, in addition to the other kind of meaning which they have, they share this characteristic, which is common to all judgements which carry descriptive meaning. [*Freedom and Reason*, 10.]

Moral judgements then are universalisable insofar as they are descriptive. But for Hare's purpose it is essential that all moral judgements be at least partially descriptive, for clearly one cannot base the rational character of morals on something which belongs to moral judgements only *per accidens*. The extraordinary thing, however, is that in *The Language of Morals* Hare states that moral judgements only sometimes have a descriptive meaning.

> Value-expressions sometimes acquire—by reason of the constancy of the standards by which they are applied—a certain descriptive force . . .

It is clear that some sentences containing the word 'ought' have a descriptive force. [*Language of Morals*, 7 and 159.]

But Hare also says:

Although the evaluative meaning of 'good' is primary the secondary descriptive meaning is never wholly absent. Even when we are using the word 'good' evaluatively in order to set up a new standard, the word still has a descriptive meaning, not in the sense that it is used to *convey* information, but in the sense that its use in setting up the new standard is an essential preliminary—like definition in the case of a purely descriptive word—to its subsequent use with a new descriptive meaning. [*Language of Morals*, 121–2.]

I do not see how this last statement can possibly be reconciled with the other two, for we cannot, short of a wild misuse of language, say that *good* has always some descriptive meaning, but that expressions which ascribe it to an object may sometimes be devoid of descriptive force. Applying the most favourable interpretation possible, however, let us assume that the last statement represents Hare's considered opinion and that the other two, insofar as they are irreconcilable with it, are to be left out of account. His theory now appears to be free from the difficulty we have been considering.

But, unfortunately, this is an illusion. For, in the first place, whenever value terms are not used to convey information, then, whether we say they have descriptive meaning or not, their use will not be governed by a universal meaning-rule. This appears immediately when we consider that the reason why one cannot assert a descriptive statement without committing oneself to a universal meaning-rule is that to do so is to infringe the principle of non-contradiction. To say that something is red but deny that anything which is like it in the relevant respects is also red is to deny that what is red is red. But if the statement: '*s* is good', does not convey any information, one does not contradict oneself by denying that anything which is similar to *s* is also good. To say that *s* is good is ex hypothesi not to say that it has certain characteristics: therefore, to say that something has the same characteristics as *s* is not to say that it is good. There is no contradiction then in asserting that *s* is good but denying the general principle, hence no committal to the general principle in making the value judgement. It follows that not all value judgements are covertly universal.

The same conclusions may be reached by a different route. If the descriptive meaning of moral judgements is due to the constancy of standards used in applying them, many moral judgements can have no descriptive meaning. Consider judgements which assert that an action is bad. There are so many different reasons why an action might be termed bad—*malum ex quocumque defectu*—that, no matter how constant one's standards of evaluation, a judgement asserting badness of an action will hardly ever convey by implication the reasons why it is bad. The same is true of judgements that an action ought or ought not to be done. There are such a multiplicity of reasons for holding that an action ought or ought not to be done that few, if any, judgements of this form could ever acquire descriptive force in the manner envisaged by Hare. Again it follows that these judgements are not covertly universal.

Now, if moral judgements do not *have* to be universalisable, Hare's whole scheme falls through. We can no longer restrict our choice of moral principles by saying that the only principles we can choose are those we are prepared to prescribe for all. Besides, there was always something very odd about his attempt to provide a rational basis of morals by means of the descriptive meaning of moral judgements. The problem of the rationality of morals arises because he regards moral judgements as primarily non-descriptive. Hence, if his solution to the problem is correct, it is superfluous, for if moral judgements have all a genuine descriptive meaning, there is no problem; it is a question, not of the rationality of morals, but of the truth or falsity of moral judgements.

But even if we overlook these difficulties, Hare's policy of founding the rational character of morals on the covertly universal nature of moral judgements is still far from satisfactory. For, in the first place, it enables one to provide a moral justification for the most odious principles imaginable. Under the nazi regime in Germany, to use Hare's own example, there was a number of people who believed that it was their duty to wipe out the Jews. Since they subscribed to the universal principle that all Jews are to be annihilated, one cannot, on Hare's theory, condemn their actions as immoral. The only condition for the validity of a moral principle laid down by Hare is that the person who accepts it must prescribe it for all. As this condition is fulfilled in the instance we are considering, the anti-Jewish principles of the nazis were, from the moral point of view, unexceptionable. We may indeed find such principles repugnant, but on Hare's theory each person has the right to choose his moral principles for himself. The nazis, after all, may have had an equally poor view of our moral outlook.

Hare's answer to this is that the nazis cannot really have universalised their desire to annihilate the Jews, for if one could have deceived a nazi into thinking that he was a Jew, it is extremely unlikely that he would have then subscribed to the principle which entailed that he and his family should be immediately transported to Buchenwald.

This is not a matter of logic; he would not be contradicting himself if he said 'Jews are such an abomination that I and my family, if we were Jews, should be sent to the gas chamber'. Our argument, as we are going to develop it, will rest, not upon logic itself—though without logic we should never have got to this point—but upon the fortunate contingent fact that people who would take this logically possible view, after they had really imagined themselves in another man's position, are extremely rare. [*Freedom and Reason*, 172.]

Hare offers no evidence in support of this 'fortunate contingent fact', but what evidence there is seems to me to point in the opposite direction. Consider a parallel case. Most people would, I take it, subscribe to the principle that crime should be punished. Would the realisation that they themselves may some day commit a crime lessen their assent to this principle? This is a question which each person can answer only for himself, but I would be extremely surprised if the majority did not answer: 'No'. Now the nazis seem to have regarded the existence of Jews within the state in the same way as we regard the existence of crime. To say that the realisation of what it would be like to be a Jew would inevitably change their outlook seems to me as implausible as saying that the realisation of what it would be like to be a criminal would make us renounce criminal punishment.

This, in any case, is not the essential point. Even if what Hare says above is true, it still does not constitute a satisfactory defence of his theory. What was wrong with the nazi policy towards the Jews had nothing to do with the supposed fact that the majority of nazis could not universally prescribe the principles on which that policy was based. Even if they could have universally prescribed it, the principles would still have been immoral. That they could not be condemned as such on Hare's theory is one of the reasons why the theory must be rejected.

There is a second objection to the founding of the rational character of morals on the universal nature of moral judgements. An action may normally be described in a great many different ways and there is nothing in Hare's theory to prevent one choosing whichever description one wishes. The result is that, for almost any action, there will be a means of describing it which will enable one to prescribe it universally. Thus the militant nazi would have described his policy towards the Jews, not as the killing of innocent people, but as the purifying of the German race; obviously he would have had no difficulty in prescribing this universally. Again, the professional burglar may not be able to subscribe to the general principle that the rights of private property can be ignored, but he may well subscribe to the principle of robbing the rich to feed the poor. There are few actions which could not be similarly justified. By describing it in a certain manner, we may subsume it under a general principle whose adoption by all would entail no disadvantages to ourselves. Morality is thus deprived of all value as a guide to human conduct.

I am not, of course, suggesting that the different ways in which an action may be described are all of equal relevance to morals. This is clearly incorrect. But it is incorrect only because there are certain forms of action which we already regard as immoral. It is because we possess a set of moral principles that we can distinguish the descriptions which are relevant to morals from those which are not. In considering Hare's theory, however, we are concerned with the *formation* of moral principles. There is no reason here for discriminating between the different possible descriptions, and this leaves us free to manipulate the descriptions at will so as to justify our actions.

8. A postscript on prescriptivism

This chapter has been so highly critical that it may give a mistaken impression of the writer's opinion of Hare as a moral philosopher. Truth, however, is not the only criterion of value in philosophy, and if Hare's theories are, as I believe, radically mistaken, his writings on the subject are invariably fresh and stimulating. That the final result is disappointing may be in large measure due to a mistaken assumption concerning the nature of meaning.

This point will emerge more clearly if we compare two passages from *The Language of Morals*:

> Value terms have a special function in language, that of commending: and so they plainly cannot be defined in terms of other words which themselves do not perform this function; for if this is done, we are deprived of a means of performing the function.
>
> Almost every word in our language is capable of being used on occasion as a value-word (that is, for commending or its opposite); and usually it is only by cross-examining a speaker that we can tell whether he is so using a word. [*Language of Morals*, 91 and 79–80.]

There is obviously a serious inconsistency here. The first passage says that commendatory terms form a special class and that the function of commending is at least part of their meaning (since it is included in their definition); the second says that almost any term can commend and that the function of commending depends on the intention of the speaker.

The confusion is due to the assumption that if a particular term is used to perform a certain function we can explain its meaning by saying simply that it is used to do so-and-so. This assumption is shared by Urmson and is, I believe, at the root of the 'functionalist' conception of moral judgement which we have been considering in this second part of the book.

The basis of the assumption is the fact that every language possesses a group of non-descriptive terms whose meaning—if they can properly be said to have a meaning—is simply the function which they perform: *if*, *and*, *this*, and *it* are among the more common members of this class. Now the statement: '*Good* is used to commend' seems on a par with: '*And* is used to connect'. Having been told what *good* does, there seems to be no further reason for asking what it means, any more than there is for asking what *and* means.

The weakness in the reasoning is revealed by Hare himself in the second passage we have quoted, where he points out that whether or not a term is being used to commend depends on the intention of the speaker. This shows that commending is a function, not of individual terms, but of expressions; the function of terms such as *and* or *if* is determined by the conventions of language, and so is independent of the speaker's intention. Commending, then, is analogous to commanding or questioning or asserting. These are functions of complete expressions, not of individual terms, and the important thing to note is that the meaning of an individual term is not in any way determined by the function of the expression in which it occurs. Consider the expression: 'It is ten o'clock'. This could be a statement, a question, or a command, according as the speaker intends it. But in any of these three uses the meaning of the individual terms remains the same. Hence, even though value terms are used to commend, this tells us no more about their meaning than Urmson's theory that they are used for grading: it no more deprives value terms of their descriptive meaning than the fact that imperatives are used to command implies that terms which occur in imperatives are non-descriptive.

There is also in Hare's thought, I believe, a parallel misapprehension concerning the function of linguistic expressions. He assumes that, because prescribing and commending are distinct from describing, an expression which is primarily descriptive or factual cannot be used to commend or prescribe.

Now there is no doubt that the basic forms of prescribing or commending are non-factual. To issue the command: 'Stand at ease', or to make the formal commendation: 'I commend so-and-so', is not to say something which could be either true or false. But we are not thereby entitled to assume that a factual remark can never be used for commending or prescribing. For we normally commend something not by means of the highly formal expression: 'I commend *x*', but by attributing to x the quality which makes it worthy of commendation. We may commend a man by saying that he is kind and generous, a book by saying that it is witty and original, a car by saying that it is reliable and economical. In fact almost any term can, as Hare points out, be used for commending. 'He is an expert cutthroat' might conceivably be a commendatory remark. But there could be no suggestion that these are not factual statements.

The same is true of prescribing. When someone asks which of two routes he should take to Brussels, we can as easily direct him by saying: 'This is much the shorter of the two', as by issuing the imperative: 'Take that one'. To say that moral judgements must be primarily non-factual since their function is to guide conduct, is to overlook the fact that information can be as effective in directing action as advice.

8
P. H. Nowell-Smith

P. H. Nowell-Smith develops his theory of moral judgement[1] in contrast to ethical intuitionism, which offers what he calls 'a theoretical system of ethics'—a system based on the idea that the purpose of moral judgement is to provide information about the non-natural properties of goodness and rightness. The chief defect of this system is that it deprives ethics of its practical character. It leaves a logical gap between believing something to be good and choosing it, between believing that an action ought to be done and doing it. If *good* and *right* denote non-natural properties, one may legitimately enquire why the presence of such a property in an object is reason for choosing it, or why its presence in an action is a reason for doing it. Neither question can be answered in intuitionist terms, but the fact that they can meaningfully be posed is enough to show the weakness of intuitionism, for as *good* and *right* are under-

[1] Nowell-Smith's theory of moral judgement is contained in his book, *Ethics*, Harmondsworth 1954.

stood in ordinary speech these questions would never have arisen.

1. The logic of adjectives

The sources of ethical intuitionism, according to Nowell-Smith, are certain views concerning the logic of language. There is, firstly, the idea that all adjectives are the names of properties, that their function is to denote. Secondly, there is the idea that every word has a meaning which is distinct from the uses to which the word is put. Following Wittgenstein, Nowell-Smith holds that both these theories are highly misleading. They are valid only for certain types of words, and since ethical terms are amongst those to which they do not apply, their effect on moral philosophy has been almost entirely disastrous.

According to Nowell-Smith's own classification, adjectives may be divided into three main classes. Descriptive terms (D-words) stand for properties: typical examples of this class are *red*, *sweet*, *soft*. The second class is composed of words which 'indicate that an object has certain properties which are apt to arouse a certain emotion or range of emotions' (*Ethics*, 72). This is the class of aptness-words, or A-words; typical examples are *terrifying*, *amusing*, *entertaining*, and *sublime*. The third class is composed of such terms as *admirable*, *damnable*, *praiseworthy*, etc. These are gerundive words, or G-words, and their function is to indicate that something *ought* to be praised, or admired, or condemned, etc.

'The operation of "good", "right", "ought", and G-words are in many respects similar to that

155

of A-words.' (*Ethics*, 84.) The latter class is of special importance, therefore, and must be studied in some detail.

There are two things which we must note about the functioning of A-words. First, their purpose is not to denote a property. To call something green or round is to say that it possesses the property of greenness or roundness. But to call something sublime or amusing is not to say that it possesses the property of sublimity or amusingness. A view from the top of a mountain, for instance, could be described completely without mentioning that it was a sublime view.

> The sublimity of the view is not part of its contents and no description of the view would logically entail the truth or falsity of 'the view was sublime'. [*Ethics*, 71.]

For A-words do not normally denote. Their principal function is to *explain* why one had a certain reaction towards something, or to *predict* that one will have this reaction towards it. If you tell someone who is about to enter a cinema that the film on show there is amusing, you are predicting that he will be amused by it; if someone asks you why you enjoyed a film and you say, 'Because it was amusing', you are explaining why you enjoyed it. Your statement 'contextually implies' that the film has certain properties which would cause the normal person to be amused, but it does not *state* that it has these properties, nor say what they are.

The mention of 'contextual implication' brings us to the second important point about A-words.

> To understand the logic of an A-sentence we must ask, not 'What does it (always) mean?', but 'What does its use in this context contextually imply?' [*Ethics*, 85.]

To ask 'What does it mean?' is to imply that it has the same meaning in every context. But if we regard *meaning* as equivalent to *use* this is not true, for A-terms have different uses in different contexts. To explain an A-term is to outline what it contextually implies in the different contexts in which it occurs. *Contextual implication* is a term coined by Nowell-Smith, and defined by him as follows.

> I shall say that a statement p contextually implies a statement q if anyone who knew the normal conventions of the language would be entitled to infer q from p *in the context in which they occur*. Logical implications are a subclass of contextual implications, since if p logically implies q, we are entitled to infer q from p in any context whatever. Contextual implication can be most easily illustrated in a case where there is clearly no logical implication. If Jones says 'It is raining', Smith is entitled to infer that Jones believes that it is raining, although 'Jones believes that it is raining' clearly does not follow logically from 'It is raining'. Conversely there is clearly no contradiction between 'It is raining' and 'Jones believes that it isn't raining'; yet it would be logically odd for Jones to say 'It is raining, but I don't believe it is'.[1]

[1] *Ethics* 81. *Logically odd* is another term coined by

The following are some general rules of contextual implication. They are not rigid rules like the rules of logical implication, for they may all be broken without the speaker involving himself in self-contradiction or absurdity:

> *Rule 1.* When a speaker uses a sentence to make a statement, it is contextually implied that he believes it to be true . . .

> *Rule 2.* A speaker contextually implies that he has what he believes to be good reasons for his statement . . .

> *Rule 3.* What a speaker says . . . (contextually implies that it is) relevant to the interests of his audience. [*Ethics*, 81–2.]

What a statement contextually implies may vary from one context to the next. For A-sentences, however, there are certain elements which seem to be contextually implied in all typical instances of their use:

> (a) *The subjective element* . . . The use of an A-sentence usually implies that the speaker has the appropriate reaction. It would be odd to say that a book was enlightening or amusing and then to go on to say that one was not enlightened or amused by it . . .

Nowell-Smith. 'I shall say that a question is "logically odd" if there appears to be no further room for it in its context because it has already been answered.' (*Ethics*, 73.) He does not explain what a logically odd *statement* is, but presumably it is a statement which contradicts something which a previous statement of the speaker contextually implies.

(b) *The predictive element.* An A-sentence is sometimes used to imply that someone would have the appropriate reaction to something if suitable circumstances arose. Thus, if I tell you that there is an amusing film at the Scala, when the question is whether you should go to the Scala or not, I am predicting that you will be amused . . .

(c) *The generalizing element.* Sensible people do not make predictions . . . except on the basis of evidence, so that a man who uses an A-sentence to make a prediction contextually implies (by Rule 2) that he has what he believes to be good reasons for making the prediction . . .

(d) *The causal element* . . . To be told that something has an A-characteristic is not to be told just what causal properties it has that give it that characteristic; but it is contextually implied that it has such properties. [*Ethics*, 85–7.]

A-sentences play a much bigger role in practical discourse than do ordinary empirical statements. This appears when we consider such activities as choosing, explaining our choice, or advising another on what to choose. The reasons for choosing something are most often expressed in A-sentences. We choose a particular book because it is amusing, a particular film because it is entertaining, a particular house because it is comfortable. The same holds true of our explanations of why we chose the way we did, and of our advice to others on what to choose.

It is instructive to consider why we use A-sentences for these purposes rather than empirical statements. If someone were asked why he chose the car he did, he might reply either with the empirical statement: 'Because it has ample leg-room', or with the A-sentence: 'Because it is comfortable'. The A-sentence is less informative than the empirical statement. 'Because it is comfortable' contextually implies the existence of certain qualities in the car, but it does not say what these qualities are. Yet, despite this, it is a much better explanation of the choice than the first statement. This is clear once we compare the questions: 'Why did you choose a car with ample leg-room?', and: 'Why did you choose a comfortable car?' The second question has a much odder ring than the first; it would leave us at a loss as to what the questioner was getting at. This shows that the A-sentence is a much more complete explanation of the choice than the empirical statement. For the A-sentence implies a pro-attitude towards the reaction in question. It is because we want cars to be comfortable, films to be amusing, books to be interesting, that we can explain our choices and advise others in the way we do.

2. The logic of moral terms

The term *good* has many of the characteristics of A-terms, but there is one significant difference. To ask: 'Why did you choose a comfortable car?', is certainly odd, and yet there are certain situations in which it would be a legitimate question —if it was a matter of choosing a car for a speed-test, for example. But to ask: 'Why did you choose

160

a good car?', seems completely out of place. The reason, according to Nowell-Smith, is that to call a car comfortable merely contextually implies a pro-attitude towards it and what is contextually implied may be withdrawn without absurdity or contradiction. But to call something good actually *expresses* that pro-attitude. To explain one's choice by saying 'I chose that car because it is good' gives even less information about the car than does the A-sentence, but as an explanation of choice it is more complete because it is more closely tied to pro-attitudes.

This is not to say, however, that 'This is good' is equivalent to 'I approve of this', or to any similar remark which merely expresses a pro-attitude.

> There is clearly a great difference between 'I approve of X' and 'X is good'; and if we say that the latter is used to express approval we may be compelled to say also that it expresses a peculiar non-natural approval. But the new model enables us to bring out this difference without recourse to non-natural approval. For we can now say that, while both sentences express exactly the same sort of approval, the latter is properly used to express this approval only under fairly stringent conditions that need not obtain when 'I approve of X' is used. [*Ethics*, 95–6.]

The 'fairly stringent conditions' mentioned here are the presence of reasons for making this choice or giving this advice whenever *good* is used for these tasks. When we explain a choice by saying that we chose this thing because it is good, we contextually imply that we had good reasons for our choice, or—to put this in another way—that the thing possesses certain objective properties which impelled us to choose it. When we advise someone to choose a particular thing by telling him that it is good, we contextually imply that we have good reasons for our advice; the same predictive and causal elements are present as in A-sentences. The use of *good* to praise or commend must be understood in a similar fashion. When we call something good so as to commend or praise it, we are not merely commending or praising. Our statement contextually implies that we have reasons for our praise or commendation, that the thing has certain unspecified properties for which we praise or commend it.

There is one use of *good* which is somewhat different from the others. When we call something good, we may be giving what Nowell-Smith terms a 'verdict' or 'appraisal'. This type of *good* sentence is unusual in that it expresses a judgement. The other uses of *good* do not assert anything which could be either true or false. They are—in the now familiar terminology of Austin[1] —performative utterances, that is, they serve to perform an action rather than affirm something to be the case. When we use *good* to choose, or to advise, or to commend, the *good* sentence has the function of choosing, advising, or commending,

[1] See J. L. Austin, 'Performative Utterances', *Philosophical Papers*, ed. J. O. Urmson and G. Warnock, Oxford 1961, 220–34. See also *How to do Things with Words*, ed. J. O. Urmson, Oxford 1962.

but not of asserting something which is either true or false. But when we use *good* to make an appraisal or give a verdict, we are making genuine assertions.

This does not mean, however, that verdicts and appraisals are not closely connected with the other uses of *good*. To use *good* to give a verdict or appraisal is to apply standards to an object; the verdict states whether or not this object fulfils the accepted criteria of goodness for objects of the same class. But standards are also involved in the performative uses of *good*. For when we use *good* to choose or to advise, our statement contextually implies standards. To say that the choice or advice is 'based on reasons' is to say that the speaker applied standards. An appraisal is implicit in the performative uses of *good*, therefore.

But, although the performatory uses imply appraisal it is not so clear that the converse is true. Indeed it is not true in any direct sense: appraisals often imply preference only in a roundabout way. For when 'good' is used to give a verdict it need neither express nor imply a pro-attitude on the part of the speaker. In such cases what a man is primarily doing with the word 'good' is *applying* those standards which are only contextually implied in the more subjective uses. Since 'good' is a Janus-word, he may, of course, be expressing his preferences or advising as well; but he need not be. The embittered schoolmaster may have no interest in the work of the examination candidates at

163

all; he may even prefer stupidity to intelligence or have a private belief that the usual criteria for intelligence are quite wrong. Nevertheless he may still apply the grading words 'good', 'fair', 'poor', and so on in accordance with the accepted criteria either from conscientiousness or from habit or from fear of losing his job.[1]

But though a pro-attitude need not be implied in the application of criteria, pro-attitudes are logically prior to criteria of goodness. For unless people had pro-attitudes towards the objects appraised, and unless *good* was first used to make choices and give advice, its use in providing verdicts and appraisals would never have arisen.

Right and *ought* are analysed according to much the same pattern as *good*. To say that an action is right is to contextually imply that it is fitting or appropriate or that it conforms to certain rules. But this alone would not be sufficient to enable *right* to play the role it does in practical discourse. For the fact that an action is in accordance with some rule is not in itself a good reason for doing it, and in certain circumstances the best thing to do is something which would ordinarily be regarded as unfitting or inappropriate. *Right* must, therefore, be directly linked with pro-attitudes. It is not entirely clear, however, whether it expresses a pro-attitude, like *good*, or merely contextually implies one. At one stage Nowell-Smith does indeed say that it

[1] *Ethics*, 170. By 'Janus-word', Nowell-Smith means a word which can perform two or more jobs simultaneously.

contextually implies a pro-attitude (*Ethics*, 186); but he later points out that *right* is always a pro-word—unlike, for example, *just*, *fair*, or *honourable*, which admit of exceptions (*Ethics*, 189). This would seem to imply that *right* expresses a pro-attitude, since what is contextually implied may be withdrawn without absurdity or contradiction.

Ought is used in the first person to express a decision and in the second to give advice. In both cases it differs from ordinary expressions of decision or advice by the fact that the speaker contextually implies that he has good reasons for what he says. *You ought* has the same function as a command, but it differs from the latter in that it would be inappropriate unless the speaker could offer reasons in support of his injunction. 'I did it because I thought I ought' implies that my choice was a reasoned one and indicates the type of reason involved, namely, that the action was in accordance with a certain rule. Here again we must invoke a link with pro-attitudes, to explain how *ought* functions in practical discourse. For to tell a person to do something is clearly to imply that you want him to do it, and the person addressed must have a pro-attitude towards doing what he ought if 'You ought to do *x*' is to provide him with a reason for doing it.

3. Meaning, use, and value terms
Nowell-Smith's theory of moral judgement is a modified form of subjectivism. But this is almost the only thing which clearly emerges from his writings on the subject. Everything else is so

shrouded in qualifications that any general characterisation must necessarily be inaccurate. The
structure of his argument is also often obscure.
It is difficult to be clear at almost every stage as to
where precisely the argument is leading and even
more difficult to be clear at the end as to how his
conclusions are connected with what has gone
before. In fact Nowell-Smith often seems to assert
his views dogmatically without offering any supporting reasons. No doubt this is sometimes
unavoidable. The answer to certain types of
philosophical problems, particularly those of conceptual or linguistic analysis, cannot be provided
with anything in the nature of a conclusive supporting argument. Usually, the only way to
appraise these theories is by searching for counter-
examples, and the main evidence for the truth of
the theories is the absence of any such counter-
examples. Astonishingly, however, Nowell-Smith
tells us that examples which are counter to his
theory must be treated with suspicion.

> The contextual implications of any use of
> 'good' are many and varied and, on occasion,
> any of them can be withdrawn, a point which
> should make us suspicious of counter-examples.
> [*Ethics*, 167.]

This ordinance is, of course, self-defeating, for if
the contextual implications of *good* are so varied
as to render dubious any attempt to provide a
counter-example, a theory such as Nowell-Smith's
which explains them in general terms must be
infinitely more dubious. As a means of forestal-
ling adverse criticism, however, it is certainly

effective, but the security achieved may in the end turn out to have been bought at too high a price. If hostile witnesses are removed from court before the trial begins, their absence is no longer a reason for believing in the innocence of the person on trial. And while it may now be very difficult to provide evidence against Nowell-Smith's theory of moral judgement, the evidence in its favour is equally scanty. Were other moralists to follow his example, the result would be a collection of conflicting and irrefutable theories. I can think of no more effective means of disposing of whatever claim philosophy still possesses to be a rational discipline.

The root of the trouble is Nowell-Smith's approach to the problem, more particularly his enthusiastic acceptance of the Wittgensteinian dictum: 'The meaning of a term is its use in language'. This leads him to reject traditional theories of moral judgement on the. grounds that they assume that moral terms have the same meaning in all contexts.

> The fact that a given expression can be used to perform many different roles is by itself sufficient to undermine or at least to make us suspicious of all arguments of the form 'When we say . . . we mean'. [*Ethics*, 98.]

More important still, it leads him to adopt the view that the nature of moral judgement can be explained only by describing the various roles which moral terms play in everyday discourse.

The old model is not just misleading: it is

wholly wrong. The words with which moral philosophers have especially to do, which are called 'value-words', play many different parts. They are used to express tastes and preferences, to express decisions and choices, to criticize, grade and evaluate, to advise, admonish, warn, persuade and dissuade, to persuade and reprove, to encourage and reprove, to promulgate and draw attention to rules; and doubtless for other purposes also. These activities form the complex web of moral discourse and our problem is to show the connexions between them and to come to understand how it is that the same word can be used in all these different ways. What a man is doing with a particular value-word at a particular time can only be discovered by examining what he says in its context, but it would be just as absurd to suppose that there is no connexion between these activities as to suppose that the same expression can only be used to do one job. [*Ethics*, 98.]

This denunciation of traditional moral theories seems to me unjustified. In offering definitions of moral terms moral philosophers were not denying that these terms have different uses. It does not seem likely that any philosopher could ever have doubted that words are used in a variety of ways —for making statements, issuing commands, asking questions, making requests, telling jokes, saying prayers, and so on. In defining a term one is not denying this. Rather, one is implying that the term in question has a primary or typical sense which is shared by most, if not all, the different uses of the term, and which must be grasped for any—even the least typical—of these uses to be fully understood. This is no doubt a debatable position, more especially perhaps with regard to philosophical terms, but one cannot refute it by pointing out that words are used in different ways.

Nowell-Smith has fallen into the same error as Urmson and Hare in confusing the function of an individual term and the function of sentences in which it occurs. To say that a term is used to denote is to describe its function *as an individual term*: to say that it is used to praise, to grade, to choose, or to advise is to describe the function of sentences in which it occurs. The two things are quite unrelated, as we have seen; almost any type of term can be used in almost any type of sentence. Terms whose function as individual terms is to denote can, like other terms, occur in sentences of various types. Moral philosophers were obviously not denying this, therefore, in implying that the function of ethical terms is to denote.

Nowell-Smith's own conception of the way in which the meaning of ethical terms is to be explained will not bear serious examination. We have seen his objection to explanations which take the form 'When we say . . . we mean . . .'; and elsewhere he speaks of the 'logical mistake of supposing that the meaning of "good" can be examined in isolation from its context' (*Ethics*, 79). But this does not prevent him from explaining the word *meaning* in isolation from its context.

The word 'meaning' is itself both vague and

ambiguous and depends more than usual on the context and purpose of the speaker. If someone asks what the meaning of a word is, he is usually asking for an explanation of the way in which the word is used. [*Ethics*, 66.]

These two sentences seem to contradict each other when taken in conjunction with what Nowell-Smith has said about ethical terms. For if we are prevented from saying what these ethical terms usually mean because of their dependence on the context and on the purpose of the speaker, the same must be true of the term *meaning*. A little later we find the statement: 'Elucidating the meaning of a word is explaining how the word is used' (*Ethics*, 67). This is equivalent to: 'When we say *meaning* we mean *use*,' a type of explanation which Nowell-Smith has himself declared to be 'wholly wrong'.

The fact is that the principle: 'The meaning of a term is its use in language', if applied consistently, would preclude any explanation of ethical terms. Whatever coherence Nowell-Smith's theory possesses derives from his ignoring the principle's implications for such terms as *meaning, use, explanation,* and *choice*. If he had been consistent and tried to describe how these are used, he would have involved himself in an endless regress. Yet their usage is hardly less complex than that of ethical terms, and it is difficult to see how the assumption that they have a fairly stable meaning can possibly be justified if a similar assumption with regard to ethical terms is wholly wrong.

170

4. The classification of adjectives

Nowell-Smith distinguishes three groups of adjectives—descriptive terms, aptness terms, and gerundive terms. We are not told whether this list is to be regarded as exhaustive, or, if it is not to be so regarded, why these three classes should have been chosen in preference to others. The grouping appears even more eccentric when it turns out that ethical terms do not come under any of these three headings; it is difficult to see the logic behind a classification which fails to include what one is expressly trying to elucidate. But whatever the truth is about the logic, the purpose of the classification is not in doubt: it is to show that not all adjectives stand for properties. Once this is clear, Nowell-Smith believes, the theory that ethical terms stand for properties will quickly lose all plausibility.

Property is such a vague term, however, that the statement: 'Ethical terms do not stand for properties', conveys little or nothing until one knows in what precise sense the term is being used. For Nowell-Smith, *property* means unequivocally *empirical property*.

> We can only hope to answer the question 'Is goodness a property?' by exhibiting the similarities and differences between 'good' and those adjectives that most typically fit what the logician has to say about properties; and these are the names of empirical descriptive properties ... To say that goodness is a property commits us to the very debatable assertion that

the logic of 'good' is like that of 'blue', 'loud' and 'round'. [*Ethics*, 51.]

To remove any further ambiguity he defines an empirical property as one whose presence and degree are detected by the senses.

We detect the presence and estimate the degree of empirical properties 'by means of the senses', by looking, feeling, tasting, and smelling; since 'empirical properties' are just those properties of which the presence and degree are discovered in this way. [*Ethics*, 51.]

Nowell-Smith hopes to prove that ethical terms do not stand for properties by showing, firstly, that A-words and G-words do not do so, and, secondly, that ethical terms have much closer affinities with A-words and G-words than with D-words. This sounds quite unexceptionable at first glance; no one would, I think, seriously suggest that goodness is at all the same sort of thing as roundness, or softness, or loudness, and in consequence, it is not extravagant to suggest that the logic of ethical terms is closer to terms such as *terrifying* or *praiseworthy* than to *loud, round,* or *soft.* However, as Nowell-Smith uses it, the classification is, I believe, seriously misleading, partly because it is inadequate—a large number, if not the majority, of adjectives do not come under any of its three headings—, and partly because of the extraordinary interpretation which Nowell-Smith gives to A- and G-terms and the sentences in which they occur. I will consider each of these points in turn.

By dividing adjectives into D-terms, A-terms, and

G-terms Nowell-Smith gives the impression that any adjective which is not a D-word must belong to the same family as A-words and G-words.

Consider, for example, the following sentences:

The view from the top was extensive.
The view from the top was sublime.

The adjective 'sublime' does not form part of a description of the view, unless we insist on making all adjectives descriptive and thereby reduce the force of 'descriptive' to vanishing point. We could give an exhaustive description of the view by enumerating its contents, and if the list contained a large number of large objects this would entail that the view was extensive. The question whether the view was extensive or not is a question of empirical fact. But the sublimity of the view is not part of its contents and no description of the view would logically entail the truth or falsity of 'the view was sublime'. It is just this that the argument against the Naturalistic Fallacy shows so clearly. Some philosophers have said that goodness is a 'consequential property', by which is meant that it is a property that something can have only if it has certain other properties. But we have already seen that the link between goodness and the good-making properties is not a logical one; a special act of awareness is needed to apprehend it. The relation between 'sublime' and those features of a landscape in virtue of which we would call it sublime is of the same type.

Consider the following conversation:

A. When I got to the top, I saw the whole plain spread out beneath me and Nanga Parbat towering above it. A waterfall that must have been at least five hundred feet high cascaded down from near where I stood into the swirling waters of the Indus.

B. What a sublime (magnificent, stirring, awe-inspiring, wonderful etc.) sight that must have been.

... The connexion between their remarks is obviously not logical entailment; yet we feel that B's comment was the natural and appropriate one to make. And this is because he is evincing the natural, appropriate emotion. [*Ethics*, 70–71.]

Nowell-Smith is obviously using *descriptive word* here to mean a word which denotes an empirical property, or whose attribution to something is logically entailed by that thing's description, i.e, by the enumeration of its empirical properties.[1] The point which I wish to make is that to define *D-term* in this way is to leave a very large number, perhaps a majority, of adjectives outside the scope of Nowell-Smith's classification. Consider, for in-

[1] This is not entirely accurate, as we learn from a footnote that '"extensive" is not strictly a "descriptive" word: for to say that a view is extensive is not to describe it. But it belongs to descriptive discourse and will do as an example' (*Ethics*, 71 *n*. 1). The distinction between a descriptive term and one which merely belongs to descriptive discourse is not elaborated further, so for the sake of simplicity I propose to ignore it and regard both types of term as descriptive.

stance, the word which Nowell-Smith puts forward as an example of a descriptive term—*extensive*. This does not denote an empirical property, nor—despite what Nowell-Smith says above—would the description of anything entail that it was extensive. *Extensive* is a relational term, and its criteria of application vary from one type of object to another—an extensive lawn, for example, would not have the same proportions as an extensive lake. No definite set of criteria is included within the meaning of *extensive*, therefore. It follows that it cannot be self-contradictory to state that an object has certain proportions but is not extensive; hence the assertion that it has certain proportions cannot logically entail that it is extensive.

Could one overcome this difficulty by defining *extensive* so that a definite set of criteria would then be included in its meaning? This is, of course, possible, but one would not then be treating of *extensive* as the term is ordinarily understood: it would then denote a definite set of criteria and would no longer be a relational term. The term as ordinarily understood is applicable to entirely different types of object, and, furthermore, allows for change in the criteria of its application without any change in its meaning. The standard for what constitutes an extensive lawn, for example, may have been quite different a hundred years ago from what it is today. But the meaning of the term has not changed. And this shows that one cannot logically deduce the applicability of the term from any statement about the lawn's extent.

This holds for all relational terms of the same type as *extensive*. But to bring out the inadequacy of Nowell-Smith's classification one has merely to consider again the passage which he puts forward as an example of descriptive writing.

When I got to the top, I saw the whole plain spread out beneath me and Nanga Parbat towering above it. A waterfall that must have been at least five hundred feet high cascaded down from near where I stood into the swirling waters of the Indus.

This contains four adjectives—*whole*, *five hundred*, *high*, and *swirling*. It goes without saying that none of these are A-terms or G-terms, and it is almost as evident that they are not D-terms. *High* has the same type of relational character as *extensive*; *whole* does not designate an empirical property of the plain, and no enumeration of the plain's empirical properties could logically entail that this was the whole plain; *five hundred* is equally clearly not the name of an empirical property, and its applicability to a collection is discovered by counting, which is not at all the same sort of thing as a deduction from the collection's empirical properties; and lastly, *swirling* is indeed an empirical term, but it is not the name of a property—it is not the same sort of term as *loud*, *soft*, or *round*—since it designates, not something which the water has, but something which it does.

I think it is not unfair to conclude from all this that Nowell-Smith's classification owes nothing to a survey of the adjectives which actually occur in language; rather it was specially fashioned so as to accord with his subjectivist theory of moral judgement.

The second aspect of the classification which I wish to examine is the peculiar interpretation given to A-terms and G-terms, and to sentences in which they occur. This has a material bearing on Nowell-Smith's theory of moral judgement, for, as we have seen, he regards ethical terms as having much the same function and characteristics as A-terms.

A-words are defined as 'words that indicate that an object has certain properties which are apt to arouse a certain emotion or range of emotions' (*Ethics*, 72). It would seem to follow immediately from this that an A-sentence—one which predicates an A-term of an object—asserts that the object has certain properties which are apt to arouse a certain emotion or range of emotions. But this is not so. Nowell-Smith repeatedly states that A-sentences merely contextually imply that the object has certain properties which are apt to arouse a certain emotion or range of emotions, but they do not assert this.

A man who calls tigers 'terrifying' contextually implies that they have certain properties which frighten people. But he does not *state* this; still less does he specify what these properties are. [*Ethics*, 90.]

But if A-sentences do not state this, what do they state? The answer is that they do not state anything; they are performative utterances, not statements of fact. To say: 'This is an enjoyable film', in the context of choice is simply another way of saying: 'I choose to go to this film', the only difference being that the A-sentence implies that one has reasons for one's choice and indicates the general nature of these reasons without specifying them. The same sentence used in the context of advice is equivalent to: 'Go to this film', the difference again being that the A-sentence implies that one has good reasons for giving this advice. The A-sentence here

> ... is not a 'statement of fact' which can be extracted from its context and pronounced true or false; it is a piece of advice that depends for its interpretation on its context. If the right contextual elements are not present, it is deceptive, inappropriate or irrelevant. [*Ethics*, 148.]

Earlier, however, A-sentences had been spoken of in quite a different manner.

> We think of 'being terrifying' as an objective property of bulls, because 'bulls are terrifying' states a fact which can be verified in the way that statements about objective properties can be verified. It is true or false independently of the reactions of the speaker and it is for this reason that we use the impersonal form of speech. [*Ethics*, 89.]

I do not see how these statements can possibly be reconciled, or indeed how the various things which Nowell-Smith says about A-terms and A-sentences form a coherent theory. For if A-sentences merely contextually imply that an object has certain properties, etc., then it cannot be the specific function of A-terms to indicate this. A linguistic expression must have a meaning (or function) of some sort before it can acquire contextual implications; hence one cannot explain the specific function of a term merely by mentioning the contextual implications of the statements in which it occurs. Secondly, if an A-sentence states a fact, then what it states is that the object in question has the ability to arouse a certain emotion or range of emotions. But if it merely contextually implies this, it is simply not a statement of fact, for what other fact is there which it could state?

Besides, the manner in which A-terms and sentences are actually used seems to run completely counter to Nowell-Smith's theory.

> If Jones says that there is an amusing or instructive film at the Super . . . the sentence is used in this context as a piece of advice and therefore constitutes a solution to Smith's problem, not something from which a solution could be deduced. But it differs from 'If I were you I should go to the Super' and from 'Go to the Super' in that it contextually implies that Jones has good reasons for giving the advice and this is but weakly implied or not implied at all in the other formula. [*Ethics*, 147.]

But there is nothing unusual in advising someone by saying: 'Although the film at the Super is amusing, I think you ought to go to the one at the Scala'. On Nowell-Smith's interpretation, this would be to simultaneously advise the person to go and not to go, and this is obviously nonsense. The same is true of A-sentences in the context of choice. There is nothing odd in saying: 'This car is more comfortable, but I shall choose the other one all the same'. On Nowell-Smith's interpretation this is equivalent to simultaneously choosing and not choosing it.

That A-sentences are indeed factual is clear from the fact that it would be contradictory to assert that a film is amusing but that it did not have the capacity to amuse people, or that a tiger is terrifying but that it did not have the ability to terrify people. It follows that when you say that a film is amusing, you are asserting that it has the ability to amuse, and this is obviously a statement of fact. A-terms are a sub-class of terms which designate capacities, potencies, powers—terms such as *fast, intelligent, active*. Nowell-Smith's tendency to regard A-sentences as non-factual seems to be at least partly due to the fact that these terms are not included in his classification of adjectives: in consequence, he is led to believe that to hold that A-sentences assert something about the object in question implies that A-terms designate properties, and this is ruled out not merely because A-terms and D-terms are distinct, but also because it makes it impossible to understand how A-sentences play the part they do in practical discourse.

If we try to construe 'amusingness' or 'instructiveness' as objective properties that do or do not reside in the film, Smith might well ask what reason there is for supposing that because the film has this property he will enjoy it, and that is what he wants to know. [*Ethics*, 147.]

The weakness of this argument may be shown by our changing the setting from advice concerning a film to advice concerning a wager at the races. Suppose that in response to Smith's request for advice, Jones tells him that Black Prince is a fast horse.

If we try to construe 'fastness' as an objective property that does or does not reside in the horse, Smith might well ask what reason there is for supposing that because the horse has this property he will win, and that is what he wants to know.

The answer, of course, is that *fast* refers, not so much to a property of the horse, as to an ability which it has. And the fact that the horse has this ability has a material bearing on whether or not it will win the race. But no one could doubt that: 'Black Prince is a fast horse', is a factual remark. And since the only difference between *fast* and *amusing* is that one designates the ability to perform a physical action, the other the ability to arouse an emotion, there is no more reason for doubting the factual character of A-sentences.

5. The analysis of *good*

Nowell-Smith's theory of value, as we have seen, is a modified form of subjectivism. The sentence: '*x* is good', he holds, is partly equivalent to: 'I approve of *x*', the difference being that the impersonal form is used only under fairly stringent conditions which need not obtain when: 'I approve of *x*' is used. This theory, he claims, puts an end to the dispute between subjectivism and objectivism by giving due allowance to both sides without committing itself to either.

> If we distinguish between the purpose for which a sentence is used and the conditions, if any, which limit the use of just this sentence for just this purpose (between what a man means by a sentence and what is contextually implied), the dispute between subjectivists and objectivists becomes clear. Briefly, the subjectivists tend to ignore the contextual background and the objectivists tend to treat this background as part of what a man actually says. [*Ethics*, 96.]

His proof for the subjective character of ethical statements is as follows:

> Just as the subjectivists are right in denying that A-words stand for special properties and explaining them in terms of people's reactions, so they are also right in connecting 'good' and 'bad' with people's desires, tastes, interests, approvals, and disapprovals. There is a logical absurdity about calling a play 'amusing' if the speaker believes that it never has amused anyone and never will; and there is the same logical absurdity in calling something 'good' without any direct or indirect reference to a pro-attitude. If the connexion between 'good' and the pro-attitude that is contextually relevant were not a logical one, a gap would emerge between calling something good on the one hand and deciding to choose it, choosing it or advising

182

others to choose it on the other, which would make these activities unintelligible. [*Ethics*, 178.]

Nevertheless there is a gap between calling something good and deciding to choose it, for otherwise the phenomenon known as moral weakness would be unintelligible. But presumably what Nowell-Smith is referring to is the fact that it never makes sense to ask: 'Why did you choose a good car?' There is no room for an explanation here, for what better reason would you have for choosing it? But this is not so of terms such as *comfortable, well-sprung,* or *economical,* for one could explain that a well-sprung or economical car is the sort of car you want. It follows that *good car* must mean 'the sort of car I have a pro-attitude towards'.

This is certainly an impressive argument, and one that might seem almost unassailable if *good* were used only to explain choices. However, once we consider the use of *good* in the context of advice, serious difficulties emerge. For if *good* expresses a pro-attitude it is difficult, if not impossible, to understand how it plays the part it does in international discourse. Not only is the fact that I possess a pro-attitude towards something not a conclusive reason why another person should choose it—it is not even a moderately good reason. For it is notorious that tastes and preferences—pro-attitudes, if you wish—vary greatly from one person to another. To persuade or advise someone to choose something one must tell him, not about one's own tastes or desires, but about the objects of his choice. *Good* could not function the way it does in the context of advice or persuasion, therefore, if its meaning were subjective.

But isn't it possible that the role of *good* in advising and persuading is due to what it contextually implies rather than what it actually expresses?

> To tell someone that something is the best thing for him to do is to advise him to do it, but not irresponsibly. The speaker implies that he has good reasons for his advice, that he knows what the problem is and that his advice is relevant. [*Ethics*, 162.]

The difficulty is, however, that if *good* expresses a pro-attitude, the fact that 'good reasons' are contextually implied adds little or nothing, since 'good reasons' are, ex hypothesi, 'reasons towards which I have a pro-attitude'. This does not render the expression any less subjective, since any pro-attitude would be based on some sort of reasons. Nowell-Smith's second rule of contextual implication is that every statement contextually implies that the speaker has good reasons for what he says.

The failure of Nowell-Smith's analysis of *good* to account for its use in the context of advice should make us look again at his argument concerning its use in the context of choice. The argument is, briefly, that since it never makes sense to say: 'Why did you choose a good car?', *good car* must mean 'car towards which I have a pro-attitude'. A serious objection to this is that we sometimes attribute *good* to things towards which we do not have a pro-attitude. A puritan who regards everything to do with the theatre as immoral would still have to admit that Shakespeare was a good dramatist; a pacifist might still agree that Napoleon was a good general.

Nowell-Smith tries to evade this difficulty by saying that such judgements are a special case; they do not express pro-attitudes, but they assert the conformity of the object to accepted standards, something which is normally only contextually implied. A linguistic analysis comes under grave suspicion, however, when it is forced to attribute different meanings to a term so as to avoid counter-examples. Occam's principle is as valid here as elsewhere. The assumption is that a term preserves substantially the same meaning in different contexts unless there are definite indications to the contrary, and such indications must be linguistic and not due simply to the exigencies of one's philosophical position. Moreover, value judgements which do not express a pro-attitude can play precisely the same role in practical discourse as the ordinary type of value judgement. The puritan we mentioned who found himself in a position where he had to choose or advise on the choice of a play would, if he were honest, be guided by his value judgements. And this shows that value judgements guide choices, not because they express pro-attitudes, but because of what they say about the objects of choice. The pro-attitude merely influences the individual to make a choice, but the *direction* of the choice is influenced by the informative content of the value judgement.

Nowell-Smith is, of course, right in postulating a logical connection between *good* and choice. But this does not necessarily imply that *good* expresses a pro-attitude. Consider, for instance, the term *efficient*. It would be just as senseless to ask: 'Why did you choose an efficient car?', as: 'Why did you choose a good car?'. Yet: 'This is an efficient car', is undeniably a factual statement. I do not wish to conclude that *good* means *efficient*. But it is clear that Nowell-Smith's explanation of the connection between *good* and choice is not the only possible one; and there are other factors, as we have seen, which render it unacceptable.

Nowell-Smith's explanation of the objective character of *good*-sentences is as follows:

But the objectivists are also right. They are mistaken in denying the points made by the subjectivists above and in thinking that goodness must be a unique, non-natural property. It is sometimes argued that if there were no such property we could not account for the fact that we use the impersonal form 'this is good' rather than the personal form 'I approve of this', and those who use this argument are inclined to forget that we have an impersonal form 'this is nice' as well as the personal form 'I like it', so that niceness would have to be an objective property too. It would indeed be puzzling to understand why we use these impersonal forms if we were just talking about or expressing our own approval; but this argument does not show that we are talking about something else, still less that this must be a unique property. We can account for the objective formula, as we did in the case of 'nice', by saying (a) 'X is good' is not only used in the context of choice and (b) that, when it is so used, it implies a great deal that is not implied by 'I approve of X' and is expressly denied by 'I happen to approve of X'. It implies that my approval is not an unusual one and that I could give reasons for it. It implies also—what is a matter of objective fact—that the object conforms to certain norms which are generally accepted. [*Ethics*, 178-9.]

Nowell-Smith here repeats the view that *good* must be a D-term for *good*-statements to be objectively true or false. This hardly requires further comment. What does require to be discussed is the question whether Nowell-Smith's interpretation of the objective character of *good*-statements allows for the fact that opposing *good*-statements contradict each other. Since, on his theory, this cannot be accounted for by what these statements express, it must be due to what they contextually imply. To argue in this way, however, is to be guilty of an elementary fallacy. For in denying a statement one does not necessarily deny what the statement implies. This is true both of logical implication and of Nowell-Smith's contextual implication. To deny that all men are dark-skinned, for example, is not to deny that some are dark-skinned. And to deny the truth of another person's statement is not to deny that he believes it to be true, for otherwise one could never challenge another's statement without implicitly calling him a liar. It follows that, on Nowell-Smith's analysis, when one person says that something is good and another denies this, their statements are not necessarily in contradiction or opposition. But since such statements do contradict each other as ordinarily understood, his analysis must be incorrect.

Nowell-Smith tries to answer this objection when dealing with *ought*-statements.

> It is true that in ordinary life we should say that Smith and Jones were contradicting each other. But this only illustrates the danger of drawing philosophical conclusions from ordinary language. 'Contradicting', which literally means 'speaking against', can be used of almost any kind of verbal disagreement; but it also has a technical logician's use which was designed to elucidate empirical discourse. And if we speak of conflicting moral attitudes as 'contradicting' we run the risk of unconsciously assimilating moral disputes to empirical ones and of inventing in the logic of moral discourse elements analogous to those which are bound up with the notion of contradiction in empirical discourse. One of these is 'correspondence with the facts'. And this is to court disaster. [*Ethics*, 195.]

But Nowell-Smith's conclusions about ethical concepts are all, confessedly, drawn from ordinary discourse. Does this process become dangerous only when ordinary discourse proves irreconcilable with his theory? His remarks on logic are also extraordinary. Its purpose, he seems to be saying, is to elucidate empirical discourse. But is it not equally applicable to the non-empirical discourse of mathematicians and philosophers? Nowell-Smith has himself stated in a different context that 'the examples they [i.e, logicians] give are very rarely drawn from practical discourse; for they have devoted almost all their attention to the logic either of mathematics or of the natural sciences' (*Ethics*, 63). In mathematical discourse, *truth* has nothing to do with 'correspondence with the facts'. I fail to see, therefore, why the application of the logical concept of contradiction to ethical discourse should be so perilous.

The fact is that opposing ethical statements *do* contradict each other in the sense in which the term *contradict* is understood in logic, that is, in the sense in which propositions are contradictory if it is logically impossible that they should simultaneously both be true together and false together. The only alternative is to deny that ethical statements can be true or false. But it is impossible to see how such a denial could be justified. For if it means that ethical statements cannot be true in the sense in which the term *true* is ordinarily understood, then it is certainly false—in everyday discourse ethical statements commonly have truth or falsity attributed to them. And if it means that they cannot be true in the sense in which empirical statements are true, then it is entirely trivial. For if ethical statements differ from empirical statements, we should naturally expect that the criterion of their truth would differ also, just as it does in the case of mathematical and philosophical statements.

6. The analysis of *ought*

Nowell-Smith's analysis of *ought* and *right* follows the same pattern and suffers from the same defects as his analysis of *good*.

> The primary use of 'you ought' sentences is to tell someone to do something in cases where it is contextually implied that the speaker has reasons for what he says. [*Ethics*, 198.]

This implies that *you ought* has a different meaning from *I ought* or *he ought*, for commands are properly used only in the second person. This in itself is sufficient to rule out Nowell-Smith's analysis since it seems undeniable that: 'You ought to do *x*', has, apart from the change in person, precisely the same meaning as: 'I ought to do *x*', or: 'He ought to do *x*'. And this is borne out by the fact that each of these three sentences, when used in a moral context, would imply *can* in the strict sense of logical implication. This would not be the case, as we have seen in the chapter on Hare, if *you ought* were a species of command.

Nowell-Smith's interpretation of: 'I ought to do *x*', as expressing a decision to do *x* with the contextual implication that I have reasons for my decision is open to the same difficulties as Hare's theory. For what we call moral weakness would be impossible if *I ought* expresses a decision. Moral weakness occurs when we do something which we believe we ought not to do. Clearly this would never happen if *I ought* entailed *I will*.

Nowell-Smith is on more solid grounds when he says that *ought* contextually implies good reasons.

If he had said rather that *ought* asserts the presence of good reasons for doing the action in question, he would, I believe, have been very nearly correct. The difficulty with this, however, is that I may have good reasons both for doing an action and not doing it. *I ought* must mean, then, that there is a conclusive reason or set of reasons for doing this action rather than any other —or, if you wish, that reason demands that I do it. This explains how *ought* can retain the same meaning whether used in the first, second, or third person, how conflicting *ought*-sentences contradict each other, and how an *ought*-sentence can have a practical character yet still be a statement of fact. Lastly, it leaves room for moral weakness, for we may recognise that there is a conclusively good reason for doing something yet, because of the influence of our passions, fail to do it.

Nowell-Smith's theory of moral judgement is, of course, largely dependent on the concept of contextual implication—on the distinction which he draws between what a statement means and what it contextually implies. If we have so far offered no comment on this, it is not because it is not open to criticism, but because it has been severely criticised by Nowell-Smith himself in a recent article. There he speaks of the doctrine as 'grossly muddled', and adds:

What I formerly called 'contextual implication' covered a number of different relations between expressions and their uses which have only this in common, that they are relations which entitle us to draw inferences and are therefore properly called relations of implication (in the ordinary, not the logician's sense), that they do not hold between propositions, statements or assertions, i.e., what someone does or might assert, and that some reference to the context in which they occur is necessary to decide whether or not they hold.[1]

The first relation of implication which Nowell-Smith distinguishes is that which enables us to infer from the fact that someone asserts something that he believes it to be true. This he terms 'pragmatic implication', and points out that, contrary to what he had previously believed, the antecedent here is not the proposition which is asserted, but its assertion by the speaker.

> The cardinal feature of pragmatic implication [is] that it is a speaker or his making a statement, not what he states, that has pragmatic implications. ['Contextual Implication', 5.]

He distinguishes two other sorts of implication which depend, to some extent, on the context in which the statement is uttered.

> The other types of relation between expressions which depend on their context, though important and, for ethical theory, more important than pragmatic implication, must be briefly dismissed. Sometimes a remark, taken out of its context, cannot be understood, and its implications will then be indeterminate ... Here the

[1] 'Contextual Implication and Ethical Theory', *Proceedings of the Aristotelian Society*, supplementary volume XXXVI (1962), 3.

context needs to be considered only in order to fix the meaning of the remark, and once this is fixed the implication is not of a peculiar or interesting kind ... Another way in which the context of a remark may be relevant to its implications is that it may be necessary to refer to its context to establish what *sort* of a remark it is, whether statement, command, threat, warning, advice and so on. ['Contextual Implication', 15.]

But if this type of implication is more important for ethics than pragmatic implication, it seems that Nowell-Smith has entirely abandoned his distinction between what an ethical statement means and what it contextually implies, for here contextual implication is simply a form of logical implication, the only difference being that what the statement logically implies depends, to some extent, on the context in which it is uttered. And if an ethical statement logically implies the presence of good reasons, etc, then that must be part of what it asserts. There is no room here, then, for a distinction between what a statement means and what it contextually implies. And neither can this distinction be upheld by appealing to pragmatic implication, for here, as Nowell-Smith confesses, the antecedent is not the statement itself but the fact that it has been asserted by the speaker.

Part 3

The 'good reasons' approach

there are standard methods of resolving it. But in ethics we must often 'agree to disagree', recognising that no reasoned agreement on the disputed question is possible. Ethical statements, they conclude, are subjective: terms such as *good* and *right* are names for subjective relations rather than for properties. (c) Finally, the 'imperative' approach denies that ethical terms are names either for objective properties or subjective relations. Ethical statements tell us what to do, not what is the case. They are really imperatives concealed under the grammatical form of statements of fact.

Toulmin's explanation for these differences of opinion is based on the Wittgensteinian dictum that disputes in philosophy arise from the failure of philosophers to command a clear view of the workings of language. Moralists have failed to take account of the full complexity of ethical statements: they have fastened on one aspect to the detriment of others.

> An ethical theory is, therefore, not just a paradox. If we reject it out of hand, on the grounds that, when taken literally, it is false, we misunderstand what its advocates are getting at. Such a theory had a certain positive value, which it would be wrong to ignore, as expressing, in its own paradoxical way, a comparison between concepts of two different kinds. This value is, however, limited; a single comparison tells one very little ... We may agree with the 'objectivist' that ethical words are 'like' words for properties—but they are not *just* like them; in

some respects, they are *unlike* them also, and his description of 'value' as a 'property of the object' is therefore only partially acceptable. They are also like, *and* unlike, words for subjective relations; and passing an ethical judgement is like, *and* unlike, exclaiming: so the other doctrines are equally unhelpful. . . . 'What is wanted' (to adapt something John Wisdom wrote in another context) 'is some device for bringing out the relation between the manner in which ethical sentences are used and the manner in which others are used—so as to give their place on the language-map.' It will be from such a description, or 'language-map', rather than from a one-sided and disguised comparison, that we shall obtain the understanding that we seek. [*Place of Reason*, 193–5.]

Thus ethical statements are like imperatives in that they tell us how to act, but unlike them in being genuine statements of fact. They are like subjective statements in that they are closely related to our attitudes and feelings, but they are unlike them in that opposing ethical statements really contradict each other.

But is not this, in effect, to embrace the objective theory? For if: 'This action is right', is a genuine statement and does not describe the attitude of the speaker, then it seems it must describe the action itself. A statement which is not subjective must be objective, and rightness must, therefore, be a property of the action. According to Toulmin, however, this dichotomy is a false one. It is based on an over-simplified view of language. The terms *good* and *right* may be meaningful and not be names in any sense. The statement: 'This action is right', is not part of the description of the action. What it asserts is not that the action possesses a certain property, but that there are good reasons for doing it.

> 'Rightness' is not a property; and when I asked the two people which course was the right one I was not asking them about a property—what I wanted to know was whether there was any reason for choosing one course of action rather than another; and, provided that they are arguing about the reasons for my doing different things, we are perfectly justified in talking of a genuine contradiction between 'N is right' and 'No not N, but M'. The idea (which the philosopher takes for granted) that, if one man attributes the predicate 'X' to anything and another withholds it, they cannot be contradicting one another unless 'X' stands at least for a *property*, is a fallacy. All that two people need (and all that they have) to contradict one another about in the case of ethical predicates are the *reasons* for doing this rather than that or the other. [*Place of Reason*, 28.]

To explain what *good* means in terms of good reasons might seem to be a case of petitio principii. But Toulmin explains that,

> ... in talking about 'a good reason', I am not talking about ethics; we can equally well (and frequently do) talk of 'a valid argument' instead, and this has far less of an ethical sound—so that even if there were any kind of circularity

here, it would be a harmless one. [*Place of Reason*, 3–4.]

2. Good reasons in ethics

The central problem of moral philosophy for Toulmin is not: 'What do ethical concepts mean?', but: 'What are good reasons in ethics?' In his view, reasoning from factual premisses to ethical conclusions is neither deductive nor inductive in character, but forms a special class of its own. Thus, from the fact that I have promised to do a certain action it follows that I ought to do it. The conclusion cannot be deduced from the premiss in the strict sense, yet the premiss is somehow sufficient to justify the conclusion.

> One point which the imperative doctrine fairly emphasises is the difference between arguments from logical, mathematical or factual premisses to conclusions of a *similar* logical type, and arguments from factual premisses to conclusions of a *different* kind, conclusions about duties or values ... Although factual reasons (R) may be good reasons for an ethical conclusion (E), to assert the conclusion is not just to assert the reasons, or indeed anything of the same logical type as R. It is to declare that one ought to approve of, or pursue, or do something-or-other. [*Place of Reason*, 55.]

The problem, then, is to discover what constitutes a good reason for judging a particular action to be right or wrong. To answer this we must first ask: 'What precisely is the role of ethics in human affairs?' According to Toulmin, ethics forms part of the mechanism which enables us to live to-

201

gether with our fellow beings. The concept of duty is completely bound up with that feature of communal life whereby we learn to renounce our claims and alter our aims when they conflict with those of our fellows. No community could exist without some means of harmonising the aims of its members; hence the so-called 'anthropological discovery' that every society recognises the absolute value of duty is really a truism.

Within each community there is a moral code of duties and prohibitions whose function is to harmonise the activities of the members of the community so as to ensure the maximum satisfaction for all. It is always a good reason for the doing of an action, therefore, that it should be enjoined by the moral code of the community to which one belongs. To say that one did something because one had promised to do so is, in the normal case, to provide a complete justification for the action, for it is a recognised moral principle that promises be kept. In some situations, however, there may be a conflict of duties, one principle demanding one course of action, another demanding the opposite. Here,

> ... one has to weigh up, as well as one can, the risks involved in ignoring either, and choose 'the lesser of the two evils'. Appeal to a single current principle, through the primary test of the rightness of an action, cannot therefore be relied on as a universal test; where this fails, we are driven back upon our estimate of the probable consequences. [*Place of Reason*, 147.]

In unequivocal cases, however, once it has been

shown that an action is in accordance with an established practice, there is no further room for the question: 'But is this really the right thing to do?'

This seems to imply that we can never properly question the moral code of the community to which we belong, but what Toulmin has in mind is not that we cannot question it, but that to do so is significantly different from questioning the morality of a particular act and demands a different type of reply. For to ask: 'Is this particular action right?', is to stay within the limits of one's moral code; it is equivalent to asking: 'Is this action justified by the moral code to which I subscribe?' To question a moral principle, however, is to question the code itself. It is similar to the problem proposed by the philosophers of antiquity who, seeing that every material object is supported by another, asked: 'But what supports the earth itself?' This is a different type of question, and a different type of reasoning is involved in its answer. There is a similar distinction in science, where at one level one may pose a problem in terms of a scientific theory, but at another level question the theory itself.

> Within the framework of a particular scientific theory, one can ask of most things, 'Is this really straight?', but the *criterion* of straightness cannot be questioned: within the framework of a particular moral code, one can ask of most individual actions, 'Is *this* really right?', but the *standards* of rightness cannot be questioned. [*Place of Reason*, 148–9.]

To question a moral principle, therefore, is to place oneself outside the moral code: there is no longer the possibility of appealing to the established moral code in justification of your answer, for it is the moral code itself which is under discussion. What is being sought are reasons why our moral code should retain this principle or, alternatively, reject it in favour of some other.

> The answer to be given will (remembering the function of ethics) be reached by estimating the probable consequences
>
> (i) of retaining the present practice, and
> (ii) of adopting the suggested alternative.
>
> If, as a matter of fact, there is good reason to suppose that the sole consequences of making the proposed change would be to avoid some existing distresses, then as a matter of ethics there is certainly a good reason for making the change. [*Place of Reason*, 149.]

We have now got, in substance, Toulmin's answer to the question: 'What are good reasons in ethics?' Individual actions are normally justified by showing that they are demanded by the accepted moral code: moral principles or actions performed in situations involving a conflict of duties can be justified only by their consequences.

> An action which is an unambiguous instance of a maxim generally accepted in the community concerned ... will be right just because it is an instance of such a maxim: but if it is an action over which there is a 'conflict of duties', or is itself a principle (or social practice) as opposed

to a particular action, it will be right or wrong according as its consequences are likely to be good or bad. [*Place of Reason*, 134.]

Toulmin's ethical system contains three elements: (a) a theory of moral judgement; (b) a theory of the nature of ethical reasoning; and (c) a criterion of good reasons in ethics. We will say something about each of these in turn.

3. Moral judgement

A moral judgement, according to Toulmin, asserts the existence or non-existence of 'good reasons'. The term *good* is being used here, he states, in a purely logical sense, and is not to be understood as having any moral connotation. This is not the only ambiguity present, however, for it is never quite clear whether the good reasons he is concerned with are reasons for doing the action or reasons for holding that it ought to be done. This confusion may easily be seen by comparing two extracts from his book.

[1] When I asked the two people which course of action was the right one I was not asking them about a property—what I wanted to know was whether there was any reason for choosing one course of action rather than another.... All that two people need (and all that they have) to contradict one another about in the case of ethical predicates are the reasons for doing this rather than that or the other. [*Place of Reason*, 28.]
[2] We have come to realise what it is that people in ethical disagreement really do have to

contradict each other about—nothing physically or psychologically 'concrete' or 'substantial', but something which, for logical purposes, is quite as solid and important—namely, whether or not there is a good reason for reaching one ethical conclusion rather than another. [*Place of Reason*, 57.]

In the first quotation a good reason is a reason for doing an action, but in the second it is a reason 'for reaching an ethical conclusion'—for concluding that an action is good, or right, or ought to be done.

This discrepancy may seem insignificant at first sight, for it could be argued that what is a good reason for holding that an action ought to be done must also be a good reason for doing it. However, the reverse is not true, and in fact the ambiguity is crucial. If it were to be resolved either way, Toulmin's position would be seen to be untenable.

Suppose, first of all, that *good reason* means unequivocally 'good reason for doing the action'. If this is the case, then *good* is not, in this context, a logical term: *a good reason* cannot mean the same as *a valid argument*, as Toulmin claims. An action cannot be the conclusion of an argument in the logical sense of *conclusion*; from an argument we can conclude only to a proposition, not to an action. We do indeed speak sometimes of a good argument, even a valid argument, for doing something, but the conclusion, strictly speaking, of such an argument, is not the doing of the action, but the judgement that it ought to be done.

But if *good* has not, in this context, a logical connotation, then it is impossible to understand how conflicting moral judgements contradict each other. We can easily conceive of an action for which there is a good reason both for doing it and for leaving it undone. The doing of a particular action, for instance, might involve the fulfilment of one promise and the non-fulfilment of another. On Toulmin's theory, then, it would be correct to say both that the action ought to be done and that it ought not to be done, which means that these judgements cannot be contradictories.

Nor is this the only awkward consequence. For if *good* reason is not a logical term, it must refer either to a morally good reason or, in the wider sense, to a good reason of any kind. To take it in the wider sense, however, is to attribute moral relevance to factors which seem to have nothing to do with ethics. The fact that I enjoy doing something, for example, is always a good reason, in the wide sense, for doing it, but it seems to have no bearing on the morality of the action. If the action was otherwise immoral, my enjoyment would not make it moral, nor would it make it immoral if it was otherwise moral. That there is a good reason, in this wide sense, for doing the action cannot be what we are asserting, therefore, when we say that an action is morally good.

Good reason must refer, then, to morally good reasons. But this immediately raises the question of circularity. It is no explanation of the morality of an action to say that it is one for which there is a morally good reason unless one explains what moral goodness is in the first place.

What of the second interpretation? According to this, the good reasons for which Toulmin seeks are not reasons for doing the action but reasons for judging that it ought to be done. This is the interpretation which Toulmin follows in practice, when he is considering the nature of moral reasoning. It is only when he is treating of the nature of moral judgement that he brings forward the first interpretation. This is not surprising for, as a theory of moral judgement, the second interpretation merits only the scantiest consideration. No one could seriously claim that the statement: 'This action ought to be done', asserts: 'There are good reasons for holding that it ought to be done'. A statement cannot be a part merely of what it itself asserts.

4. Ethical reasoning

At this stage of the argument Toulmin might well claim that the principal part of his work remains untouched by this criticism. The fundamental problem of ethics is not what ethical concepts mean, but what are good reasons in ethics.

> We must give up the traditional oblique approach of asking, first, 'What *is* goodness?' and 'What *is* rightness?' and attack our central problem from scratch . . . We shall have to go right back to the beginning, to the first form in which we asked our question: 'What kinds of argument, of reasoning, is it proper for us to accept in support of moral decisions?'. [*Place of Reason*, 63–4.]

This sounds not unreasonable at first sight. One could, presumably, work out criteria for correct reasoning in mathematics by examining the sort of arguments accepted by mathematicians, while remaining uncommitted as regards the nature of mathematics. But there is a serious reason for not adopting a similar method for working out criteria for moral reasoning—there is no unanimity within morality, neither as regards the validity of arguments nor as regards the truth of conclusions. Before working out criteria for moral reasoning, how is one to know whether a particular argument is valid or not? The whole purpose of Toulmin's investigation is to enable us to distinguish between valid and invalid arguments in morals. But if we are unable to do this before beginning the investigation, then obviously the enterprise will get nowhere.

Besides, can the quest for criteria for distinguishing between good and bad arguments in morals be regarded as the central problem of moral philosophy? Is there any reason for regarding moral arguments as having a different logical character from those encountered in other fields of enquiry? Toulmin's contention, as we have seen, is that moral judgements are of a different logical type from purely factual ones, and that the derivation of an ethical conclusion from factual premises is not, therefore, a deductive inference:

Although factual reasons (R) may be good reasons for an ethical conclusion (E), to assert the conclusion is not just to assert the reasons, or indeed anything of the same logical type as R. [*Place of Reason*, 55.]

Now this presupposes: first, that ethical judgements are of a different logical type from non-ethical ones: and secondly, that we do sometimes argue from purely factual (i.e, non-moral) premisses to a moral conclusion. About the first assumption one can say immediately, not that it is right or wrong, but that it is wholly unjustified on Toulmin's part, for he has stated explicitly that he is tackling the problem of ethical reasoning from scratch, without first asking: 'What is goodness?', or: 'What is rightness?' If he does this, he clearly cannot *assume* that moral judgements are of a different logical type from non-moral ones, since the chief point of asking: 'What is goodness?', etc, is to examine the propriety of this assumption.

Moreover, Toulmin's previous remarks about the nature of moral judgement seem to run counter to his theory that ethical reasoning is non-deductive. For he holds that ethical statements are genuine assertions and, to that extent at least, factual in character. Since, for him, however, ethical statements are of a different logical type, they must also have a 'non-factual character' which distinguishes them from purely factual remarks. Now if this non-factual character is not a factor in the derivation of ethical conclusions, then there is no reason for believing that the process is other than deductive. But if it is a factor, then it seems that the process cannot be a logical one in any sense. For if what an ethical statement asserts could be derived from the factual premisses in a strictly deductive manner, the non-factual character of the statement could not render this process invalid; whereas if it could not be so deduced, it is impossible to see how the non-factual character could cause the process to be, in any sense, logically valid, since the premisses are, ex hypothesi, purely factual.

Thus it seems that if the non-factual character of ethical statements plays a part in the derivation of ethical conclusions, the connection between premisses and conclusion must be psychological, rather than logical, and the objective criteria which Toulmin is looking for are simply a chimera. But if it does not play a part, ethical reasoning has no special character, and the search for objective criteria is unnecessary.

The second assumption which Toulmin makes is that we sometimes derive moral conclusions from non-moral premisses. There is, of course, a real problem here, for if we deny the correctness of this assumption, we must, to avoid an infinite regress in moral reasoning, postulate some moral principles which are somehow self-evident or without need of support. But even if there are such, it is difficult to see how they can play the role in moral reasoning which is demanded of them.

The first to pin-point this problem was David Hume, and his expression of it is still worth quoting:

In every system of morality which I have hitherto met with, I have always remarked, that the author proceeds for some time in the ordinary way of reasoning, and establishes the being of a God, or makes observations concerning human affairs; when of a sudden I am surprised to find that instead of the usual copulations of propositions, *is*, and *is not*, I meet with no proposition that is not connected with an *ought*, or an *ought not*. This change is imperceptible; but is, however, of the last consequence. For as this *ought*, or *ought not*, expresses some new relation or affirmation, it is necessary that it should be observed and explained; and at the same time that a reason should be given, for what seems altogether inconceivable, how this new relation can be a deduction from others, which are entirely different from it.[1]

From the fact that I have promised to do *a*, for example, it follows that I ought to do it. If there is no moral principle covertly contained in the premisses, there is the problem of how an *ought*-statement can legitimately be deduced from an *is*-statement. If, however, one holds that the moral principle: 'Promises ought to be fulfilled', is implicitly contained in the premisses of the argument, one must explain how this principle is arrived at. One could perhaps have recourse to a self-evident moral principle, such as: 'One ought to do what is right', or: 'One ought to avoid doing what is wrong'. The trouble with this, however, is that the knowledge that a promise ought to be kept seems to be more immediate than the knowledge that to keep a promise is right and not to keep it is wrong. It is difficult to see what basis one could have for the judgement that failure to

[1] D. Hume, *A Treatise of Human Nature* III, I, i.

keep a promise is wrong beyond the fact that one ought to keep one's promises; to try to derive the second judgement from the first, therefore, is to argue in a circle.

A more fruitful approach to the problem could be made, I believe, by examining the dichotomy between moral statements and statements of fact. Many so-called 'purely factual' statements have in fact moral implications. The statement: 'I promised to do *a*', may seem purely factual, but on examination it can be seen to have a moral import. For to promise is to confer a right on another person, and a right is obviously something which makes sense only in a moral context.

I hope to deal more fully with this problem in the final chapter. For the moment it is sufficient to point out that Toulmin's treatment of moral reasoning is of no help in this matter. His account of what constitutes good reasons in ethics makes moral reasoning entirely deductive. The judgement that an individual action ought to be done can be justified, according to him, only with reference to the general principles of the community's moral code, while moral principles can be justified only with reference to the rule that we ought to adopt the principle which will produce the best results. But if there is always an *ought*-statement included in the premisses in moral reasoning, the question of how *ought* is derived from *is* does not arise.

5. The criterion of good reasons
For Toulmin, as we have seen, there are two sorts of good reasons in ethics. At the level of in-

dividual actions, to provide a good reason is to show that the action in question is an example of a practice demanded or permitted by the moral code of one's community. This view seems to me to be highly misleading. For, in the first place, it seems to imply that the scope of one's moral principles is bounded by the limits of one's community. This is clearly incorrect. Moral principles are normally looked on as governing the relations between all men and as having equal validity for all. To interpret the principle: 'Promises ought to be kept', as meaning: 'Promises made to members of one's community ought to be kept', is obviously absurd.

It might be thought that this is an unfair interpretation, for a community's moral code, while binding only on members of the community, might be universal in scope—that is, its rules might bind members of the community in their relations with others whether these are members of the community or not. This, however, is to overlook the fact that Toulmin's explanation of ethical reasoning is based on his theory that morality makes sense only in the context of community life.

The only context in which the concept of 'duty' is straightforwardly intelligible is one of communal life—it is, indeed, completely bound up with this very feature of communal life, that we learn to renounce our claims and alter our aims where they conflict with those of our fellows ... And we can fairly characterise ethics as a part of the process whereby the desires and actions of the members of a community are harmonised. [*Place of Reason*, 133 and 136.]

This implies that a community's moral code governs only the relations between members of the community, which is certainly incorrect as an interpretation of how moral judgements are actually understood and of how moral arguments are actually conducted. This appears immediately when one raises the question: 'Whence arises the obligation to obey the community's moral code?' On Toulmin's theory, there must be a moral principle to the effect that the moral code of one's community ought to be obeyed. Without this, the fact that a particular action is sanctioned by the community's moral code is no longer a good reason for doing it or for holding that it ought to be done. However, this principle cannot be a *part* of the community's moral code, for then it becomes quite useless—to say that one ought to obey the community's moral code because there is a principle in the code to that effect is to beg the question. The principles of morality cannot, therefore, be identified with the moral principles of one's community, and Toulmin's conception of moral principles as valid only for the members of a community is clearly untenable.

At the second level of ethical reasoning—that which concerns principles rather than actions—, justification for a principle, according to Toulmin, consists in showing that its adoption will produce the best results. This theory, is, of course, in one sense, undeniable; a valid moral principle will obviously produce better results than any

215

alternative, for its adoption will produce actions which are right, whereas failure to adopt it will result in actions which are wrong. In this sense, however, the theory is trivial and can no longer function as a criterion for valid moral principles. If the theory is to have content, the term *best results* must be given a definite interpretation. This Toulmin provides when he states

> Except when there is reason to believe that an existing principle could be superseded by another involving less suffering and annoyance on the whole, we are 'obliged' to embrace it. [*Place of Reason*, 169.]

But the theory is not now self-evident and needs to be justified. In fact, not merely is it not self-evident—most people would, I believe, regard it as false. For it completely overlooks one of the most important elements in morality, that of human rights—one could not, for example, deprive an innocent person of his life because the amount of suffering and annoyance in the world would thereby be lessened. Whatever one may think of this principle, therefore, it is certainly not self-evident. And since Toulmin has no justification to offer for it, it is difficult to see why he appealed to it in the first place. There is little point in justifying a moral principle by a broader principle which is itself unjustifiable.

In a more recent article he tries to avoid this difficulty by arguing that the principle is not a moral principle, and so does not require justification after the manner of an ordinary moral principle.

216

The principle of utility . . . is presented as a test, not for single deeds but for general practices, not as a moral rule itself but as a tribunal before which legal and moral rules have to answer.[1]

This reply seems more verbal than real. A tribunal has the same need for credentials as a moral principle has for justifying reasons. If it has none, then there is no reason why we should be bound by its decisions.

[1] S. E. Toulmin, 'Principles of Morality', *Philosophy* xxxi, 117 (1957), 146.

10
Kurt Baier

Moral judgements, according to Kurt Baier,[1] have four main logical features: (a) they can be mutually contradictory; (b) they are capable of guiding a moral agent in the search of the morally right thing to do; (c) there must be good reasons why a moral agent should do the morally right thing rather than the opposite; and (d) we can know whether a course of action is right or wrong even though we cannot perceive it by means of the senses. None of the traditional ethical theories, he claims, can account for all four. Emotivism is incompatible with (a). Naturalism and non-naturalist intuitionism cannot accommodate (b), since for them moral judgements state facts, and a fact by itself is logically compatible with any sort of behaviour. Ideal law theories fail to account for (c)—the main reason why we obey a law is that disobedience is morally wrong and this would no longer be a reason if morality and law were

[1] Baier's views are contained in his book *The Moral Point of View*, Ithaca (NY) 1958.

identical. All other theories are incompatible with
(d).

1. Value judgements

Baier's own theory is designed to accommodate
all these logical features. Moral judgements, he
states, are practical judgements, that is to say, they
provide answers to the question: 'What shall I do?'
But this does not mean that they cannot be true or
false. For the person who asks: 'What shall I do?',
is not asking for orders. He is looking rather for
information. His question might be paraphrased
as: 'What is the best thing for me to do?'

This assumes that value judgements *do* provide
information. But Baier sees no reason to doubt
this. Those who look on value judgements as non-
factual usually base their opinion on the supposed
fact that they cannot be verified. But this is simply
an error due to an absurdly narrow conception
of what verification involves.

Philosophers rely on a highly specialized model
of empirical verification. They think of it as
verification by looking, listening, touching, or
sniffing. It should have occurred to philosophers
that often a good deal more is involved than
that. Thus, I may claim that the Union Theatre
has 500 seats. But I cannot verify this by looking, listening, touching, tasting or sniffing. It
should, therefore, be declared not to be empirically verifiable. No one has ever objected to
counting as a non-empirical way of verifying
propositions. Nor, strangely enough, to measuring or weighing. Yet these latter methods in-

219

Many value judgements can be verified without difficulty. The proposition: 'This is a good fountain-pen', for example, may be verified by using the pen for a short period. The criteria for what constitutes a good fountain-pen are generally accepted and easily recognised. Not all value judgements are as easily verified as this, of course. Sometimes there is disagreement as to what constitutes the criteria of goodness in the type of object in question. But this may also occur in disputes which are not concerned with values. When there is a dispute as to which of two houses is the bigger, for example, one person may be using volume, the other floor-space, as the criterion of size. Here the discovery that they are using different criteria ends the disagreement. The people involved are really making different factual claims, and this has been obscured by the fact that they are using the same verbal formula. But in value disputes the discovery that different criteria are being used, while it may clarify the dispute, does not end it. For a value judgement is something more than a factual claim. When we evaluate a thing, we do not merely say something about its properties—we also say something about the *appropriateness* of certain lines of behaviour in relation to a thing with such properties. Hence, to have different criteria of evaluation amounts to

220

giving different advice. We can always ask, therefore, of the criteria used in evaluation: 'Are these the *right* criteria?'

Value judgements, then, unlike non-value judgements, cannot be confirmed by a simple process of verification. For we must show not merely that the object possesses the criteria of goodness, but that these are the right criteria. The latter process Baier terms 'validation'. To establish conclusively the truth of a value judgement we must verify it by showing that the relevant criteria are present and validate it by showing that these are the right criteria.

But can one ever objectively validate a value judgement? The judgement that these are the right criteria is itself a value judgement which needs to be validated, and so on ad infinitum. This suggests that validation is a question of acquiring an attitude rather than of discovering a truth, and that value judgements are ultimately subjective in character.

Baier offers no full-scale rebuttal of this argument. He contents himself with pointing out that there must be something wrong with it, since some value judgements can be conclusively verified and validated:

Could anyone deny that 'Landy is the best miler in the world to-day' is capable of both verification and validation? Could anyone deny that, at any rate, the criteria mentioned for comparing and ranking milers are the right ones?... And what is true of this case is also true of all cases involving purposes. Roughly speaking, the proper criteria for evaluating cars, fountain pens, milers and so on are determined by the purpose of the thing, activity or enterprise in question. [*Moral Point of View*, 80.]

2. The best thing to do

What the moralist is concerned with is, of course, the criteria for evaluating actions. For Baier the question: 'What shall I do?', is a request for a value judgement. The speaker wishes to find out what he ought to do or, equivalently, what is the best thing for him to do. This is shown by the fact that it makes no sense to say: 'I know that this is *the best* thing to do, but what I want to know is *what shall* I do'. The first part of the statement answers the question posed in the second part. Now the best thing to do is the action which is supported by the best reasons. Reasons are relevant facts. We decide what facts are relevant by having recourse to what Baier calls 'consideration-making beliefs'. A fact is a consideration in a practical problem if it constitutes a reason for or against doing something. Consideration-making beliefs are rules of reason which give certain facts the status of reasons. Thus the fact that I enjoy doing something is a reason for doing it. This is a consideration-making belief which gives the fact that something is enjoyable the status of a reason in practical deliberation. If I enjoy doing something, then, and provided that there is no reason against doing this thing or in favour of some alternative action, that action is the best thing for me to do.

The fact that I have a reason for or against entering on the proposed line of action *does not entail* that I ought or ought not to enter on it—it merely 'presumptively implies' it. That is to say, it must be taken to imply that I ought or ought not to enter on it unless, later on, in the weighing of considerations, I find some that are weightier than this one. In that case, the original presumptive implication has been rebutted. [*Moral Point of View*, 102.]

It must be noted that the truth of consideration-making beliefs is not relative to particular situations or particular persons. This sounds paradoxical at first, for it is well known that people have different tastes, so that what seems a good reason to one person for doing something may not seem so to another. Thus, the fact that there is good fishing at Fort Fairlie is a good reason for one person to take a holiday there, but not for another. But this is to confuse considerations with consideration-making beliefs. That there is good fishing at Port Fairlie is a good reason for taking a holiday there if one enjoys fishing, but not if one does not. The consideration-making belief is that if one enjoys doing something one has a reason for doing it. And this is equally true for everyone.

These consideration-making beliefs or rules of reason are of three different kinds: individual rules, social rules, and moral rules. Individual rules concern such things as enjoyment, desire, and self-interest—that I enjoy doing something, that it satisfies a desire on my part, that it serves my interest, are all good reasons for doing it. Social rules are based on law, custom, and religion, while moral rules need no characterisation to be recognised.

In particular situations there may, of course, be a conflict of rules, individual rules of reason favouring one course, social rules favouring another. Here one must have recourse to 'rules of superiority', that is, to beliefs about the superiority of one type of reason over another. Reasons of self-interest, for example, are usually taken as superior to reasons of mere pleasure or enjoyment, and reasons of law, morality, or religion as superior to reasons of self-interest. But there is considerable uncertainty about whether and when law is superior to morality, religion to law, and morality to religion.

Moral rules of reason or moral convictions are usually called moral principles. It is a central point in Baier's theory that these moral considerations are capable of being either true or false. A distinction must be made, however, between 'absolute morality' and 'true morality'. There is only one absolute morality; there may be many true moralities. Absolute morality is that set of moral convictions which are true in all contexts. True morality is those moral principles which are true in a particular society, but which might not be true in others; their truth is relative to the social institutions which actually obtain. And since different societies may have different social institutions, there may be a number of different moralities. But every true morality must contain as its core the principles which belong to absolute

morality. The other principles which it contains
are the result of applying absolute moral principles to the specific conditions of a particular
social order. Thus, the principle: 'It is wrong to
misuse social institutions', is part of absolute
morality; but the same cannot be said of the
principles: 'Stealing is wrong', 'Adultery is wrong',
'Promise-breaking is wrong', for these refer to the
misuse of certain social institutions which a given
society may not have.

3. The moral point of view
How can we tell whether a particular moral principle is true or false? For Baier, a moral principle
is true if it is seen as required or acceptable from
the moral point of view. This is the point of view
'of an independent, unbiased, impartial, objective,
dispassionate, disinterested observer . . . a God's-
eye point of view (*Moral Point of View*, 201). An
individual is moral if he always views the facts of
a practical problem from the moral point of view,
and if he allows moral considerations to override
all other considerations when making his decisions
—that is, if he makes the moral point of view
supreme.

Baier regards the moral point of view as having
two essential features. The first is that to adopt the
moral point of view is to act in accordance with
principles. Moral principles are not merely rules
of thumb—one cannot discard them when they
happen to conflict with one's aims and desires. A
rule is not a *moral* rule if it admits of exceptions;
a moral principle is not something which one may
discard whenever it is convenient. There is indeed

a sense in which it would be true to say that a moral principle admits of exceptions, but this is only because the rule has been incompletely stated. The exceptions which the rule admits of are really part of the rule. Moral principles are also peculiar in that they are meant for everyone. They are not in any sense the code of a privileged group. Only those rules which are capable of being taught universally can be moral rules. Therefore the rule: 'Always assert what you think not to be the case', could not be a moral rule, for to teach it universally would be to frustrate its purpose: if it were adopted, the only difference that would result would be that negative assertions would be understood as positive, and vice versa.

The second essential feature of the moral point of view is that the principles which it sanctions are for the good of everyone alike. A principle is for the good of everyone alike if the conduct it permits is 'reversible', that is, acceptable to a person whether he is at the giving or receiving end of it.

Conduct which is not 'reversible' in this sense is absolutely immoral in that it would be immoral at any time or in any context. But there are also, as we have seen, moral principles which are true only in certain circumstances. This is due to the fact that, in a social setting, a line of conduct which causes no harm when done by one may cause great harm when done by many; here, though the conduct is 'reversible', it is not for the good of everyone alike. No harm is done if one person walks across a lawn, for example, but the

226

lawn is ruined if everyone does. But the fact that a particular line of conduct would be harmful if done by many is not in itself sufficient to show that it is immoral. To remain celibate, for instance, is not immoral, yet if everyone did so the human race would die out. Baier formulates three conditions which, if fulfilled with regard to a certain line of behaviour, show that this behaviour should be prohibited by the morality of the group: (a) the consequences of behaving in this way would be harmful if everyone did it; (b) all are equally entitled to engage in it; and (c) engaging in this sort of behaviour is an indulgence, not a sacrifice.

If a line of conduct fulfils these three conditions *and* is prohibited by the morality of the group, then it is correctly regarded as immoral by the members of the group. But it is not immoral if it is not prohibited by the morality of the group, even though it fulfils these conditions and should be so prohibited; nor is it immoral if it is prohibited by the morality of the group but does not fulfil these conditions.

But why should we adopt the moral point of view? If acting morally means, as it sometimes does, acting contrary to self-interest, then by adopting the moral point of view we are doing ourselves more harm than good. The answer is that to reject the moral point of view is to make self-interest the supreme principle of practical deliberation. And a world in which everyone puts self-interest first would be what Hobbes called a 'state of pure nature', where life is 'solitary, poor, nasty, brutish, and short'. It is obvious that this world is much inferior to one in which morality takes precedence. Reason demands, therefore, that we adopt the moral point of view and allow our actions to be guided by moral considerations.

> The very *raison d'être* of a morality is to yield reasons which overrule the reasons of self-interest in those cases when everyone's following self-interest would be harmful to everyone. Hence moral reasons are superior to all others. [*Moral Point of View*, 309.]

Baier's approach to the problem of moral judgement is significantly different from that of other writers whose views we have examined in that it does not presuppose a theory of meaning. His procedure, so far as one can judge, has been to examine moral language and moral concepts as they actually function in everyday discourse without making any attempt to force them into a preconceived pattern. And this is surely the correct approach to the problem. The theory of meaning should be the final result of the application of linguistic analysis to different types of discourse, not an attempt to formulate an a-priori model to which all significant discourse must conform. The analysis of ethical terms must show what they actually mean, not what they *ought* to mean in the light of prevailing semantical theories.

But, whatever the reason, Baier's theory is by far the most convincing account of moral judgement to be produced by a member of the English analytic school. I do not think that it is entirely satisfactory, but its defects are more in the nature of lacunae than of positive errors. Thus, the treatment of value judgement is excellent in so far as it goes, but it is incomplete. This prevents Baier from fully substantiating his claim that moral judgements are objectively true or false. Again, his analysis of *ought* is, I think, generally acceptable—an action ought to be done if there is a reason for doing it, or, where there are reasons for and against, if the reasons for doing it outweigh those against. But there is no satisfactory explanation of why certain facts *are* reasons. To invoke 'consideration-making beliefs' is merely to place the problem one stage further back. And having no explanation of what constitutes a moral reason, Baier must invoke a 'moral point of view' to account for the fact that moral judgements can be true or false. But if morality depends on a 'point of view', then, however good a description one may give of this, it is impossible to give a satisfactory explanation of why one's actions should always be governed by morality—of why we ought to adopt this point of view.

In my criticism, then, I will concentrate on two main issues: the claim that moral judgements are objectively true or false, and the moral point of view.

4. Can moral judgements be objectively true or false?

To demonstrate the truth of a value judgement one must, according to Baier, both validate and verify it, that is to say, one must show both that the criteria of value are present (or absent) and that these are the right criteria. The difficulty arises in connection with validation. How is one to distinguish between correct and incorrect criteria? If there is no objective test, if it is simply a matter of choice as to which criteria one uses, value judgements cannot be regarded as objectively true or false.

Baier provides no general solution to this problem. He points out instead that is certainly possible to obtain correct value criteria for objects which have a specific purpose:

> The proper criteria for evaluating cars, fountain pens, milers and so on are determined by the purpose of the thing, activity or enterprise in question ... Anyone who claims that safety, reliability, comfort, and the like are *not* appropriate criteria of excellence in cars simply does not know what he is talking about. [*Moral Point of View*, 80–81.]

I think Baier has here oversimplified matters a little. It is not at all clear that there is general unanimity concerning the criteria for evaluating objects of this kind. Consider cars, for example. Some people regard speed and acceleration as all-important; others take no account of this when evaluating cars (economy is what they look for); while still others evaluate cars almost exclusively according to comfort. This case is, in fact, very similar to the non-value dispute where one person uses the volume of a house, the other its floor-space, as the criterion of its size. There is not just one correct set of criteria for evaluating cars any more than there is for estimating the size of houses. The criteria you use will depend on what you look for in a car, and when people look for different things and so have different criteria, the disagreement between them may be more verbal than real.

But Baier is, of course, partly right, for not all value disputes are so easily settled. When people dispute about the value of a painting or of a poem, for example, one cannot say simply that they look for different things in a poem or picture and hence have different value criteria. The disputants would, on the contrary, claim that the difference in criteria is just what the dispute is about, for there are certain things which one *ought* to look for in a work of art, and hence certain criteria which one *ought* to use in evaluating it. Here one must validate one's criteria.

Baier is mistaken, however, in thinking that this sort of problem occurs only in connection with value judgements. Consider, for example, a dispute on the question as to whether a particular individual is sane. This sort of problem often arises in courts of law, but it may also arise in conversation. Different individuals, different psychiatrists even, may use conflicting criteria for judging whether or not a person is sane, but the discovery that the criteria being used are different will not end the dispute. In this case also you must validate your criteria before you can be said to have proved conclusively that your judgement is correct. The validation may take different forms, but to have any plausibility it must be based on the meaning of the term *sane*. And this is equally true of the validation of value criteria—it must be based on the meaning of *good*. But since

Baier has offered no definition, analysis, or even characterisation of its meaning, his proof that value judgements are objectively true or false is radically incomplete.

But this is not the end of the story, for his treatment of moral judgement is largely independent of what he has said concerning value judgements—that is to say, he does not try to validate the criteria of moral evaluation by showing that they follow from the purpose of human activity. Instead he claims that the truth of moral judgements follows from the truth of 'consideration-making beliefs'. If this is correct, and Baier can show that consideration-making beliefs are objectively true or false, he has indeed proved his case.

Here is how he argues in support of the claim that consideration-making beliefs are objectively true or false.

> The function of consideration-making beliefs ... [is] to serve as major premises in practical arguments. These arguments are supposed to yield true answers to questions of the form 'What shall I do?' or 'What is the best course of action open to me?' Premises of argument are true if the argument is valid and the conclusion is true. We can infer that the premise is true if the argument is valid and if it is true that the course of action recommended in the conclusion of the argument is the best course open to the agent. The matter is considerably simplified by the fact that, at this point, we are dealing merely with prima facie reasons. In order to determine the truth of the conclusion

we have only to find out whether the recommended course of action is the best, *other things being equal*, that is, whether it is better than its contradictory or its contrary.

Our practical argument runs as follows:

(i) The fact that if I did *x* I would enjoy doing *x* is a reason for me to do *x*

(ii) I would enjoy doing *x* if I did *x*

(iii) Therefore I ought to do *x* (other things being equal).

Hence our consideration-making belief (i) is true (since the argument is valid) if our conclusion (iii) is true. [*Moral Point of View*, 300–301.]

There are two defects in this argument. The first is that it involves a petitio principii. On Baier's analysis the truth of judgements of the form: 'I ought to do *x*', depends on the truth of a consideration-making belief or beliefs. One cannot, therefore, prove the truth of the consideration-making belief by arguing from the truth of the *ought*-judgement, for one could not know that the *ought*-judgement was true unless one already knew that the consideration-making belief was true.

The second defect may be explained as follows. Consider the following syllogism:

(i) The fact that the moon is made of green cheese is a reason for me not to tell lies.

(ii) The moon is made of green cheese.

(iii) Therefore I ought not to tell lies (other things being equal).

This is a valid syllogism according to Baier's analysis of *ought*. And the conclusion is certainly true. On Baier's reasoning, then, the premisses must also be true. In fact, the premisses are (ludicrously) false, so there must be something wrong with the reasoning. Baier has made an elementary logical error in thinking that the premisses of an argument are true if the argument is valid and the conclusion is true. There is no difficulty, as we have just seen, in constructing false premisses which yield true conclusions.

5. Morality and the moral point of view

There seems to me to be a fundamental ambiguity in Baier's treatment of the moral point of view. It is never made clear whether this is the point of view which is actually held, or the one which ought to be held, by people who wish to be moral. The ambiguity conceals a difficulty, for I do not see how either alternative could be justified.

Let us consider it, first of all, as the point of view which is actually held by those who wish to act in accordance with morality. The difficulty here is that there are often conflicting views on whether a particular line of action is or is not moral, and it is impossible to understand how these could have arisen or how they could be maintained if we all share the same moral point of view. Consider, for example, the problem of suicide. There would be no reason for regarding the taking of one's life as absolutely immoral if Baier's conception of the moral point of view is correct, and he himself states that suicide is wrong only in certain special circumstances.[1] But, in fact, many people regard suicide as wrong in itself, hence wrong in all circumstances. It is obviously not a question of different social institutions giving rise to different moralities: their conception of the moral point of view cannot be the same as that of Baier's. The same point could be made with regard to the morality of such things as abortion and euthanasia; most of those who regard them as immoral regard them as absolutely immoral, as immoral for all times and in all societies. The conclusion is that if Baier's description of the moral point of view is valid, then it must be regarded as the point of view which people *ought* to adopt, rather than the one which they actually do adopt, when considering moral problems.

But what sort of *ought* are we concerned with here? It cannot be a moral *ought*, for this would be to beg the question at issue: if one did not already accept Baier's conception of the moral point of view, one would have no reason for accepting his moral principle that one ought to adopt it. Yet if it is not a moral *ought*, the only alternative seems to be that it is an *ought* of self-interest—that one ought to adopt Baier's conception because by doing so one is serving one's own interest. But if this is the case it is no longer a moral point of view, but rather a refined version of the point of view of self-interest. And if the reason why we ought to adopt the moral point of

[1] See, for example, *The Moral Point of View*, 211–14 and 228–30.

view is because it serves our own interest, we need be moral only so long as it is in our interest; whenever morality and self-interest conflict, we have no longer any reason for obeying the dictates of morality.

One can make precisely the same objection to Baier's explanation of why we ought to be moral:

> The universal supremacy of the rules of self-interest must lead to what Hobbes called the state of nature. At the same time it will be clear to everyone that universal obedience to certain rules overriding self-interest would produce a state of affairs which serves everyone's interest much better than his unaided pursuit of it in a state where everyone does the same . . . We are now looking at the world from the point of view of *anyone*. We are not examining particular courses of action before this or that person; we are examining two alternative worlds, one in which moral reasons are always treated by everyone as superior to reasons of self-interest and one in which the reverse is the practice. And we can see that the first world is the better world, because we can see that the second world would be the sort which Hobbes describes as the state of nature. This shows that I ought to be moral, for when I ask the question 'What ought I to do?' I am asking 'Which course of action is supported by the best reasons?'. [*Moral Point of View*, 309–10.]

But if the sole reason for acting morally is that my interests are better served in a world in which people obey the dictates of morality than in a state

236

of pure nature, morality is clearly subordinate to self-interest. Hence I would have no reason for acting morally if it can be shown that I would serve my self-interest better by not doing so. And even if it is true that my self-interest is better served in a world where moral rules are observed, it still does not follow that one's self-interest is always better served by acting in accordance with morality. For by choosing to act immorally in a particular instance, I do not thereby bring about a state of pure nature. At most I merely contribute to bringing it about. So whenever I find myself in a situation such that an immoral course of action would not contribute, or would only contribute slightly, towards bringing about a state of pure nature, whereas to act morally would gravely injure my own interests, reason would clearly demand that I act immorally; the reasons for so doing would undeniably outweigh the reasons against.

It seems, therefore, that one cannot formulate a satisfactory criterion of morality in terms of a moral point of view alone. For experience tells us that people have different moral viewpoints. And if it is claimed that this is the point of view which ought to be adopted by all, one is either begging the question or subordinating morality to self-interest.

Part 4

The nature of moral judgement

11
The logical status of moral judgements

1. The question of intention

Three opinions are possible concerning the logical status of moral judgements. One may regard them:

a. as non-factual in character, that is, as having a function other than that of conveying information;

b. as expressing subjective propositions, that is, as conveying information about the feelings or attitudes of the person who makes the judgement;

c. as expressing objective propositions, that is, as conveying information whose truth or falsity is independent of the inner dispositions of the person who makes the judgement.

These three opinions appear to be mutually exclusive, but several of the writers whose views we have been considering endeavour to sustain two of them simultaneously. Stevenson's two patterns of analysis, for example, is an effort to combine (b) and (c), and Hare tries to combine

241

(a) and (c) by claiming that moral judgements, though primarily prescriptive, have a subordinate descriptive meaning. Both Hare and Stevenson seem, however, to have confused the meaning of ethical terms with the criteria of their application, and it could be argued with some plausibility that the view that moral judgements belong to two of these categories at once is fundamentally incoherent. In any event, this problem need not detain us, since the question of whether moral judgements possess a secondary function is really of little importance for ethics. If moral judgements are non-factual or subjective in their primary function, the fact that they may acquire a secondary descriptive meaning would not render ethics any less subjective; and if the primary function of moral judgements is to express objective propositions, then their truth-value will not be affected by any secondary function they may happen to possess.

In this chapter, I wish to propose two theses concerning the logical status of moral judgements. The first is that the theory that moral judgements are non-factual is an untenable one. There is no evidence of any consequence in its favour, and it seems to be totally irreconcilable with the manner in which moral judgements are spoken of and expressed in ordinary language. The second thesis is that the subjectivist-objectivist dispute in ethics has hitherto been misconceived; the real point at issue is not the meaning of ethical terms, but the criteria used in applying them.

The truth of the first thesis can be decided by examining what moral judgements are intended to express. Those who deny their factual character do so on the grounds that, though they look like statements of fact, they are really imperatives— or expressions of feeling, or prescriptions (in Hare's sense), or something of that kind. Now, while it is permissible to say that moral judgements are not what they seem to be, it is not permissible to say that they are not what they are intended to be (unless one holds that they are meaningless). If they are really imperatives, for example, then they must be intended to be imperatives. It is true that one might conceivably utter an imperative without intending to do so, but this would be because one had used a form of words which one did not intend to use, or had used words which one did not fully understand. But no one could reasonably hold that this is what habitually occurs when we make a moral judgement. If one holds that moral judgements are non-factual, one is committed to holding that they are not intended to be factual. What one cannot hold is the type of view which says that moral judgements, though intended to express something factual, are really imperatives disguised in propositional form.

How are we to discover what moral judgements are habitually intended to express? It might seem that intentions are private phenomena which can be ascertained only by introspection, and hence that each individual must answer for himself as to what he intends. If this were so, the only scientific approach to our problem would be a statistical survey based on the introspective findings of individuals. It is unlikely, however, that such a survey would yield any satisfactory result. The difficulty is that we do not always accept avowals of intention as accurate even though their sincerity may be unquestioned. Thus, a person may quite sincerely deny that he intended to express contempt, when in fact his words clearly indicate that such an intention must have been present. A poet may be doubtful as to what he intended to express in a certain passage—literary critics sometimes fancy themselves as better guides to an author's intentions than the author himself. When Ayer stated in *Language, Truth and Logic* that moral judgements are expressions of feeling, he must have believed that, in uttering moral judgements, he intended only to express his feelings; yet how many would agree that he had correctly described his intentions? But if philosophers cannot be trusted on this issue, there is little point in consulting the man in the street to whom, more than likely, the question has never previously occurred.

In this matter, therefore, the best guide to intention is not introspection, but the manner in which the intention is expressed in language. In ordinary discourse, there is usually little or no difficulty in recognising the speaker's intention. We do not have to ask him after each sentence whether he intended that sentence as an expression of feeling, a command, an assertion, or a question. His intention is apparent from the form of speech employed. There are characteristic speech-forms which have specific functions in language—a characteristic interrogative form for asking questions, an imperative form for issuing commands, a propositional form for expressing propositions and so on—and the employment of one of these is as indicative of what the speaker intends to say as the employment of a tool or instrument is of what he intends to do.

Now one of the most obvious things about moral judgements is that they are always expressed in propositional form. We convey our moral judgements by saying such things as: 'Euthanasia is always wrong', 'Hitler was an evil man', 'Your duty in these circumstances is to obey'.[1] It would be very difficult to understand why the propositional form is always used if we do not intend to express a proposition. If our intention is something else, we would surely use a non-propositional form of words. There are, of course, certain expressions which are not intended to express propositions even though they are couched in propositional form. 'You will assemble on the square at seven o'clock to-night', for example, might be used, not as a prediction, but as a command. But I do not think we can draw any parallel between this type of expression and moral judgements. For there *is* an imperative form which is the one usually employed for expressing commands, but there is no other way of expressing a moral judgement except in the form of a proposition. And this strongly suggests that expressions of moral judgement are intended to be, and are understood as, factual remarks.

There is further evidence which points to the

[1] The evidence which I cite here is taken from Peter Glassen, 'The Cognitivity of Moral Judgments', *Mind* LXVIII, 269 (1959), 57–72.

same conclusion. Not only do we express moral judgements in propositional form, we ask questions on moral issues as if they were matters of fact. We say such things as: 'Is euthanasia always wrong?', 'Was Hitler really an evil man?', 'Is it your duty in these circumstances to obey?'. It is perhaps not impossible to provide an explanation of these questions which is in conformity with the emotive or prescriptive theory of moral judgement. What is certain, however, is that this explanation would never have occurred to anyone who was not trying to make the facts of ethical discourse conform to a preconceived theory. Outside of ethics, we never pose questions in this manner unless they concern matters of fact. The obvious inference is that, when the same type of question is posed in ethics, the issue involved is also factual.

A third piece of evidence worth considering is the fact that we commonly apply such terms as *true, false, correct*, and *mistaken* to moral judgements: 'It is not *true* that euthanasia is always wrong', 'You are *mistaken* in thinking that Hitler was an evil man', 'It is *incorrect* to say that your duty is to obey'. This seems to show quite conclusively that moral judgements are intended to express propositions, for if we commonly predicate truth or falsity of moral judgements, then in making a moral judgement we must intend to express something which is either true or false, and if we label them as 'correct' or 'mistaken', then we must intend them to convey something which could be either mistaken or correct.

This evidence, taken in its entirety, seems to

246

me to rule out the possibility that moral judgements are not intended to express propositions. If one still wishes to deny their factual character, one would be forced to fall back on the plea that they do not succeed in expressing genuine propositions. But this is something which is for the moment beside the point. All that we are concerned with here and now is whether moral judgements are intended to express propositions. If, as the evidence indicates, they are so intended, then it cannot be true to say that they are really prescriptions or imperatives, or expressions of feeling. Moral judgements cannot, any more than other forms of discourse, have a logical character which they are not normally intended to have. Hence to claim at this stage that they do not express genuine propositions is to claim that they are abortive utterances, that they do not express anything.

We have now reached the second stage of our discussion. The next question is: What sort of propositions are moral judgements intended to express, that is, are they intended to be subjective or objective in character? This question is not decisive for the subjective-objective controversy in ethics, but in answering we will clear the air and perhaps see the nature of the dispute more clearly.

Here again there are several items of evidence to be considered.[1] The first item was previously mentioned as having been made the basis of an

[1] For this evidence I am again indebted to the article by Peter Glassen.

argument by G. E. Moore. People are commonly said to differ in opinion or to hold contradictory opinions on moral issues. Moore thought that this is sufficient to disprove subjectivism in ethics, but this may be to claim too much. It does constitute an effective argument against the type of subjectivism which Moore was concerned with, that is, the theory which attributes subjective meanings to ethical terms, but, as we shall see shortly, subjectivism may be formulated in such a way as to leave it outside the scope of Moore's criticism. What his argument undoubtedly does rule out is the possibility that moral judgements are intended to be subjective, since opposing moral judgements obviously would not contradict each other, nor would they be described as contradictory, if they were intended merely as subjective remarks.

The second point is that we commonly say such things as: 'I *believe* that euthanasia is always wrong', 'I have *come to the conclusion* that Hitler was an evil man', 'I am *of the opinion* that your duty in this situation is to disobey'. This is not the language of subjective discourse. To be convinced of this, one has merely to consider such remarks as: 'I believe that I dislike pop art', 'I have come to the conclusion that I disapprove of the mini-skirt', 'I am of the opinion that I am opposed to racial discrimination'. Even if one could devise a situation in which these statements make sense, one would still be faced with the difficulty of explaining how it is that expressions which are commonly used in moral discussion can only with the greatest difficulty be made to bear sense in subjective discourse. The only reasonable explanation seems to be that moral judgements are intended to be objective.

The final piece of evidence is the use of abstract nouns derived from ethical predicates. We say such things as: 'The goodness of the man was evident from his actions', or: 'I am in doubt, not concerning the efficacy of the action, but concerning its rightness'. It is difficult to see why we should speak of the goodness or the rightness of an action unless we intended our judgement that an action is good or right to be a judgement about the action itself and not merely about our attitude towards it.

Almost as significant as the evidence we have produced is the complete absence of evidence pointing in the opposite direction. There is nothing in moral discourse to indicate that moral judgements are not intended to express objectively true propositions, and those who favour subjectivism in ethics never attempt to bring forward such evidence. According to Stephen Toulmin,

> The variation in ethical judgments and standards, both between individuals within a community and between members of different communities, is the main evidence produced in favour of subjective ethical theories. [*Place of Reason*, 33.]

But this fact, though important in itself, has no bearing on what we intend when we utter moral judgements. There can be little doubt then that moral judgements, whether they succeed in being objectively true or not, are at least intended to be such.

2. Meaning and criteria

Nothing that has been said up to now implies, however, that subjectivism is false, for even though moral judgements are intended to be objective, they might turn out to be merely subjective. This seems to contradict something which we have previously laid down, namely, that a form of expression cannot possess a character which it is not normally intended to possess. How could moral judgements be subjective in character if they are not normally intended to be subjective? The answer is that for moral judgements to be objective they must not only be intended to be objective, but they must also fulfil a certain condition—the application of moral terms must be governed by objective criteria. No such condition is demanded for commands, questions, expressions of feelings, and the like. Hence there is no possibility that, through failure to fulfil this condition, they would acquire a different logical status from the one which they are intended to have. But the judgement: 'This action is morally wrong' will not be objective unless the application of the term *morally wrong* is governed by objective criteria. If it is not, then the judgement will concern merely the attitude of the speaker towards the action.

This point may be illustrated by an example which has nothing to do with ethics. A lady who describes a hat as 'nice' intends to make an objective statement about the hat. (This is evident from the fact that she would regard her statement as contradicted by someone who denies that the hat is nice.) Roughly speaking, what she means is that the hat has a pleasant appearance. But her reason for calling it nice is that it appears pleasant to her. This in itself would not imply that her judgement is subjective. Our reason for calling something sweet, for example, is that it tastes sweet to us, but since most people have similar taste-sensations, the average individual's sensations provide objective criteria for the application of gustatory terms. The sensation of sweetness which a substance provides, though private in an obvious sense, is public in the sense that it can be verified by almost everyone. Consider now the case of an individual whose taste-sensations change so radically that they no longer coincide even remotely with those of other people. In such a situation we would say that his judgements of taste were false rather than subjective, for there *are* objective criteria for the application of gustatory terms. But no such criteria are available for the term *nice*—at least, not as far as ladies' hats are concerned. There would be no point, therefore, in branding the lady's judgement as false; what we would say rather is that, though intended to be objective, it really conveys nothing more than that the hat appears nice to her.

It is important to note that *nice* does not have here a subjective meaning. To suppose that it has would be to envisage the absurd situation in which a term would have a meaning which nobody who uses it ever intended it to have. One could, of course, object that to regard *nice* as having an objective meaning is to envisage an equally paradoxical situation—that of a judgement possessing a logical status which nobody who makes it ever intends it to possess. But the two cases are not strictly parallel. The meaning of a term is a matter of convention; it possesses the meaning which those who use it ordinarily intend it to possess. But for a judgement to be objective, as we have seen, more is required than that those who make it should intend it to be objective. If a term lacks objective criteria of application, its predication of an object will never result in an objective judgement, no matter what the person who makes the judgement intends.

Now the only way, it seems to me, in which subjectivism in ethics can plausibly be presented is by saying that moral judgements, though intended to be objective, are rendered subjective by the absence of objective criteria for the application of moral terms. This, on the face of it, is a not unpersuasive theory: but, so far as I am aware, it has never been seriously put forward. Subjectivists invariably assume that the evidence cited by Toulmin indicates, not that the application of moral terms is governed by subjective criteria, but that moral judgements are intended to convey information merely about the inner dispositions of the speaker, and hence that moral terms are to be given a subjective interpretation. Objectivists, for their part, assume that subjectivism has been disproved once they have cited the evidence which we have earlier presented to show that moral judgements are intended to be objective. Since both assumptions are false, it is hardly surprising that the whole subjectivist-objectivist dispute has shed singularly little light on the nature of moral judgement.

252

The key to the dispute then is the criteria which govern the application of moral terms. But before we go on to consider these, we must be clear in our minds as to what constitutes objective criteria and what subjective. There is a temptation to say that the difference between the two is that objective criteria are 'public' in the sense that their presence can be verified by everyone, whereas subjective criteria are 'private' in the sense that their presence can be verified only by the person making the judgement. If this is correct, then we will have to say that at least some of the criteria used in the application of moral terms are objective. When we call an action wrong because it was the deliberate telling of an untruth, for example, or an individual good because he is honest, kindly, and truthful, we are using criteria whose presence can be verified by all. But this would be a wholly unconvincing demonstration of the objective character of moral judgement. For a subjectivist could immediately reply that though these criteria are public, they are not objective, since their role as criteria is conferred on them by the individual who makes the judgement. It is because we disapprove of lying that we regard it as morally wrong, but if we were to change our attitude, then the fact that an utterance was a lie would no longer seem to us to be a reason for describing it as immoral. There is, therefore, the subjectivist would go on to say, no means of distinguishing legitimate criteria for the application of moral terms from criteria which are illegitimate. This means that we are free to use whatever criteria we please, and so moral judgements are, in the last resort, subjective.

Whatever we may think of his general position, we must, I believe, agree with the subjectivist in holding that criteria will not be objective merely because they are public. For the fact that they are public does not rule out the possibility that the connection between the term and its criteria of application is subjective in the sense that one may use the term in accordance with whatever criteria one pleases without being guilty either of false-hood or the misuse of language. For moral judge-ments to be objective, therefore, there must be some means of distinguishing legitimate criteria for the application of moral terms from those which are illegitimate. This demands that moral terms be objectively linked to their criteria of application; the connection between the two must be something which we recognise rather than create for ourselves.

At first glance, there appear to be only two ways in which a term and its criteria of applica-tion can be objectively connected. The first is when there is a logical connection between the two—when the presence of the criteria logically entails the judgement ascribing the term to what-ever object or situation is in question (the equian-gularity of a triangle, for example, constitutes this type of criterion for the term *equilateral*). We will label these 'logical criteria'. The second is when the connection between the two is con-tingent—when we know from experience that these criteria are present only when the judgement ascribing the term to an object or situation is true (an abnormal temperature, for example, provides this sort of criterion for the ascription of the term *ill*). We will call this second type 'empirical criteria'. There are also criteria which may be described as imperfect instances of logical or empirical criteria. These are present whenever the judgement ascribing the term to an object or situation is true, but they do not guarantee its truth, since they may also be present when it is false. They do not constitute a third type of criteria, but are more properly regarded as members, though inadequate ones, of one or other of the two categories already mentioned.

The existence of synthetic a-priori truths would provide a third type of objective connection between terms and criteria, but this would have no bearing on the problem that we are considering unless there are synthetic a-priori moral principles. The character of moral principles renders this most unlikely, however. Synthetic a-priori truths are by definition true independently of experience, and therefore true in all circumstances, whereas moral principles almost invariably admit of exceptions. A moral principle would have to be extremely general to avoid the possibility of a situation in which one would be entitled to contravene it. It is, however, a truism in ethics that differences between moral philosophers are almost always centred on the most general principles of morality; there is usually widespread agreement, even amongst those who propound very different moral systems, with regard to less general principles. But a principle whose truth is frequently disputed can hardly be true a priori. It seems, then, as if those principles which are universally accepted cannot be synthetic a-priori because they admit of exceptions, whereas those which are sufficiently general to avoid exceptions cannot be synthetic a-priori because they are not universally accepted. The only moral principles which could plausibly be regarded as synthetic a-priori, therefore, are purely formal principles such as: 'Good ought to be done and evil avoided', and these clearly could not provide criteria for the application of moral terms to actual situations.

Are we to say, then, that, leaving synthetic a-priori propositions out of account, there are only two types of objective criteria for the application of terms? To do this would be to fall into the trap of placing too much reliance on a-priori reasoning, for if we examine the criteria which we actually use in the application of terms, we will find that there are some which are neither logical nor empirical in character and yet have all the appearance of being objective. Consider the term *tall*, for example. Let us say that a man is tall if he is more than six feet in height. The characteristic of exceeding six feet in height is then a criterion for the application of the term *tall* to men. It is not a logical criterion, however; the expression: 'X exceeds six feet in height', does not entail that X is tall; if it did, anything which exceeds six feet in height would be tall, and this is obviously absurd as applied to buildings, say, or to mountains. But neither is it an empirical criterion, since tallness is not something we perceive, and so we could not know that an individual is tall unless we first possessed a criterion of tall-

256

ness; the criterion of tallness is logically prior to the judgement that an individual is tall, and therefore cannot be based on that judgement. The truth is that this criterion is partly logical in character and partly empirical. It is based on two things: first, the meaning of the term *tall*, the fact that *tall* means 'of a height notably exceeding the average height of members of the same class'; and secondly, the empirical fact that the average height of men is somewhat less than six feet. Since these two facts constitute the connection between term and criterion, and since both are clearly objective, there is no reason for doubting that logico-empirical criteria are also objective.

We now have three types of objective criteria, but only two—logical and logico-empirical criteria —need to be taken into account when examining the logical status of moral judgements. Moral terms do not admit of purely empirical criteria of application, since moral judgements are never based on observation alone. Our immediate task, then, is to consider whether the meaning of moral terms permits the existence of objective logical or logico-empirical criteria for their application. To do this we will examine the meaning of one basic moral term: *good*. This might seem an insufficient basis for establishing any clear conclusion. On the other hand, it would hardly make sense to suggest that the application of *good* in moral contexts is governed by criteria which have a difference status from the criteria used in the application of other moral terms. This appears particularly unlikely when we consider how closely linked is the application of *good* to that of other basic terms such as *ought, right,* and *duty*. If we know that an action is our duty, or is right, or is one that we ought to do, then we also know that it is morally good, whereas if we know that an action is not morally good we also know that it is not right, that we ought not to do it, and that it is one which we have a duty to avoid. This seems to establish beyond doubt that the criteria which govern the application of *good* are similar in character to those which govern the application of other moral terms, and hence that by examining the meaning of *good* we will provide ourselves with sufficient evidence for determining the logical status of moral judgements.

3. The meaning of *good*

What we are aiming at here is something in the nature of a definition of *good*. This approach has been out of fashion since Wittgenstein, in his *Philosophical Investigations*, described the search for definitions of the concepts of ethics and aesthetics as 'a hopeless task'. He went on to say:

> In such a difficulty always ask yourself: How did we *learn* the meaning of this word ('good' for instance)? From what sort of examples? In what language-games? Then it will be easier for you to see that the word must have a family of meanings. [*Philosophical Investigations*, para. 77.]

Since this was written, moralists have been chary of offering definitions of ethical terms. Instead they have usually restricted themselves to saying something about the different ways in which these terms are used. But the result has been so un-illuminating as to force us to think again about the implications of Wittgenstein's remarks.

No one could, I think, seriously question the dictum that many of the words used in everyday speech have not one but a whole family of meanings attached to them. Wittgenstein used the word *game* to illustrate this, but to avoid the fault, which seems endemic to philosophy, of sticking always to the same set of examples, we will use a different, though equally commonplace, term. Let us consider for a moment the different ways in which the word *head* is used. We speak of the head of a river, the head of a society, a head of steam; a headmaster, a headland, a headrace, headquarters; of being headstrong, of having a good head (e.g, for heights), of eating someone's head off, of heads or tails (when tossing a coin), and so on. It is doubtful if the word *head* has the same meaning in any two of these examples, but neither has it in any one instance a meaning which is not related in some way to all the others. The word has, therefore, not a common meaning, nor a set of entirely unrelated meanings, but 'a complicated network of similarities, overlapping and criss-crossing'—a family of meanings.

From this Wittgenstein concluded that the search for definitions is a hopeless task, since the purpose of a definition is to outline the meaning which is common to all the different uses of a term. But *is* this in fact the purpose of a definition? The dictionary definition of *head* is 'the uppermost part of an animal's body',[1] and since

[1] *Chambers's Twentieth Century Dictionary*.

the lexicographer immediately goes on to add that the term is used to refer to 'the brain; the understanding; self-possession; a chief or leader; a headmaster; principal; the place of honour or command; the front or top of anything', he can hardly have intended his initial definition to describe what is common to all the different uses of the term. What his definition refers to rather is the 'basic' or 'primitive' meaning of the word, the meaning from which all its other uses are derived. This 'basic' meaning illuminates all the others, since it enables us to perceive the relationships between them. In fact, without a grasp of this basic meaning we would never be able to make sense of these relationships. How otherwise would one grasp, for example, that the same term, without being equivocal, could be used to refer both to the intelligence and to a point of land jutting out into the sea?

Wittgenstein's metaphor of a family of meanings helps to bring out this point. What constitutes a family is not the resemblances between the members—different families can have similar features and different terms similar meanings—, nor the fact that they all possess the same name—unrelated namesakes are just as likely to turn up as equivocal terms—, but the fact that they are all descended from the same stock. And to know the parents is to have an unrivalled insight into the resemblances between the children.

The moralist who examines the different uses of *good* but refuses to commit himself to a definition is like a cartographer who depicts the surface of the earth in a series of almost disconnected oval strips. He sacrifices overall perspective for the sake of accuracy of detail, and he is, of course, perfectly justified so long as he is concerned only with the details. But in philosophy, unless one has an understanding of the essential features of a concept—the basic meaning of a term—, a knowledge of the less essential details is of little value. Definitions are like Mercator's Projection—they are misleading only so long as one remains unaware of their limitations. But if one recognises that a definition cannot hope to sum up the different uses of a term, but is intended rather as a description of its basic or primitive meaning, then the search for an accurate definition of *good* will appear as a task which is not only not hopeless, but even indispensable. Wittgenstein's theory of meaning will then be understood, not as ruling out the possibility of a valid definition, but as providing a warning against allowing definitions to blind us to the complexity of language.

There is one other preliminary point to be considered before attempting an explanation of the meaning of *good*. G. E. Moore's refutation of the 'naturalistic fallacy' has often been thought to rule out the possibility of a legitimate definition of *good*, and though few would now accept the argument as it stands, it still influences ethical thinking. The argument is as follows:

> The hypothesis that disagreement about the meaning of good is disagreement with regard to the correct analysis of a given whole, may be most plainly seen to be incorrect by consideration of the fact that, whatever definition be

offered, it may always be asked, with significance of the complex so defined, whether it is itself good. [*Principia Ethica*, 5.]

This argument may be paraphrased in the following terms: If we define *good* as meaning 'x, y, and z', the question: 'Is x, y, and z good?', is always a significant question. But this would not be so if 'x, y, and z' is the correct definition, for it is clear that questions of the form: 'Is a puppy a young dog?', or: 'Is a brother a male sibling?', are not significant questions to anyone who understands English. If one understands the meaning of the word *puppy* one knows already that it means 'a young dog'; if one did not know this, one could not be said to understand the meaning of the word. Now since we do understand what *good* means, and since the question: 'Is x, y, and z good?', is always a significant question, it follows that 'x, y, and z' cannot be the correct definition. And this means that *good* is indefinable.

It has recently been suggested that Moore's argument does not rule out the possibility that a correct definition of *good* may eventually be put forward.

It may be granted ... that this argument is effective in regard to many, or most, or all definitions of the concept offered in the past. But, the objection may be raised, how do we know that this argument would work in absolutely all cases?[1]

But if there is a definition of *good* to which

[1] George C. Kerner, *The Revolution in Ethical Theory*, London 1966, 19.

Moore's argument does not apply, how is it that philosophers have spent such a long time wrangling over its correct definition? If the question: 'Is *x*, *y*, and *z* good?' is ever lacking in significance, this can only be because '*x*, *y*, and *z*' is quite obviously and self-evidently the correct definition of the term. But why then have the philosophers been so long blind to this fact? To admit that the argument is effective against previous definitions is as good as admitting that the term cannot be defined.

In fact, however, Moore's argument does not really tell against any definition of *good*. The argument is based on the assumption that the understanding of what a term means includes the ability to recognise a correct definition of it. Now this is true of a great many terms, but it is not true of all. It is untrue in particular of those terms which are at the centre of philosophical discussion. We all know what *truth* means, for example. But does this mean that we would immediately recognise a correct definition of it? If it did, then it is extremely difficult to account for the philosophical controversies which have devolved on this very issue. The reason why we do not always recognise the correct definition of a term whose meaning we understand is that analytic statements are not always self-evident. Analyticity is a logical attribute, self-evidence a psychological one. The statement: 'The square on the hypotenuse of a right-angled triangle is equal to the sum of the squares on the other two sides', is, if geometry is the purely deductive science it claims to be, analytic; but, as schoolboys know to their cost, it is certainly not self-evident, and to query its truth would be to ask a significant question. The same is true of definitions of such concepts as *goodness* and *truth*. That it would always be possible to question significantly the correctness of a term's definition does not imply, therefore, that the term is indefinable.

In seeking the correct definition of *good* we will begin by considering the type of statement which describes something as 'a good *x*' where *x* denotes the class to which the thing belongs. We have already noticed one peculiarity about this type of statement.[1] When we describe an animal as a black horse, our statement is equivalent to the two separate assertions that the animal is black and that it is a horse; the fact that it is black is quite independent of the fact that it is a horse. But when we describe someone as a good singer, say, our statement cannot be broken up in the same way. We are saying not that the individual is good and that he is a singer, but that he is good considered as a singer. This is a peculiarity which *good* shares with relational predicates such as *tall*, *heavy*, *small*, and so on. To describe an animal as a small horse is not to assert that it is both small and a horse, for it may not be small when considered under a different category—as an animal, say, or as a member of a particular breed. This peculiarity seems to belong to relational predicates alone, and it is difficult, if not impossible, to conceive how it could attach to a term which denotes a non-relational attribute, so

[1] See pp. 119–20 above.

264

the fact that *good* possesses it seems sufficient indication that *good* is itself a relational predicate.

The next step is to discover what are the terms between which the relation holds. In the case of *small* the terms are this particular object's dimensions and the standard dimensions of objects of the same type. What corresponds to this in the case of *good*? R. M. Hare has drawn our attention to the fact that there are certain types of things to which *good* is never applied. 'We do not speak of good wireworms. This is because we never have any occasion for choosing wireworms and therefore require no guidance in so doing.' (*Language of Morals*, 127.) This fact is significant, but Hare's explanation of it is incorrect. There are objects which we never have occasion to choose but to which *good* is often applied.[1] Thus we speak of a good father, or of a good head for crosswords, even though these are not possible objects of choice. The reason why we do not speak of good wireworms, good hurricanes, good headaches, good diseases, etc, is not because we have no occasion for choosing these things, but because we have no use for them; they perform no useful function as far as we are concerned. This indicates that one of the terms of the relation which *good* denotes is the function of the object whose goodness is in question. But since, as we have just seen, we evaluate objects as members of a class, the function we are referring to is not any function which the object happens to possess, but the function of the class of objects to which it belongs. The other term of the relation

[1] See pp. 131 2 above.

must then be the way in which this particular object carries out that function.

We have now arrived at the following position. To say that something is a good x is to say that it carries out, or is capable of carrying out, the function of an x. The main difficulty with this definition is that certain types of things to which *good* is applied cannot plausibly be said to possess any function. For example, we speak of events as being good ('It was a good thing that you were at home when he called'), and we also speak of good luck and good news. But it hardly makes sense to say that an event which occurs by chance has a function to fulfil, and it is doubtful if anyone would be tempted to explain good luck or good news by saying that they fulfil the function of a piece of luck or an item of news. These are admittedly exceptional instances—further examples of the same sort of thing would be difficult to come by—, but they do not seem to be 'off-colour' or even extended uses of the term, so it is not easy to see how we are to reconcile them with our proposed definition.

This difficulty can, I believe, be resolved by taking into account some other uses of the term *good*. We speak of certain things as good *for* other things—medicine is good *for* the sick, moisture *for* the soil, exercise *for* the middle-aged, and so on. What all these expressions have in common is this: they imply a need on the part of the person or thing for whom the other thing is good. We never speak of x as being good for y unless we believe that y has a need which x is capable of satisfying. It is because the sick need medicine that medicine is good for them—obviously it isn't good for those who do not need it. When the bible tells us that it is not good for man to be alone, it implies that man has need of a companion. The need which is implied by the expression *good for* is not necessarily directed specifically towards the thing which is termed good. 'Guinness is good for you' does not imply (though it may suggest) that you have a need for Guinness; what it does imply is that you have a need which Guinness is capable of satisfying. In other words, 'x is good for y' implies not that y needs x specifically, but that x is capable of satisfying y's need.

There is another use of *good* whereby we speak of a thing, not as a good x, nor as good for y, but simply as 'a good'. Health, happiness, and knowledge, for example, are spoken of in this way. Does *good* have here the same meaning as in those contexts in which we speak of x as good for y? When we speak of something as a good, do we mean that it is good for people in general, there being no point in saying for whom it is good when we mean that it is good for everyone? But if this were true, it should be possible to say that happiness is good for you, or that health is good for you, and there is an obvious air of absurdity about these remarks. Nevertheless, the statement that something is a good seems to imply a need for this thing on the part of people in general, just as the statement that x is good for y implies a need on the part of y. We are all obviously in need of health, happiness, and knowledge, and we seem to speak of these things as goods because they satisfy human needs. But why then does it not make sense to speak of happiness as being 'good for you'? The answer, as I see it, is that we speak of something as 'good for you' only when this thing is a means to one's happiness or health or well-being in some form, that is, when this thing possesses instrumental goodness. But we speak of something as 'a good' only when it is intrinsically good, and not when it is good merely because it is a means to something else. The absurdity which surrounds the remark: 'Happiness is good for you', arises not from the fact that *good* has a different meaning when applied to happiness and to Guinness, but from the implicit suggestion that happiness is good because it is a means to something else. When we speak of something as 'good for x' and of something else as 'a good', the word *good* refers in both instances to the ability to satisfy a need, but there is a question here of two different kinds of need. The need implied by the first expression is a need for something as a means to something else, but the need implied by the second is a need for something for its own sake.

We now seem to be saddled with two definitions of *good*. To say that something is a good x is to say that it fulfils, or is capable of fulfilling, the function of an x, while to say that something is 'a good', or is good for someone, is to say that it satisfies, or is capable of satisfying, a need on the part of people generally or on the part of the individual referred to. There is, however, a close connection between the two definitions, and the first may be said to have grown out of the second.

In the first definition, the term *function* refers not to what the thing does or is designed by its nature to do, but to the use which man has for this thing —that is, to its ability to satisfy some human need. The bee, for instance, besides collecting honey, builds honeycombs, pollinates flowers, and performs mysterious dances, but we judge him to be good or bad solely in terms of his honey-making ability, for this is the only one of his performances which relates to human needs. The reference to a need implied by the use of *good* is indirect, therefore, when you designate something as a good member of a class. What you are saying is that this thing fulfils the function of an x, or—which amounts to the same thing—satisfies the criteria used in evaluating xs, but this function and these criteria are themselves based on the need which xs satisfy.

The exceptions which we noted to our first definition can now be satisfactorily explained. A piece of luck will sometimes satisfy a need, but there is no specific need which luck as such satisfies. The same is true of events and items of news. It makes no sense, therefore, to speak of the function of these things, and in describing them as good we are not, despite appearances, evaluating them as members of a class. What we are saying, rather, is that this event, piece of luck, or item of news happens to satisfy someone's need; the reference to a need is direct where the form of the statement would lead one to believe that it is indirect.

Before going further with our argument, it is as well to consider two objections which are sure to arise. The first is that, though we have now given an explanation of what *good* means in different contexts, we have come nowhere near proving that this explanation is correct. This is undoubtedly true, but it hardly constitutes a valid objection, for a conceptual analysis of the kind we have given is not really susceptible of proof. The best that one can do is to provide some evidence in favour of the analysis—something which has been done in this instance—, and after that the question of the validity of the analysis is the question of whether or not it makes sense of the way in which the term is used in ordinary speech.

The second objection is that we have explained the meaning of *good* in terms of two other concepts: *function,* and *need.* But these concepts are themselves so imprecise as to make doubtful what exactly our definition amounts to. The answer is that, if a concept is vague, as ordinary-language concepts usually are, it can only be defined by means of concepts which are themselves vague. To define an imprecise concept such as *good* by means of concepts which are clear and precise is to distort it. As to leaving *function* and *need* undefined—well, the process of definition must end somewhere. If we were to define these two terms, the same problem would arise with regard to the terms used in their definitions. You must assume at some stage that the terms employed in a definition will be intelligible to the reader without further explanation. Now it could hardly be claimed that the terms *function* and *need* would not be understood by anyone who understands

English, and since we are not claiming to use them in any sense other than the sense which they enjoy in everyday speech, further elucidation of them would seem to be unnecessary.

4. The criteria of goodness

The next question is: Does the meaning of *good*, as we have explained it, admit of objective criteria for its application? This is a question which will have to be answered piecemeal and we will begin at the level at which difficulties are least likely to arise, that of instrumental goodness. Every judgement of instrumental goodness presupposes two other judgements: a causal judgement, and a judgement of intrinsic goodness. The judgement: 'Exercise is good for the middle-aged', for example, presupposes, first, that exercise is conducive to the health of middle-aged people and, secondly, that health is 'a good'. The causal judgement, however, could normally be verified by purely empirical methods and so may be presumed to be objective. The issue depends, therefore, on the logical character of judgements of intrinsic goodness. If they are objective, the criteria which govern the application of *good* in judgements of instrumental goodness will also be objective.

What criteria do we use in deciding whether or not something is intrinsically good? On the assumption that our analysis of the meaning of *good* is correct, this question is equivalent to: How can one tell whether or not we need something for its own sake? One way of answering this question, though not perhaps the only one, is by considering the connection between need and

271

desire. A desire is always accompanied by a need. This is a matter of logic, not a question of mere contingent fact. A state in which one desires something but needs nothing is inconceivable, for to desire is to be dissatisfied with one's present condition, and to be dissatisfied is to be in need, if of nothing else, at least of an awareness that one's dissatisfaction is groundless.

But even though a need always underlies desire, needs and desires, as we know, do not always coincide. Some factor—a circumstance or trait of character—may intervene between the need and its conscious expression, with the result that the desire misrepresents the need. The more general the desire, however, the less likely that its character has been influenced by some individual trait or circumstance, and if the desire is universal, the possibility of such influence is almost non-existent. If people universally and invariably desire something, that desire cannot be due to some individual peculiarity, but must represent a genuine need on their part. A universal desire for something for its own sake seems, therefore, to constitute an objective logico-empirical criterion for the application of *good* in judgements of intrinsic goodness. That a need always accompanies desire is a matter of logic; that the desire is universal is empirical evidence that this particular desire accurately represents the underlying need. This empirical evidence may not provide an absolutely conclusive proof of the conclusion we have drawn from it, but in the absence of evidence to the contrary it is *sufficient* evidence in the sense of leaving no further room for reasonable doubt. And as no evidence to the contrary seems to be forthcoming with regard to such things as happiness, health, and knowledge, there is no reason for regarding the judgements which describe these as intrinsically good as other than objective.

This brings us to the third type of *good*-judgement, that in which something is described as a good member of a class. The judgement: 'A is a good *x*', is based, again on the assumption that our analysis of *good* is correct, on the following three presuppositions: (a) that A is an *x*; (b) that Xs have a specific function; and (c) that A fulfils this function, or at least is capable of fulfilling it. If these three judgements are objective, then the value judgement which is based on them must also be objective. Now the second presupposition seems to be the only one whose objectivity could seriously be questioned, since the first is objective if there is any such thing as an objective judgement, and the truth of the third could normally be settled by purely empirical, and therefore objective, methods. There are, no doubt, certain functions whose fulfilment could not be decided empirically, and this would create problems for the objectivity of value judgements in this area. But investigation of exceptional instances such as these is obviously outside the scope of the present inquiry. It is sufficient for our purpose if it is true to say, as I think it is, that *as a general rule* the question of whether something fulfils, or is capable of fulfilling, a particular function, is a purely empirical matter.

The question of the objectivity of this type of

value judgement is therefore reduced to this: Are judgements which assign a function to members of a class objective? When we state what a thing is for, are we stating an objective fact about it, or are we merely expressing a decision to use it in that way? We are stating a fact whenever the object is designated by a functional term, that is, a term whose meaning can be explained only by saying what the object in question is for. Functional terms are used mostly to refer to human artefacts and to individuals who perform special tasks. We would not know what the word *razor* means, for example, unless we knew what a razor is for, nor would we know what *plumber* means unless we knew what a plumber is supposed to do. The function is built into the meaning of the word. Consequently, the statement which assigns a function to something described by a functional term is not only objective, but is in fact analytic; the fact which it asserts is a fact about the term which describes the object and not about the object itself.

This means that *good* admits of logical criteria when we speak of something as 'a good *x*' and *x* is a functional term. To say that one's razor consistently provides a close, comfortable shave, but is not a good razor, is to contradict oneself; to take that statement seriously would be to reveal ignorance either of the meaning of the word *razor* or of the meaning of the word *good*. Hence the fact that the razor consistently provides such a shave logically entails that it is good. But not all functional terms have so clearcut and stable a meaning as the word *razor*. The term *house*, for example, has such a wide range of application

274

that it can be defined only in the most general terms. Consequently, the logical criteria provided by this definition for the application of the word *good* to houses are insufficient for the evaluation of any particular house. Here we would have to use two different sorts of criteria, one sort logical, the other not. The question then is (and this is the same question as that concerning the objectivity of statements which assign a function to objects which are described by non-functional terms): Are these non-logical criteria objective?

We will take the word *tree* as an example of a non-functional term. Does the statement: 'The function of a tree is to provide shade in summer', have any claim to be objective? Obviously it isn't entirely subjective, since there are at least two ways in which it could be objectively false—if trees were incapable of providing shade, or if the provision of shade was entirely unrelated to human needs. The statements: 'The function of a tree is to provide one with a close, comfortable shave', and: 'The function of a tree is to enable spiders to build cobwebs between the branches', are both objectively false, for example. (The last statement might conceivably be true if the tree is being considered as created by God for a special purpose, but *tree* would then be a functional term.) There is no question, therefore, of the objectivity of the judgement ascribing *a* function to a tree, since what this asserts is that the tree has a capacity which we, directly or indirectly, avail ourselves of, something which can be decided empirically. There is, however, a certain subjectivity about the judgement which speaks of *the* function of a tree, since here the speaker has chosen one of the many functions which could legitimately be ascribed to a tree and given it a special status.

But does this fact mean that the statement: 'That is a good tree', is subjective? This question can best be answered by taking account of a parallel situation. Consider the statement: 'That is a tall tree'. The speaker may mean that it is tall considered as a tree simply, but he is more likely to mean that it is tall considered as a certain sort of tree—as a member of this plantation, for example, or as belonging to a certain species or age-group. In other words, the speaker is free to choose the category according to which he is judging the tallness of the tree, and the fact that he has a certain limited choice in this matter does not take anything from the objectivity of his judgement. Now the freedom to choose the category according to which one is judging the tallness of the tree seems to be exactly parallel to the freedom to choose the function according to which one judges its goodness. The choice is limited in the one case by the fact that the tree belongs only to a certain number of categories, and in the other by the fact that only a certain number of functions can be attributed to it. In both cases the speaker must, to make himself fully clear, indicate which category or function he is concerned with, though this will sometimes be clear from the context. Finally, in both cases the terms *tall* and *good* are applied in accordance with criteria which are logico-empirical in character, derived both from the meanings of the terms *tall* and *good* and from the empirical facts that trees of this kind have a standard height and objects of this kind perform a particular function. Both sets of criteria seem to have precisely the same character and since no one, I believe, would want to deny that *tall* is applied in accordance with objective criteria, the criteria which govern the use of *good* in judgements of this kind must be regarded as objective.

The position, therefore, is as follows: When we describe something as a good *x*, the word *good* is applied, at least as a general rule, in accordance with objective criteria; these criteria are for the most part logical in character when *x* is a functional term and logico-empirical when it is non-functional. The question now is: How does the application of *good* in moral judgements fit into this pattern?

In moral contexts, we apply the word *good* to actions, motives, intentions, consequences, and—finally—to persons. These are clearly not functional terms, so the application of *good* would here appear to be governed by logico-empirical criteria. But now a serious difficulty arises. When you describe something as a good *x* and *x* is a non-functional term, you are free to choose the function according to which you evaluate the thing, always provided the thing can properly be said to possess this function. But this is not true of moral judgements. A human action may have all kinds of functions attributed to it, but this does not entitle you to decide its moral goodness in accordance with whatever function you please. It is not a question of the subjectivity or objectivity of moral judgements, for if you could choose the function these judgements would in fact be objective just like other value judgements. It is a question rather of the significance of the word *moral*. If it has any significance—and whether you are a subjectivist or an objectivist, you will have to agree that it means something—, then the moral goodness of an action means its goodness from a definite point of view and not from any point of view you please.

Does it not seem, then, that *moral* is itself a functional term, and that consequently we could determine the function of an action from the moral point of view by asking: 'What does *moral* mean?'? This sounds plausible in theory, but it does not seem to work out in practice. It does not seem possible to decide the meaning of *moral* on the basis of linguistic considerations alone, and to introduce considerations of a different kind would be to presuppose the point at issue. Suppose, for example, we say that *moral* refers to the ability of an action to produce pleasure, and that it is in accordance with this function that we must make our moral judgements. This view cannot be based on purely linguistic considerations, since certain types of pleasures are commonly regarded as morally evil, and this would be absurd if the meaning of *moral* is as we have just described it. The view that *moral* refers to the ability of an action to produce pleasure must, therefore, be due to the fact that one regards actions which produce pleasure, or the maximum amount of pleasure, as morally good. Now this is itself a moral judgement, and it will not be objective unless *good* is here applied in accordance with objective criteria. But, since the criteria for the application of *good* in moral contexts are ex hypothesi derived from this judgement, there are no objective criteria available for the judgement itself, and this can only mean that the judgement is subjective. It follows inevitably that *good* in moral contexts is applied in accordance with criteria which have no objective basis.

It might seem that this problem is due to the definition of *moral* which we have supplied, and that if *moral* were defined differently, the problem would disappear. But this is not so. A definition of *moral* is never morally neutral. It could never be based, therefore, on purely linguistic considerations. How you define *moral* depends on your moral outlook, on the basic principle of your moral system. The meaning of *moral* cannot, then, provide criteria for this basic judgement, and this seems to imply that the judgement is nothing more than an optional postulate—something which depends ultimately on the decision of the individual. If this is so, the criteria used in the application of moral terms are not, in the last resort, objective.

12
The ultimate criterion of morality

1. Statement of the theory

The argument we have been considering has such enormous implications for ethics that it merits the closest consideration. Its basic premiss is that, since moral characteristics are not observable, the terms which designate them require criteria for their application. Since we do not perceive the goodness of an action, we need some test or criterion to enable us to decide whether or not an action really is good. Now the application of moral terms to particular actions is governed by criteria provided by universal moral principles. If we accept the principle: 'Lying is immoral', then the fact that an action involved the deliberate telling of an untruth is an indication that it is immoral—an infallible indication if we regard the general principle as universally valid. But criteria are also required for the making of general moral judgements, and these must in turn be derived from moral judgements of an even more general character. This process cannot continue indefinitely, however. We must eventually arrive at an ultimate criterion. (Whether there are one or several ultimate moral criteria is of no account as far as this argument is concerned.) Let us call this ultimate criterion *C*. The judgement that actions which are in accordance with *C* are morally good is itself a moral judgement. For it to be objective, the term *good* must be applied here in accordance with objective criteria. But clearly there are no objective criteria available for this purpose since, ex hypothesi, *C* is the ultimate moral criterion. This means that this judgement is not so much a judgement as a decision to regard actions which are in accordance with *C* as morally good, and actions which are contrary to it as morally evil. The ultimate criterion of morals is therefore subjective. It follows that there are no objective criteria available for the application of moral terms.

This argument seems to me to be effective against the criteria of morality put forward by the classical systems of ethics. The scholastic theory that the ultimate moral criterion is human nature and the hedonist theory that it is pleasure, to take two fairly obvious examples, are both open to the objection that we could not know that actions which are in accordance with human nature or which produce pleasure are morally good unless we possessed some more ultimate criterion. The protagonists of these theories are then faced with the dilemma of saying either that there is a more ultimate criterion of morality, or that the question of what criteria to use in applying moral terms is a matter which each individual must decide for himself. And it looks as if the second alternative would have to be accepted in the long run, since to accept the first is merely to place the problem one stage further back.

But is the argument universally effective? Is it true of any possible moral criterion that the judgement that actions which are in accordance with this criterion are good is subjective unless *good* is here applied in accordance with objective criteria? There is in fact one way of evading the argument. If it is self-evident that actions which are in accordance with *C* are morally good, then it is no longer necessary that *good* be applied here in accordance with objective criteria for the judgement to be objective. To circumvent this argument, therefore, we must produce a moral criterion whose status is self-evident.

There is in fact such a moral criterion, and it is one which is constantly used and appealed to in moral judgement and moral discussion. When we say that killing of the innocent is wrong because each of us has a moral right to life, or that we ought to pay our income tax because the state has a moral right to demand a share of our incomes, we are using rights as a criterion of morality—we are appealing implicitly to the principle: 'The rights of others ought to be respected'. Now this principle, as is clear as soon as one reflects on it, is self-evident; it does not bear arguing about, nor could one coherently deny it. It could not be true to say that one has a moral right which others are not obliged to respect, because a right which does not impose this obligation on others is simply not a moral right. To

282

assert that an individual has a right to something and simultaneously deny that others are obliged to respect that right is to say nothing; it is take away with one hand what one is giving with the other.

But does the fact that this principle is self-evident mean that it is empty of content? Is the statement: 'A has a right to x', identical in meaning with: 'We are morally obliged to leave A in peaceful possession of x'? If it is, rights cannot function as a criterion of morality, since we could not then know that A has a right to x unless we also knew that we are morally obliged to leave him in peaceful possession of x, and this would mean that another moral criterion would be required to enable us to make this latter judgement. That this is not so is, however, clear from the fact that rights sometimes conflict. The fact that A has a right to x does not logically entail that we are morally obliged to leave him in peaceful possession of it, for the reason that A's right to x may conflict with someone else's right to it, and if the latter's right is the more pressing of the two, then it is morally permissible for him to deprive A of x. It would be morally permissible, for instance, to deprive a person of his car, even if he is unwilling to part with it, so as to bring a badly injured man to hospital. The fact that A has a right to x does not, therefore, entail that we are morally obliged to leave A in peaceful possession of x, since, in this instance, the first statement is true and the second false. And if one statement does not logically entail another, the two cannot be identical in meaning.

Let us see now what precisely is involved in the claim that rights constitute the ultimate criterion of morality. The content of this theory can, I believe, be set out in the following three theses:

a. When there is no conflict of rights, an action is morally good if it meets, or helps to meet, the obligations arising out of another's right; it is morally wrong if it violates another's right.

b. When there is a conflict of rights, an action is morally good if it meets, or helps to meet, the obligation arising out of the right which takes precedence; it is morally wrong if it violates that right.

c. When an individual performs an action which he has a right to do, his action is morally permissible, though not necessarily morally good.

Each of these theses requires a certain amount of explanation and justification.

a. The phrase: 'meet the obligations arising from another's right', is not identical in meaning with: 'respect another's right'. There are two ways in which another's right is respected. The first is by doing that which respect for the right demands; the second is by merely avoiding anything which would violate the right. The difference between the two is exemplified by the difference between paying one's debts and not killing someone. In both cases there is question of moral obligation, but in the first instance, the obligation requires the doing of something positive, in the second instance, the negative action of merely refraining from doing something. The phrase: 'meets the obligations arising from another's right', as I am using it, is reserved for actions of the first type. But the corresponding phrase: 'violate another's right', is understood in a broader sense; it is intended to cover both the failure to meet the obligations arising from another's right and the doing of that which the obligations arising from another's right requires you to refrain from. It covers, in other words, both the failure to pay one's debts and the committing of a murder.

What the first thesis asserts is that, when there is no conflict of rights, an action which meets the obligations arising from another's right is morally good and an action which violates that right is morally wrong. But what about actions which merely refrain from that which would violate another's right? These are morally indifferent in themselves, but they may acquire moral value from the motive of the agent. This sounds debatable in the abstract, but it becomes evident once you consider particular instances. My refraining from killing someone, for example, is not something which deserves praise; it is not morally meritorious and therefore not morally good, since to kill someone may have never entered my head. To suggest that it is morally good is equivalent to suggesting that I earn merit every minute of every waking hour by refraining from doing something which it may never have occurred to me to do. But suppose a person is tempted to commit murder and refrains from doing so. Is not his action morally good? The answer is that it depends on his motive. His action is morally good if he refrained from a good motive; if not, his action has no moral value. But in the first case the goodness of the action is derived entirely from the motive and not from the action itself. This is clear once you consider that what he did is no different from what he has always done, namely, that he refrained from committing murder. The only difference is that, following the temptation, his refraining was consciously motivated. Any value which his refraining now has must, therefore, be due to the motive, since it cannot be due to the act itself which up to now had no moral value. On the other hand, an action which positively meets the obligations arising from another's right, such as the payment of a debt, since we cannot reasonably speak of it as morally indifferent, is morally good. It may, of course, be deprived of merit by being done from an unworthy motive, such as the fear of the consequences of non-payment, but the fact that we use the word *deprived* here signifies that the unworthy motive dispossesses the action of a value which would otherwise accrue to it; the moral value of the action derives at least partially, therefore, from the nature of the act itself.

The two ways of respecting another's right are not, then, morally equivalent. The positive fulfilment of the obligations which arise from another's right is morally good; the mere negative refraining from violating another's right is morally indifferent, but may acquire moral value from the motive of the agent.

b. The second thesis introduces the notion of a conflict of rights. This is much more complex than it sounds, since there are several kinds of rights and, consequently, several ways in which rights can conflict. There is the right to do something (e.g, the right to marry, or the right to choose a vocation); the right to something which one has not yet got (e.g, the right of a worker to his salary); the right to remain in the peaceful possession of one's material goods; the right to remain in peaceful possession of one's personal faculties, such as life and bodily integrity. The last two may seem too similar to merit separate classification, but this is not so. The manner in which we possess our personal faculties is quite different from the manner in which we possess material goods. This is clear from the fact that we are free to relinquish our bodily integrity only if there is a justifying reason, whereas we are free to relinquish our material possessions whenever there is no serious reason to the contrary. Even if one disagrees with this moral principle, the fact that it is widely accepted shows that the two cases are dissimilar, and that their morality requires separate consideration.

When rights conflict, therefore, the conflict may have different characteristics in different instances. In some cases the maintenance of one right necessarily involves the complete suppression of the other, as, for example, in the case of income tax— the right of the individual to that portion of his income which goes for income tax is completely suppressed once the tax has been collected. In other instances, the maintenance of one right involves merely the temporary suppression of the other, as in the requisitioning of a car to bring someone to hospital. This is something which has to be taken into account when deciding which right takes precedence, since the complete suppression of a right is obviously a more serious matter than its temporary suppression.

How is one to decide, then, which of two conflicting rights takes precedence? There is one approach which can be ruled out immediately, even though it might seem plausible enough in the abstract. One cannot draw up a list of rights in order of precedence showing which rights take precedence over which. It might seem, for example, that the right to life would automatically take precedence over the right to private property, but consider the situation in which a person's life is only slightly endangered if another's right to his property is maintained, whereas the second individual will suffer grave material loss if his right to his property is not maintained. In this situation we would, I believe, say that it is the second individual's right which takes precedence.

The reason why we would do so is highly significant. The loss of life is a more serious matter than the loss of material goods, but the slight endangering of a life would usually be a less serious matter than a grave material loss. This indicates that when rights conflict, the question to be asked is not: 'Which right, considered in the abstract, takes precedence over the other?', but: 'Which party will suffer most loss through the suppression or temporary suspension of his (or their) right?' The answer to this question will not, however, be always decisive. One must ask: 'Is the right whose suppression causes least loss of such a kind that

288

it can be legitimately suppressed?' The reason for this second question is that some rights, such as the right to life, are commonly regarded as inviolable. (Whether this position is justified is something which will have to be discussed later.) Thus it would not be morally permissible to kill someone, even if by doing so one would save the lives of several others, and their lives cannot otherwise be saved. The inviolability of human life, as it is commonly understood, is not, however, absolute. It is only the lives of the innocent which are inviolable, and even this does not render immoral actions which merely prejudice the life of another and for which there is sufficient justification. Thus it would be morally permissible to endanger the life of another provided there is a sufficiently grave reason for doing so. Hence one cannot assume that the right to life takes precedence when it conflicts with another right. One must determine, first, whether it is the life of an innocent person which is at stake, and, secondly, whether the maintenance of the other right involves the loss of life or the mere endangering of it, and, if the latter, whether there is sufficient justification.

The results of this discussion may be summed up as follows: When rights conflict and neither right is inviolable, then that right takes precedence whose suppression or temporary suspension involves most loss for the party concerned. But is this satisfactory for all conflicts of rights? Could one not envisage a situation in which one individual would have a much better right to something than another, yet the loss of the thing would mean much more to the second individual than to the first? The payment of income tax, for example, is usually a more serious matter for the individual citizen than its loss would be for the state, but the right of the state here seems to take precedence.

This objection gains most of its plausibility from a confusion between a conflict of claims and a conflict of rights. When two people lay claim to the same thing, each may have a prima-facie right to it, but usually only one has a real right to it; the resolution of the conflict involves determining, not which of the two parties will sustain the greater loss through being deprived of the object in dispute, but which of the prima-facie rights is the real right. When there is a conflict of genuine rights, on the other hand, its resolution involves determining, not which of the rights is the better founded—since both are genuine, they must be equally well founded—, but which party will sustain the greater loss through the suppression or temporary suspension of his right.

The income tax issue involves, of course, a conflict of genuine rights, but it must be remembered that the conflict is between the right of the state and the right of, not one, but all its citizens. If the state's right does not take precedence, then it has no title to any revenue from income tax, and this would be a much more serious matter for the state than the payment of income tax is for its citizens, since what the individual citizen pays comes, at least in theory, from his *superflua*.

A final point is that, while it is usually easy to determine which of two conflicting rights takes precedence, at times it may be difficult and perhaps even impossible. One cannot rule out the possibility that two conflicting rights may have equal claims to precedence, and that if they are rights to something which cannot be divided, then a resolution of the conflict would, at the theoretical level, be impossible even in principle. But this should not surprise us unduly. It is merely another reminder that morals are not akin to mathematics, and that, in acute cases of conflict, one must fall back on the criterion proposed by Aristotle—the judgement of a man of practical wisdom.[1]

c. The third thesis lays it down that an action which one has a right to do is morally permissible but not necessarily morally good. We are speaking here, of course, of strictly moral rights, and not (say) of purely legal ones; and, secondly, we are speaking of actions considered in themselves, that is, apart from the motives of their agents. Some may be disposed to question this thesis on the grounds that if one has a moral right to do something, then it must be morally good. That this is false can, however, be shown quite easily. Every action which is not morally wrong is one which its agent had a right to do. If it were possible to do something which one has not a moral right to do and not be guilty of immorality, the statement: 'He had no moral right to do what he

[1] Aristotle, *Nicomachean Ethics*, 1107a. In this context it is interesting to note that one of the older ecclesiastical journals invites its readers to send in moral problems 'for solution'. This seems to place moral problems on the same level as crossword puzzles.

did', would be an empty formula, since the sole point in making it is to indicate that the action was immoral. It follows, therefore, that any action which is not immoral is one which the agent has a right to do. But not every action which is not immoral succeeds in being morally good. This fact is hardly susceptible of proof, but I do not think it requires it, since to deny it would be to attach moral value to such trivialities as lighting a cigarette or chewing a piece of gum. And to admit that these are instances of morally indifferent actions is to admit that actions which one has a right to perform are morally permissible but not necessarily morally good.

2. Defence of the theory
The theory that rights constitute the ultimate criterion of morality is open to attack from three sides. It could be claimed: (a) that rights are not really a moral criterion; (b) that they are not an *ultimate* criterion; or (c) that they are not the *sole* ultimate criterion of morality. Let us see how much weight is to be attached to each of these objections.

a. The denial that rights constitute a moral criterion of any sort could take one or other of two forms. It could be claimed either that there is no such thing as moral rights, or that, though they exist, they cannot function as a moral criterion. But the second position, as we have seen already,[1] seems utterly untenable. If moral rights are not a criterion of morality, then they are nothing. If the

[1] See pp. 282–3 above.

statement that a person has a moral right to something does not imply that others have a duty to respect that right, then it tells us nothing at all.

To continue to deny that moral rights can function as a criterion of morality involves, therefore, falling back on the first position and adopting the view that moral rights are non-existent. But is this view any more coherent than the other? The denial that there is any such thing as a moral right implies that no one has a right to do anything. It could not be claimed, I think, that this is a reasonable position, but is it even meaningful? When we deny that someone has a right to do something, it is always on the ground that by doing this thing he will infringe someone else's right. In fact, this seems the only reasonable ground on which the existence of a right could be denied, for to say that an action will not infringe any one else's right is equivalent to saying that there is no reason for denying the agent's right to do it. It follows that when we deny that an individual has the right to do something, we are implying the existence of a right on the part of someone else. The denial that anyone has a right to do anything makes no sense, therefore. It is like saying that every statement is false; the content of the statement rules out the possibility that the statement might itself be true.

Could one evade this consequence by saying that the denial that there is any such thing as a moral right is not quite the same thing as the denial of the existence of a particular right in a context in which the existence of rights is taken for granted? There is a sense in which this is true, for the person who denies the existence of a right in a particular case intends to imply that, by doing this thing, the agent would be acting immorally, whereas the person who denies that there is any such thing as a moral right can hardly intend to imply that every human action is immoral. But though he does not intend it, this is what his statement does imply in fact. For an action would not be morally permissible unless the agent had a right to do it. To say that an action is morally permissible, but that the agent had no moral right to do it, is, no matter how one interprets the second half of the statement, to contradict oneself. One cannot hold, therefore, that there is such a thing as a morally permissible action without conceding the existence of moral rights.

b. The second way in which one could object to the theory we have been advocating is by claiming that, though rights do constitute a criterion of morality, they do not constitute the ultimate criterion. This is a common enough position among writers in the scholastic tradition, who usually claim that rights are derived either from law or from duty. Here is a typical statement of the first position:

> Right, then, is a result of law. It springs from law simultaneously with duty. Right and duty are the two *termini* of the one relation created by law.[1]

If this were correct, then we could know of the

[1] Michael Cronin, *The Science of Ethics*, Dublin 1909, 660.

existence of a right only through knowing of the existence of the law which confers it, and consequently it would be law rather than rights which would constitute the ultimate criterion of morality.

One cannot, of course, seriously question that some rights are derived from law. The state, for example, can confer certain rights on its citizens —the right to free health services, the right to free education, and so on. But this is not the point at issue. The question which we must consider is whether rights *as such* are derived from law, that is, whether there can be such a thing as a moral right which is not derived from law. The answer is evident once you consider that law itself must be based on a right. If the lawgiver does not have the right to legislate, then what he propounds will not be a genuine law, and so will not give rise to rights. Thus, it cannot be true to say that all rights derive ultimately from the natural law, for unless God has the right to impose this law on his creatures, the law itself would have no binding force. Instead of rights presupposing law, therefore, it is the reverse which is the case; law as such presupposes a right.

Could one adapt the scholastic position to meet this objection by saying that it should be understood to mean that all *human* rights are derived from law? But though this avoids the objection, it weakens the position considerably, for if it no longer asserts that rights *as such* are derived from law, it is difficult to see what grounds there can be for ruling out the possibility of a human right which is not derived from law. Furthermore, the modified version of the theory is itself open to objection. There are certain human rights which cannot plausibly be regarded as being derived in any sense from the natural law. Consider the right to act in accordance with one's conscience, for example. Since one's conscience may err, this involves the right to act contrary to the natural law when one erroneously thinks that that is the right thing to do. But it hardly makes sense to say that the right to act contrary to the law is itself derived from the law. It follows that the natural law cannot be regarded as the ultimate source of human rights.

The alternative scholastic theory is that rights are derived from duties; my right to do something, according to this, derives from the duty which devolves on others of not hindering me from doing it. As before, what this asserts is that rights *as such* are derived from duties; it is refuted, in other words, if it can be shown that there is one right which is not so derived. Consider now what happens when one makes a promise. When A promises to give something to B, B acquires a certain right to that thing. The theory which we are considering asserts that B's right is derived from A's duty to fulfil his promise. But this view cannot be upheld because A's duty is derived from the fact that he has made this promise, and the promise cannot be understood except as the transfer of the right to B. The promise is prior to the duty which arises from it, and therefore the right which is transferred in the course of the promise is prior to the duty to fulfil the promise. Instead of B's right being derived from A's duty, it is the reverse which is the case.

If we consider other instances of rights and correlative duties we will see that this is not an isolated instance, but that rights *as such* are more basic than duties. The right to life, for example, can hardly be represented as deriving from the duty to treat human life as sacred and, as a general rule, inviolable; the duty here obviously derives from the right, not the right from the duty. When a person gains possession of something, we describe the event by saying that he acquires rights over it. It would certainly be very odd to describe it by saying that what has happened is that a duty has been imposed on others to leave him in peaceful possession of this item. This has, of course, occurred, but it is a consequence of the initial event, not an essential part of it. Here too it is the right which is fundamental, the duties which are derivations.

But there is a more fundamental argument against the view that rights constitute the fundamental criterion of morality. The question of whether or not someone possesses a particular right is usually resolved by an appeal to criteria. If it is a question of the rights of the citizen, we appeal to the constitution or to civil law; if it is a question of whether or not someone owns something, we seek for a document which would show his title to possession. The constitution, civil law, and documents such as wills are instances, therefore, of criteria which enable us to determine the presence or absence of rights. But if rights are a consequence of these criteria, are not these criteria themselves criteria of morality? This would entail that rights do not constitute the ultimate moral criterion.

This argument loses its force once it is realised that in appealing to criteria to establish the existence of a right one does not thereby leave the realm of rights. It would make no sense to say that it is not rights but such things as wills and civil laws which constitute the ultimate moral criterion, since a will is the conditional transfer of rights, and a civil law of the kind we are considering the conferring of a right. These cannot be put forward as rival moral criteria, since they are merely conventional means of expressing the giving of a right; were it not for their connection with rights, they would have no moral significance.

There are, however, certain rights which cannot be conferred, such as the right to life, to bodily integrity, to choose one's vocation. The individual does not acquire these, but possesses them from the beginning of his existence. For this reason they are more difficult to account for than the rights which he acquires from some outside agency. How do we know, in the first place, that the individual possesses these rights: Is this judgement self-evident, or do we need criteria to arrive at it? Secondly, what is the basis for these rights in the individual? Perhaps the best way to approach these problems is by first considering the question: Why do persons possess rights while material things do not?

A right is that which limits the extent to which a being may be possessed. This is not the most obvious statement one might make about the nature of a right; nevertheless, it expresses a fact whose truth can, I believe, be easily perceived by anyone who reflects on it. (The limit which a right places to possession is, of course, moral, not physical.) A material thing, because it has no rights, may be possessed totally; its owner may, in principle at least, use it as he pleases, and even destroy it if he so wishes. A person, on the other hand, can be possessed only to a very limited extent. We do, indeed, speak of a state possessing its citizens and of parents possessing their children, but this sort of possession is nowhere near absolute, and falls far short of the possession one might exercise over a material thing. The reason is that a person is an individual who possesses himself. (By *himself* we understand not merely his body, but his life, faculties, and destiny.) Non-persons may be treated purely as means because they can be totally possessed, but persons must be treated as ends because we cannot possess them in anything more than a relative sense, and therefore are not free to use them as we wish. The attitude to persons which morality demands of us is similar to the attitude which it demands of us with regard to the property of other people. If I own a book, I may mark it, or remove some of its pages, or even treat it as waste paper. But if I borrow a book, I may not do any of these things; the borrowed book must be treated with respect, since my use of it is strictly limited by its owner's rights. The respect due to persons is similar to this. We may *use* them to a limited extent—as, for example, when we get someone to do something for us—, but we may never transgress the rights which a person possesses over himself; in other words, we must always treat persons as ends in themselves, and never purely as means.

The terminology of the last sentence is Kantian, and what we have been saying is in fact very similar to what Kant said in his ethics, for when you respect a person's rights you are treating him as an end in himself, and furthermore you are acting on a maxim of a kind which you can will should become a universal law. To act out of respect for another's right to his life or property is to show respect, not merely for *his* rights, but for the right to life or property as such; it is to act, therefore, in accordance with a universal principle. The theory of rights as the fundamental criterion of morality has a good deal in common, then, with Kant's Categorical Imperative, but it avoids certain difficulties inherent in the latter. For Kant lays it down that we are to act *only* on that maxim which you can will that it should become a universal law, and this seems to imply that it would be immoral to act on a maxim such as: 'Always smoke a cigar after dinner', which is perfectly harmless in itself, but is not the sort which one could will should become a universal law. Another well-known difficulty in Kant's theory arises from the fact that it is usually possible to describe an action in several different, but equally valid, ways. The Categorical Imperative must then be interpreted as saying *either* that an action is immoral if none of its alternative descriptions enables us to bring it under a maxim which one could will should become a universal law, *or* that it is immoral if each of its descriptions does not enable us to bring it under such a maxim. Neither interpretation is acceptable, however. The first would prevent us from regarding any action as immoral—Hitler could have described the destruction of the Jews, not as the killing of millions of innocent people, but as the purification of the German race, and he would have had no difficulty in willing as a universal law the maxim: 'Do everything in your power to purify the German race'. The second interpretation would compel us to regard as immoral every action which has a bad effect, no matter what good effect it produces.

The theory that rights constitute the ultimate moral criterion avoids both these difficulties. It avoids the first by asserting, not that every action must be done out of respect for the rights of others, but that every action which impinges on another's interests must respect his rights; clearly this leaves room for actions which are morally indifferent. It avoids the second by asserting that if any possible description of an action shows it to violate another's right and there is no question of a conflict of rights, then that action is immoral.

We have compared the respect due to a person to the respect due to another's property, but there are certain differences between the two which must also be mentioned. The first is that the respect due to another's property is not based on anything intrinsic to the thing, but on the fact that it is owned by someone else, while the respect due to a person is based on the fact that he possesses himself; the individual who possesses and the being which is possessed are here identical. The second, and more important, difference is that in certain circumstances one may treat another's property as if the owner had no right over it; it would be permissible, for instance, to destroy another's property to save a life. But a person may never be treated in this way. According to the common estimation, nothing could ever justify the deliberate killing of an innocent person. One might be tempted to explain this by pointing to the differences in value between a human life and a material object; a material object may be sacrificed for the sake of some greater good, but human life is so valuable that no good could ever justify someone being deliberately deprived of it. This solution will not work, however. For one thing, two human lives are more valuable than one, and this should mean that it would be permissible to murder an innocent person if by so doing you saved the lives of several others. Secondly, it doesn't take account of those situations in which the deliberate taking of life is permissible: self-defence, for example. The life of a guilty person is no less valuable than that of an innocent person, and if you rule out the deliberate destruction of the second because of the value of human life you have no valid reason for permitting the deliberate destruction of the first.

The real solution of this problem seems to me to lie in the distinction between a person's possession of himself and his possession of things external to himself. My right to things external to myself is relative in the sense that it does not rule out the possibility that, without my relinquishing my right in any way, someone else may acquire a greater right to them. If someone needed my property for his immediate survival, then his right would obviously supersede mine. The reason for this is that my right is based on inheritance, or purchase, or something similar, and this clearly does not rule out the possibility of someone acquiring a superior right to the property. My ownership of myself, on the other hand, is inherent in the sort of being which I am. My title to ownership of myself is the best possible—I *am* myself; there is no distinction here between the possessor and the possessed, and no possibility therefore of anyone acquiring a right over me which would supersede my own.

This again seems to be part of what Kant means by speaking of persons as 'ends in themselves'. To recognise a person is not merely to recognise a bearer of rights; it is to recognise one who bears an inviolable right over himself. It is impossible to be a bearer of rights without being a person; if one possesses any rights, then one must possess an inviolable right to oneself. All one's rights could not be relative in the sense of being capable of being superseded, for if one is capable of possessing anything, one must possess oneself. It would make no sense to say that one has this capacity but does not possess oneself, for the title to self-possession would be far more compelling than any title one might acquire to anything other than oneself. That one possesses any right implies, therefore, that one is the source of a moral absolute.

But if a person's right to life is inviolable, how can it ever be permissible to kill another deliberately? (I do not wish to commit myself here on the vexed questions of the morality of warfare or capital punishment, but hardly anyone will deny that one is allowed to defend oneself if unjustly attacked, even if this involves killing the aggressor.) The answer seems to be that it is the aggressor who has placed his own life in jeopardy by attacking the other; he has thereby brought it about that his life is no longer inviolable. It is not that another's right supersedes his own, but that he himself has relinquished the inviolability which attaches to his life. A combatant in warfare seems to be in a similar position, though in his case the relinquishing of his inviolable right to life does not necessarily have any guilt attached to it. One could also make a case for saying that a person guilty of murder or treason has also relinquished his inviolable right to life. Here the situation is not so clear—but then it is not so clear that capital punishment is ever morally permissible.

c. The third possible objection to the theory that rights constitute the ultimate criterion of morality is that, while they do constitute an ultimate criterion, they are not the only ultimate criterion. This would be not so much an objection to the theory as an extension of it, but either way the issue is of sufficient importance to merit careful examination.

The question of whether there are one or several ultimate moral criteria is not one which can be answered a-priori. If any moral criterion is such that it is self-evident that one ought to act in accordance with it, or that actions performed in accordance with it are morally good, then it is an ultimate criterion, and the question of whether there is one or more of these is something which cannot be settled in advance. There is, however, a reason for thinking that rights cannot be the only ultimate criterion of morality. There are numerous actions which are morally good but not morally obligatory. If I decide to devote my life to the service of the poor, for example, my action is morally good, but not one which I am morally obliged to do. But if one accepts rights as the only ultimate moral criterion, then one must hold that the only actions which are morally good are those which fulfil the obligations which arise out of another's rights. This implies that the only morally good actions are those which are morally obligatory, and since this is incorrect rights cannot be the only ultimate criterion of morality.

This objection, as A. I. Melden has pointed out,[1] is based on a confusion between two distinct notions: an obligation-meeting action, and an obligatory action. There is little difficulty in showing that these two notions are not identical. If they were, then in a situation in which one cannot meet one's obligations to A without failing to meet one's obligations to B, one cannot avoid failing to do what one ought to do; whichever course of action is taken, one omits an action which one is morally obliged to perform, and this means that one cannot avoid incurring moral guilt. But this is obviously incorrect. When one is faced with a conflict of rights, one's duty is to meet the obligations arising from the right which takes precedence. By failing to meet the obligations

[1] A. I. Melden, *Rights and Right Conduct*, Oxford 1959.

arising out of the less pressing right, one is not acting immorally, hence an obligation-meeting action is not necessarily morally obligatory.

There seem to be two ways in which one can perform an obligation-meeting action which is not at the same time obligatory. The first is when there is more than one way of meeting an obligation. A husband is obliged to express his love for his wife. If he gives her a present, he is helping to fulfil this obligation, but his action is not one which he is morally obliged to do, since there are several ways in which his love could have been equally well expressed. The second way is when one fulfils one's obligations beyond the measure to which one is strictly obliged. The individual in wartime who volunteers for a particularly dangerous task provides an example of this. He is thereby helping to meet the obligations which devolve on him as a citizen, but the fact that he has volunteered shows that this is a task which he is not morally obliged to perform. These are two instances, then, of actions which are morally good, but not morally obligatory.

But does the confusion which we have pointed out deprive the objection of all its force? The confusion arises out of the attempt to make the objection stronger than it actually deserves—the thesis that rights constitute the ultimate criterion of morality does not imply that for an action to be morally good it must also be morally obligatory. But the objection may be given a milder formulation which would avoid this error. This can be done as follows: If rights are the only ultimate moral criterion, then there are certain areas of morality which would have to be regarded as having in reality no significance for morals. The first of these is moral ideals. A moral ideal may be defined as a rule of conduct (using the term *rule* in the wide sense) which, if lived up to, gives behaviour a moral value which it would not otherwise possess, but which one is not morally obliged to live up to in the sense that neglect of this ideal does not of itself constitute immoral behaviour. The christian commandment to love is such a moral ideal; to live up to it would be to give to one's behaviour an added moral value, but to depart from it is not in itself to act immorally—one could not reasonably claim that if my behaviour towards someone shows that I do not love him in the same way as Christ loved his disciples, my behaviour is thereby shown to be immoral. But the christian commandment to love has nothing to do with rights. No one could seriously claim that he has the right to be loved by others as Christ loved his disciples, nor in acting towards others in accordance with the christian ideal could we be said to be merely meeting, or helping to meet, the obligations which arise out of their rights; no doubt we are doing this, but we are also doing a great deal more. It follows that if rights constitute the sole ultimate moral criterion, then the christian commandment to love is not really a moral ideal.

The second area of morality which I wish to consider comprises those actions, virtues, and vices whose primary impact is on the person who performs or possesses them and whose effect on others is merely indirect. A typical example of this is the virtue of temperance, its opposite vice of intemperance, and the actions connected with both. No one who is not concerned to make the facts conform to a preconceived theory would be tempted to deny that temperance is a moral virtue. But if we regard rights as constituting the sole ultimate moral criterion, we are committed to holding that the moral value of temperance is based entirely on the effect which it has upon others. This view is not by any means devoid of plausibility, and I do not see any way in which it could easily be disproved. But it involves a narrowing of the traditional scope of morality and seems to make it impossible to provide a solution of one of the central problems in ethics: Why do we want to be moral? For these reasons—the second will be discussed in the final section—I believe that this view must be rejected.

3. Why are we moral?

We now find ourselves in a dilemma. If we say that there is more than one ultimate criterion of morality, we seem to be dividing morality into a number of unrelated segments. But if we continue to maintain that there is only one ultimate moral criterion, then we are arbitrarily narrowing the scope of morality. There is, however, a way of avoiding both these consequences. In the last chapter we came to the conclusion that *good* has two basic, but not unconnected, meanings: when we speak of something as 'a good x', we mean that it is capable of fulfilling the function of an x; and when we speak of something as 'a good', we mean that it is capable of satisfying a need. The connection between the two is due to the fact that the function of a thing is derived from the need which it satisfies. This implies that when we speak of a morally good action we are evaluating the action according to a function which is itself derived from some need which morally good actions satisfy. Up to now, we have been considering morality merely from the point of view of the ultimate moral criterion—from the point of view, in other words, of the function which an action must fulfil in order to be morally good. If we ask ourselves: 'What is the need which underlies this function?', we may find a solution to the problem which now concerns us.

That morally good behaviour does satisfy a need on the part of the agent is something we could know independently of the analysis of ethical predicates which was put forward in the last chapter. For unless we needed to be moral, unless we benefit in some way by being moral and deprive ourselves of something by acting immorally, moral behaviour would be simply irrational. This might be questioned on the grounds that it makes self-interest the sole rational motive for behaviour, but this would be a misinterpretation. What we are saying is that no one freely does something unless he wants to do it, and he will not want to do it unless the doing of it affords him satisfaction. The first part of this statement is a logical truism, since it would be self-contradictory to assert that you freely chose something which you did not want to do, and the second part of the statement is true of all rational behaviour, since it would be irrational to want to do something which you believe will not afford you the slightest satisfaction. The reason why we are slow to accept that it would be irrational to want to do something which will not afford you any satisfaction is that it seems to brand altruistic behaviour as irrational, and this we naturally find unacceptable. But this conclusion is incorrect. An altruist is not a person who performs actions which help others but provide him with no satisfaction; rather, he is a person who gets satisfaction out of helping others. This satisfaction is not, of course, the motive for what he does; he is motivated by the desire to help others, but he possesses this desire because helping others provides him with satisfaction.

But why do we need to be moral? What is the fundamental reason for behaving morally? If we ask simply: 'Why do we want to be moral?', we can easily provide a number of answers. We want to be moral to gain the good opinion of others, to get on in the world ('honesty is the best policy'), to avoid the trouble which would result from immorality, and so on. But none of these can be the fundamental reason for wanting to be moral, for these are reasons which might not be operative for a particular individual. It might be the case that I am anxious to gain the good opinion of others, for example, and that my behaviour is constantly shaped by this factor; but it might equally be the case that the opinion of others is a matter of almost complete indifference to me. But everyone wants to be moral—a complete indifference to morality would be regarded as a sub-human characteristic. There seems to be a necessary connection between being human and wanting to be moral, and there must therefore be a fundamental reason for being moral which is operative for everyone.

This fundamental reason has been interpreted in different ways by different moralists, but the most widely accepted interpretation is that which could be described as the 'What would happen if everyone did the same?' theory. This points out that a world in which everyone behaves morally is far preferable to one in which moral considerations are disregarded. It is in everyone's interests, therefore, to help towards bringing about such a world, and to avoid anything which would contribute towards bringing about a state of pure nature. Now, since we all naturally want to bring about a state of affairs which is better for everyone including ourselves, we all have a reason for being moral. Clashes between morality and self-interest are due to the fact that we are prone to take account of only our short-term interests. A clash between morality and enlightened self-interest would be impossible, since the two are identical.

This theory does provide a genuine reason for being moral, but I do not think that it is the fundamental reason we are looking for.[1] It asserts that the fundamental reason for being moral is based on the causal connection between immoral behaviour and a state of pure nature. But is this connection always present? Does an immoral

[1] I have already touched on this point on pp. 139–50 above.

action always influence others to behave immorally? It seems to me that the reverse is often the case—that an immoral action may just as easily repel the onlookers, so that they are strengthened in their resolve to avoid such behaviour. Does it make sense to say that the sight of a person committing a murder or drinking himself into a state of stupor would tend to induce the onlookers to behave in a similar way? If it does not, then the theory implies that as far as these actions are concerned, there is no moral reason for not acting immorally. But even when this causal connection is present, all that it implies is that the action will *help* to bring about a state of pure nature. In others words, when a person is tempted to perform an immoral act, the only reason for resisting the temptation is that, if he performs the act, he *may* contribute to bringing about a state in which moral considerations are disregarded. If this were really the case, could one ever be blamed for acting immorally so as to further one's interests?

A second and even more damaging criticism of the 'What would happen if everyone did the same?' theory is that it implies that immoral behaviour is harmless if it is not found out. People are unlikely to be influenced by something of whose existence they are ignorant, so it is obvious that an immoral action will not contribute in any way towards bringing about a state of pure nature if either its existence or its immoral character can be successfully concealed. This means that I have no moral reason for refraining from committing a murder if I have good reason for believing that I can either conceal the victim's body where it will never be found, or that I can contrive to make the murder look like an accident. But this consequence is so absurd that the theory which implies it hardly merits further discussion.

The weakness of the theory we have just been considering stems from the fact that it explains why we want to be moral in terms of a characteristic which belongs to the class of immoral actions rather than to individual members of the class. Immoral actions considered as a class obviously tend to bring about a state of pure nature, but the same cannot be asserted, or can be asserted only in a very weak sense, about individual immoral actions. But to explain why we want to be moral is to explain why we want to be moral in particular instances, and not merely why we want people to behave morally as a general rule. The explanation must be based on a characteristic which belongs to individual actions; it must show, in other words, why it is in the agent's own interests not to perform individual actions which, though immoral, are likely to have desirable effects.

In the second book of the *Republic*, Adeimantus addresses Socrates as follows:

All of you who profess to sing the praises of right conduct ... have never denounced injustice or praised justice apart from the reputation, honour and reward they bring; but what effect either of them in itself has upon its possessor when it dwells in his soul unseen of gods or men, no poet or ordinary man has ever yet explained.[1]

A twentieth-century Adeimantus would have grounds for making the same complaint, but not all the blame for this should be assigned to the moralists. There is something mysterious about morality, and it may not be possible to explain, in absolutely clear-cut terms, what is the fundamental reason for being moral and why moral considerations outweigh all others. This is no doubt an unacceptable position for those who believe that 'everything that can be said, can be said clearly', but it is worth pointing out that in the *Tractatus Logico-Philosophicus*, where that statement first appeared, Wittgenstein asserted that 'ethics cannot be expressed' (6.421). He went on to say:

> 6.422 The first thought in setting up an ethical law of the form 'thou shalt . . .' is: And what if I do not do it? But it is clear that ethics has nothing to do with punishment and reward in the ordinary sense. This question as to the *consequences* of an action must therefore be irrelevant. At least these consequences will not be events. For there must be something right in that formulation of the question. There must be some sort of ethical reward and ethical punishment, but this must lie in the action itself.

What Wittgenstein is saying here, one point excepted, seems to me to be both true and im-

[1] Plato, *The Republic*, 366.

portant. One cannot explain morality in terms of the good effects produced by moral behaviour and the bad effects produced by immoral behaviour. It is of the essence of morality that its demands are absolute, that no consideration can ever provide a justification for acting immorally. But if morality is desirable because of its effects, one could not rule out the possibility of a situation in which the bad effects of acting immorally are either altogether avoidable or else insufficient to outweigh the damage to one's interests which would result from not acting immorally. What one cannot accept, therefore, is the type of theory which says that the fundamental reason for being moral is that by acting immorally we are risking our eternal damnation or helping to bring about a state of pure nature. On the contrary, the fundamental reason for being moral is that virtue is its own reward and vice its own punishment. And I would want to add, not that—as Wittgenstein seems to say—the nature of this reward and punishment cannot be expressed in language, but that it cannot be *fully* expressed.

But if this reward and punishment cannot be fully expressed, how can we be sure that it even exists? What is obscure is the *nature* of the reward and punishment, not their existence. Their existence cannot seriously be regarded as doubtful, since it is something which is brought home to us constantly in our everyday lives.

Whoever debases others is debasing himself. That is not a mystical statement but a most

315

realistic one, which is proved by the eyes of any Alabama sheriff.[1]

But the most palpable evidence for it is to be found, not in the eyes of others, but within ourselves. We know that when we act immorally, we are thereby debased. The self-abasement is not just an effect of the immoral action, something which generally follows but might conceivably not follow; as Wittgenstein says, it resides in the action itself. It would be as senseless to speak of a person performing an immoral action and not being debased as it would be to speak of a doctor curing a patient and the latter not recovering.

To say that this reward and punishment exist but that their nature cannot be explained is not a satisfactory position, however. For one thing, if we knew nothing about their nature, we could not even know that they exist, since we could not identify them. And secondly, without some idea of what this reward and punishment consist in, we will be at a loss to know why ethical considerations take precedence over all others—why we are never justified in acting immorally, no matter what the consequences.

The question of the nature of this reward and punishment becomes more accessible if we rephrase it in the form: Why are we necessarily debased in the performance of an immoral action? To act immorally is, primarily, to violate the rights of another, to treat him as a non-person. Why does the refusal to recognise the personality

[1] James Baldwin, *The Fire Next Time*, Harmondsworth 1964, 73.

of another involve the debasement of oneself? To answer this, we must take into account certain facts about the nature of personality. An individual becomes a person through his membership of a community of persons. A human being who is deprived of all contact with other humans will never get beyond the animal level or develop specifically human characteristics. This is borne out by the fact that man, so far as history can tell us, has always lived in groups, and that when he is brought up apart from human society—as in the case of children reared by animals or left in extreme isolation—his behaviour is such as to 'leave little doubt that without contact within a human group, man can hardly develop those characteristics which we call human and that life in a group is indispensable for the human being'.[1]

As the individual cannot become a person apart from society, so neither can he function as a person apart from it. By being removed from society, the individual is deprived of what is essential to the exercise of his personality—he can no longer communicate. One becomes a person by coming into contact with other persons as persons —by learning, that is, to communicate. Man is a person because he is a language-using animal. But to one who is cut off from society language is as useless as money. He may indeed play at communicating by talking to himself, but this would eventually become as meaningless as playing at buying and selling. Cut off from society the individual's personality would atrophy from lack

[1] Samuel Koenig, *Sociology*, New York 1957, 17.

317

of exercise in much the same way as his muscles would atrophy if he were prevented from using them. This is not to say that an individual might not use language significantly while living in absolute isolation. But its significance would be due to some link, real or hoped for, with the society from which he is cut off. He might read Dickens, as Tony Last did unwillingly in the jungle, or write an account of his experiences, as Francis Chichester did aboard the *Gypsy Moth.* In both these instances, however, the individual is still linked with society. The reading acquires its significance from the society in which it was written, and the writing from the society to which, he hopes, it will eventually be communicated. If the isolated individual were to merely write for himself alone and to read only what he himself had written, his use of language would have no more significance than his talking to himself. And in all these activities—even talking to himself—the use of language provides a link with the society from which he is cut off, since his language is a product of that society and reflects its structures.

The exercise of one's personality requires, therefore, that one acts as a member of the community of persons. This necessarily involves treating the other members of the community as persons. When one violates the rights of another and so treats him as a non-person, one places oneself outside the community of persons and thereby deprives oneself of the status of a person. It is in this that the debasement inherent in immorality consists. This is, admittedly, difficult to understand, and one might be tempted to say that it is true only in a metaphorical sense. An immoral action does not, after all, prevent you from functioning as a member of the community of persons, so how can it be said to place you outside that community? The answer to this is extremely difficult, and it is here that the element of 'mystery' which I mentioned earlier enters morality. There are, however, impressive reasons for accepting that immorality does deprive you of your status as a member of the community of persons in a real, and not merely a metaphorical, sense. Consider, first of all, how society reacts to criminal behaviour. It invariably removes the criminal from society by imprisoning him. It treats him, in other words, as if he were deprived of his membership of the community. Secondly, it treats him as if he had lost his status as a person, as if he no longer had possession of himself, and deprives him of his liberty and the control of his destiny. Crime and immorality are not, of course, identical, but a serious crime is almost always an immoral act, and it would hardly make sense to say that what society is reacting against is its criminal and not its immoral aspect. Besides, a community often spontaneously reacts in a similar way to one whose immoral behaviour is not punishable by law—they remove him from society by shunning him.

The attitude of society to immorality is paralleled by the guilty one's attitude to himself. The guilt which he experiences is not just a fear of consequences—if it were, it would be indistinguishable from the feeling of a person who is wrongly accused. Guilt indicates an awareness of present debasement which is independent of possible consequences.

> Analyse the feeling of remorse in the soul of a desperate criminal. You might mistake it at first for the dread of punishment ... But look closer. What the fellow wants is not so much to evade punishment as to wipe out the past, to arrange things just as though the crime had never been committed at all. When nobody knows that a thing exists, it is almost as if it were non-existent. Thus it is the crime itself that the criminal wants to erase, by suppressing any knowledge of it that might come to the human ken. But his own knowledge persists, and note how it drives him more and more out of that society within which he hoped to remain by obliterating the traces of his crime. He, knowing what he is, feels more isolated among his fellow-men than he would on a desert island; for in his solitude he would carry with him, enveloping and supporting him, the image of society; but now he is cut off from the image as well as the thing.[1]

The alienation from society which is involved in immoral behaviour, like immorality itself, admits of degrees. But it is seen most clearly in the extreme case of murder. Here the guilty one has treated another as a non-person in an absolute sense. He has subordinated his victim completely to his own ends and in doing so has removed himself in an apparently permanent fashion from the

[1] Henri Bergson, *The Two Sources of Morality and Religion*, New York 1956, 17–18.

community of persons. It is this which accounts for the popular feeling of revulsion towards a murderer, for the tendency to regard him as a monster, a non-person—not an attitude to be commended, but evidence of an unreflecting awareness of what is involved in immoral behaviour.

There is much in this that is still obscure, but the central features of the situation are, I believe, sufficiently clear for us to perceive why we need to be moral and why moral considerations take precedence over all others. Since it is our personality which makes us what we are, anything that threatens it is contrary to our interests. And no value which we could obtain by subordinating morality to self-interest could possibly outweigh our membership of the community of persons, since this is the foundation and indispensable condition of all human values. It follows that in practical affairs, moral considerations always take precedence. Secondly—and this brings us back to the problem which was raised at the beginning of this section—since personality is central to morality, anything which bears on the development of personality has a moral character. This enables us to regard certain ideals of conduct as genuine moral ideals and to attach moral value to actions which bear directly only on the individual who performs them. Nor does this involve an appeal to a second ultimate criterion of morality. Rights and personality are not distinct criteria, since to respect another's rights is to show respect for him as a person. A statement of someone's rights is a statement of what respect for him as a person requires as a minimum. Rights constitute the ultimate criterion of our moral obligations, but to understand the source of these obligations and of all moral value, we must go back to the concept of personality which underlies that of right.

What then of the difficulty concerning moral criteria which was posed at the beginning of this chapter? Is the statement: 'Every action done out of respect for the person is morally good', self-evident? If it is, how are we to explain the various ethical theories which posit a different source of moral value? If it is not, we are faced with the old problem of the subjectivity of moral judgements. It is obviously not self-evident in the way in which: 'The rights of others ought to be respected', is self-evident, since its denial does not involve one in immediate self-contradiction. I would suggest, however, that its denial does involve a contradiction of a similar type to that involved in the denial of a theorem of geometry. The contradiction is not apparent on the surface, but is nonetheless present since respect for the person is what morality is about. And this last assertion expresses not just an ultimate decision, but an objective judgement, since it is entailed by the acceptance of rights as an ultimate moral criterion. One cannot coherently deny that one is morally obliged to respect the rights of others, and to accept that position is to place the person at the centre of morality.

Bibliography

List of books and articles discussed, quoted and cited.

ARISTOTLE, *Nicomachean Ethics*, Loeb edition, trans. H. Rackham, London, Heinemann (1926).

AUSTIN, J. L., *How to do Things with Words*, ed. J. O. Urmson, London, OUP (1962).

—— —— *Philosophical Papers*, ed. J. O. Urmson and G. Warnock, London, OUP (1961).

AYER, A. J., *Language, Truth and Logic*, London, Gollancz (1936); and Harmondsworth, Penguin (1946).

—— —— *Logical Positivism*, Glencoe, Glencoe Free Press (1960).

—— —— 'On the Analysis of Moral Judgements', *Horizon* XX, 117 (1949); reprinted in *Philosophical Essays*, London, Macmillan (1954).

—— —— *Philosophical Essays*, London, Macmillan (1954).

—— —— 'The Vienna Circle', *The Revolution in Philosophy*, ed. G. Ryle, London, Macmillan (1956).

BAIER, Kurt, *The Moral Point of View*, Ithaca (NY), Cornell UP (1958).

BALDWIN, James, *The Fire Next Time*, Harmondsworth, Penguin (1964).

BERGSON, Henri, *The Two Sources of Morality and Religion*, New York, Henry Holt (1935); and Garden City (NY), Doubleday (1956).

BLACK, Max, *Language and Philosophy*, New York, Cornell UP (1950).

CARNAP, R., *Philosophy and Logical Syntax*, London, Kegan Paul (1935).

CRONIN, Michael, *The Science of Ethics*, Dublin, Gill (1909).

DUNCAN-JONES, Austin, 'Critical Notice of *Ethics and Language*', *Mind* LIV (1945).

EWING, A. C., *The Definition of Good*, New York, Macmillan (1947).

FEIGL, H. and Sellers (eds), *Readings in Philosophical Analysis*, New York, Appleton-Century Crofts (1949).

FLEW, Antony (ed.), *Essays in Conceptual Analysis*, London, Macmillan (1952).

—— —— *Logic and Language* II, Oxford, Blackwell.

GEACH, P. T., 'Good and Evil', *Analysis* XVII (1956).

GLASSEN, Peter, 'The Cognitivity of Moral Judgments', *Mind* LXVIII, 269 (1959).

HARE, R. M., *Freedom and Reason*, London, OUP (1963).

—— —— *The Language of Morals*, London, OUP (1952).

HUME, David, *An Inquiry Concerning Human Understanding*, ed. L. A. Selby-Bigge, London, OUP (1888).

—— —— *A Treatise of Human Nature*, ed. A. D. Lindsay, London, Dent (1911).

KANT, Immanuel, *Groundwork of the Metaphysic of Ethics*, trans. H. J. Paton, London, HUL (1948).

KERNER, G. C., *The Revolution in Ethical Theory*, London, OUP (1966).

KOENIG, S., *Sociology*, New York, Barnes & Noble (1957).

MALCOLM, Norman, *Ludwig Wittgenstein*, London, OUP (1958).

MARSH, R. C. (ed.), *Logic and Knowledge*, London, A. & U. (1956).

MOORE, G. E., *Principia Ethica*, London, OUP (1903).

—— —— *The Refutation of Idealism*, *Mind* XII (1903), reprinted in *Philosophical Studies*, London, Routledge (1922).

—— —— *Ethics*, Cambridge (1912).

MELDEN, A. I., *Rights and Right Conduct*, Oxford, Blackwell (1959).

NOWELL-SMITH, P. H., 'Contextual Implication and Ethical Theory', *Proceedings of the Aristotelian Society*, supplementary volume XXXVI (1962).

—— —— *Ethics*, Harmondsworth, Penguin (1954).

OGDEN, C. K. and I. A. Richards, *The Meaning of Meaning*, London, Routledge (1922).

PLATO, *The Republic*, trans. Davies and Vaughan, London, Macmillan (1950).

ROBINSON, Richard, 'The Emotive Theory of Ethics', *Proceedings of the Aristotelian Society*, supplementary volume XXII (1948).

ROSS, David, *The Right and the Good*, London, OUP (1930).

RUSSELL, Bertrand, *Introduction to Mathematical Philosophy*, London, A. & U. (1919).

—— —— 'Knowledge by Acquaintance and Knowledge by Description', *Proceedings of the Aristotelian Society* XI (1910–11); reprinted in *Mysticism and Logic*, London, A. & U. (1918).

—— —— *Mysticism and Logic*, London, A. & U. (1918).

RUSSELL, Bertrand, 'On Denoting', *Mind* XIV (1905); reprinted in *Logic and Knowledge*, ed. R. C. Marsh, London, A. & U. (1956).

—— —— *Our Knowledge of the External World*, London, Open Court Publishing Co. (1914).

—— —— 'The Philosophy of Logical Atomism', *Monist* XXVIII–XXIX (1918–19); reprinted in *Logic and Knowledge*, ed. R. C. Marsh, London, A. & U. (1956).

—— —— *The Principles of Mathematics*, London, CUP (1903).

—— —— 'The Relation of Sense-Data to Physics', *Scientia* (1914); reprinted in *Mysticism and Logic*, London, A. & U. (1918).

—— —— 'The Ultimate Constituents of Matter', *Monist* XV (1915); reprinted in *Mysticism and Logic*, London, A. & U. (1918).

RYLE, Gilbert (ed.), *The Revolution in Philosophy*, London, Macmillan (1956).

SCHILPP, P. (ed.), *The Philosophy of G. E. Moore*, Evanston, Library of Living Philosophers (1942).

STEVENSON, C. L., 'The Emotive Meaning of *Ethical* Terms', *Mind* XLVI (1937).

—— —— *Ethics and Language*, New Haven, Cornell (1944).

—— —— 'Letter', *Mind* LXX, 277 (1961).

—— —— 'Moore's Arguments against Certain Forms of Ethical Naturalism' *The Philosophy of G. E. Moore*, ed. P. Schilpp, Evanston (1942).

—— —— 'The Nature of Ethical Disagreement', *Readings in Philosophical Analysis*, ed. H. Feigl and Sellers, New York (1949).

STRAWSON, P. F., *Introduction to Logical Theory*, London, Methuen (1952).

STRAWSON, P. F., 'On Referring', *Mind* LIX (1950); reprinted in *Essays in Conceptual Analysis*, ed. A. Flew, London, Macmillan (1956).

TOULMIN, Stephen, *The Place of Reason in Ethics*, London, CUP (1950).

—— —— 'Principles of Morality', *Philosophy* XXXI, 117 (1957).

URMSON, J. O., 'On Grading', *Mind* LIX (1950); reprinted in *Logic and Language* II, ed. A. Flew, Oxford, Blackwell (1953).

WARNOCK, Geoffrey, 'Analysis and Imagination', *The Revolution in Philosophy*, ed. G. Ryle, London, Macmillan (1956).

WITTGENSTEIN, Ludwig, *Philosophical Investigations*, Oxford, Blackwell (1953).

—— —— *Tractatus Logico-Philosophicus*, London, Routledge (1922), new translation by Pears and McGuiness (1961).